SO YOU CAN TELL

Prisoner 48378
Auschwitz

faiga burman
with
simon wajcer

TESTAMENT EDITION

Published in 2004 by WhiteSir Press,
Montreal, Quebec
Canada

www.whitesirpress.com
simonwajcer@videotron.ca
ISBN 0-9683224-1-7
Printed and bound in Canada

Cover design S. Wajcer
Cover graphics R. Stratulat
Text design and page composition R. Stratulat

www.soyoucantell.com
history/holocaust
burman/wajcer
Testament Edition

SO YOU CAN TELL

By
Faiga Burman
and
Simon Wajcer

SO YOU CAN TELL ©
Published by WhiteSir Press

SO YOU CAN TELL

'...Do not become embittered by wailing and tears. Speak of these matters with calmness and serenity ... pour forth your words and cast them into letters. This will be the greatest retribution you can wreak on the wicked ones. Despite the raging wrath of our foes, the holy souls of our brothers and sisters will then remain alive. These evil ones schemed to blot out their names from the face of the earth; but a man cannot destroy letters. For words have wings; they mount heavenly heights and they endure for an eternity.'

Rabbi Nachum Yanchiker,
ed. The Assembly of Rabbis of the
Reform Synagogues of Great Britain

London and Oxford:
Oxford University Press, 1977, pp. 256-57,
Widner Library, Harvard Yivo Library, N.Y.,
Hebrew University Library

FOREWORD

The writing of this book was an act of love: the love of family, love of our people, love of humanity and love of life. It follows the biblical and Talmudic tradition of recording. To record is to remember. To remember is to be spiritually armed to recognize and to resist hatred and evil.

My collaboration in the realization of this book stems from an unremembered moment in my childhood when I innocently asked, 'What is that number on your arm, Mother?' I am still learning the answers to that question.

As my mother's first-born I am the first of my family to receive her oral history. Over the years she has told it to all her children and grandchildren and I have heard her story many times over. Yet, no matter how many times I have heard it, I cannot retain many of its details. These events, the murder of my mother's family, and countless others, were not witnessed by me; they are not seared into my mind like they are into my mother's. I have the unconscious ability to block them out so that they do not drive me mad. My mother does not have that luxury. She cannot forget. She has to tell. She was given a sacred mission to live: so you can tell.

I grew up and lived among many Holocaust survivors. I heard their stories and have read numerous Holocaust survivors' testimonies; I realized that my mother's story was unique in the annals of Holocaust literature. Her story is a paradigm of the Holocaust that befell the Jews of Poland. She is one of the very few who survived every hell point on that paradigm: the bombing of Warsaw, persecution under the Government General, the Warsaw Ghetto and its destruction, the concentration camps of Maydanek and of Auschwitz, and the Death Marches.

My mother was thirteen years old when the war started, the youngest child of a large Jewish family. A family which was not rich yet not poor, not orthodox yet not without faith, not insulated but not assimilated; they had close relations with their Polish neighbors. Hers was a family which was part of a clan that numbered in the hundreds of souls. When she was liberated by the Soviet Red Army, she was nineteen years old, and the sole survivor of her family.

Not many other people survived the same horrors she did, and of those very few have written about their ordeals. Even fewer have displayed the memory and recall that she has. Her vivid and detailed testimony provides not only a rare first-hand insight into the hell that so very few survived, but also into the thinking and beliefs of those close to her who did not survive. The perceptions and re-actions of her family members and their neighbors to the forces and events that they were swept up in answered many of my own questions about how the Holocaust was perpetrated.

This testimony is not only my mother's story but it is also my legacy, the legacy of my brother, my sisters, my nieces and my nephews. It is also the legacy of every human being. Her story reveals universal and timeless truths about the human condition. It shines a penetrating light on the mechanisms of evil and hatred. How the hatred of one man for another is rooted in envy and jealousy and how that generates the lies to vilify, dehumanize and de-legitimize the other so that their rights, their goods and their property can be stolen and ultimately, that they can be murdered. More lies then justify the murder and yet more lies deny that any of it ever happened. The cycle of envy, jealousy, hatred, lies, theft and murder has not ended. We have seen it repeated again in Rwanda, and once again it is being perpetrated against the Jews under the guise of anti-Zionism.

To believe that the Holocaust was an aberration in human history is wishful thinking. To ignore the truths to be drawn from *'So You Can Tell'* is to default to future disaster. The battle against anti-Semitism, against one man's irrational hatred of another, must be fought in every generation. *'So You Can Tell'* must be told today and to the generations to come, not only because it is our history, but because it can arm them with the understanding to prevent future Holocausts.

Simon M Wajcer

INTRODUCTION

Auschwitz Prisoner: 48378

More than fifty years have passed since the Holocaust ended. During this time I have not lived a single day or night without unbidden flashbacks and recurring nightmares that wrack me with painful memories and overwhelm me with depression and guilt.

> ... I am seventeen years old, huddling with my sister and her seven year old daughter, my niece Felunia, beside the rail road tracks at Maydanek. We have barely crawled out of the fetid cattle car that has brought us here from the *Umschlagplatz* and now my sister is pushing me away, crying, begging me to leave them, to line up in the last labor unit being formed from our transport. To live while they died. Through her tears she is saying, "Do whatever you can to survive, so you can tell." ...

I survived Hell. I am a living witness to its existence. Yet today, there are people who deny that such horrors ever happened. It is a time when our youth refuses to believe that human beings would ever subject other human beings to such suffering again.

I have struggled for the strength and courage to deliberately invoke the terror and horror that those events seared into my memory and to record them in written words.

My witness is just one story. Six million other stories will never be told. My family, my neighbors, my friends, and the people whose names I never knew, who did not survive, must be remembered by my children, my grandchildren and the future generations to come. This testament is dedicated to the memory of my sister, Channa, and is the fulfillment of my promise to her; to tell what happened to the Jewish people ... to anyone who will listen.

SO YOU CAN TELL

BOOK ONE

A WORLD IN TWILIGHT

March 1, 1926 – September 1, 1939

Menashe, my older brother, vomited and convulsed to the moment of his death. Father and Mother watched their infant's death throes in helpless anguish. Menashe had poisoned himself by eating an unknown substance. He was only eighteenth months old. His death was a terrible loss for the family. Father could not accept the cruel loss of this joyous child who at such a young age was already dancing and displaying various talents. Father became suicidal. I was conceived to replace Menashe. I was conceived to console the family, to heal my Father.

I was born on March 1, 1926, in Grodzisk Mazowiecki, a small Polish city where my family lived. Both of my parents were in their late thirties at the time of my birth. I was my mother's seventh child. I was also her last child. My mother and I were inseparable; wherever Mother went, I went. I could not bear to be away from her. She was the core of my life. Whatever she did, I was always at her side, observing and listening. I never tired of hearing Mother's stories. I was immersed in her love and wisdom, and her words and actions resound through my life to this day. Father and the entire family doted on me. I came into a world that was in its twilight. A world that soon would be no more than smoke billowing from crematorium chimneys.

Before World War II my family had lived in Grodzisk Mazowiecki for many generations. My ancestors fleeing persecution in the rest of Europe arrived in Poland during the sixteenth century, some 350 years after King Boleslaw issued the Statute of Kalisz in 1264 A.D. which welcomed and protected Jews.
According to the oral tradition of our family, we had come from Germany where we had sojourned after fleeing the persecution of the Spanish Inquisition. Approximately 4,000 of Grodzisk Mazowiecki's 30,000 citizens were Jews. We took great pride in our city and were passionate Polish patriots.

Grodzisk Mazowiecki, which we simply referred to as Grodzisk, was a small, bustling city approximately 27 kilometers south-west of Warsaw and approximately 70 kilometers north-east from Lodz. Grodzisk had all the amenities of a much larger city, plus a commuter train to Warsaw, that made it the hub for a ring of smaller towns and hamlets located in the surrounding villa-sprinkled, pastoral landscape. Grodzisk was our home.[1]

Mother, Chava Domb, was born to Sarah Feigenblatt and her husband, David Domb, in 1887, in the town of Rawa. Shortly after Chava's birth her parents moved to Grodzisk, 72 kilometers away. When Mother was only a year old, her father, David Domb, was killed by an army sentry while returning to his base from leave.

There was never any explanation of the circumstances surrounding his accidental death and grandmother Sarah never received a pension or any other form of compensation for the loss of her husband. She became a penniless widow and Mother began the struggle that was life for a fatherless child. All her life Mother longed for a father she never knew.

Grandmother Sarah remarried. Her new husband, Menashe Slak, was a Talmudic scholar. His vocation assured Sarah a life of perpetual pregnancy and poverty. Sarah bore him six children. In 1892 she gave birth to twins. They died in their infancy. In 1893 she gave birth to a son, Milech. Milech was followed by three daughters: Schifra in 1896, Raizel in 1904 and Rachael Leah in 1906.

To ease Sarah's ever increasing poverty, Mother, Chava, was brought up by her paternal grandmother, Chaia. Chaia fed her and sent her to school. When she was twelve years old Chava apprenticed herself into the hosiery trade. With her meager earnings she helped her mother put food on the table for her half-brother and three half-sisters. Chava also paid for her own Jewish education. Despite her poverty, she learned to read and write.

Chava grew up to become a strikingly beautiful young woman. Her jet-black hair, flashing dark eyes and perfect white teeth caught everyone's eye. I never tired of hearing Mother's story about how she and Father met at a Jewish community social function and fell in love. Her prince charming was Mordechai Burman, a sweet, soft-spoken, well-educated, good looking young man from a well-to-do family. He was kind and honest to a fault. He could not, and would not, lie. His blond hair and ever present smile, which caused his green eyes to twinkle, enchanted everyone. Everyone loved him and affectionately called him Motta. Chava and Motta were the same age, in their late teens, when they met. They both worked in the hosiery business.

Mordechai's parents, Faiga Brandstein and Moshe Burman, were prosperous army uniform manufacturers. They were far from overjoyed about their son's choice of a poor, fatherless girl. A girl without a dowry. They forbid him to marry her.

Chava and Mordechai eloped when they were nineteen. They married in Rawa, among her family, and then returned to Grodzisk. Chava's mother-in-law would not accept her and refused to speak to her. A short while later, Chava bore Mordechai, their first child. He was named David, after her deceased father. David died in infancy. Mother was very hurt by the loss of her first child. Mordechai's parents never saw this much-mourned child because they were so bitter about the marriage. Mordechai began to resent his parents' attitude towards his young wife but Mother would not allow any rift to develop between Mordechai and his parents. She always told him, 'They are your parents, they want the best for you, like every other parent.' And she always sent him to visit them. Even though they would not accept her, Mother bore no malice towards Mordechai's parents.

When Mordechai turned twenty-one he was drafted into military service by the Russian Army.[2] Thanks to his musical ability he was posted as a drummer with an orchestral unit stationed in Odessa, a resort town on the Black Sea. Fortunately Chava's maternal first cousin, Surka Kanterovitch, had a restaurant in Odessa. Surka invited Chava to come and stay with her, so that she could be close to her husband. Being in the orchestra meant that Mordechai was on leave almost every night. Chava was soon pregnant again.

In 1910 Chava gave birth to another boy and to assure his survival she named him Chaim, the Hebrew word for life. After the birth of Chaim, Chava and Mordechai returned to Grodzisk. By now Mordechai's father was deceased and his mother was ill. She was also plagued with guilt for never having seen her son's lost child, David. She realized that she had made a grievous mistake and she now wanted to be close to her new grandson. She asked Mordechai to bring his wife to her. When Chava went to see her, Mordechai's mother asked Chava to forgive her. Chava did. Mordechai's mother was very happy with her son's wife and new family. From then, until her death several years later, they were very close. She left Mother all her jewelry.

Mother always told me these stories on Friday nights when all the older children were out and the house was quiet. Only she, the Bubbeh, as we called my maternal grandmother Sarah, and I would be home. As I listened to

Mother's stories, they broke my heart. I could not imagine someone not liking my mother. I pitied her; I could not understand that she had never known her father. On Saturdays I would accompany her on her visits to see her father's brother. He was a pious man. A tall, good-looking, bearded man. I would say to her, 'Your Tata must have looked like him. She would answer, 'Yes, that is what everyone says.'

Mother sensed that I felt hurt by the rejection she had endured from my paternal grandparents. But she was never bitter, and she gently explained to me that of all my paternal grandmother's six children, Father was the apple of her eye, the most loved child. He was always at her side. He was the only one still living in the same city as his parents. All her other children were living in different cities and one son had emigrated to Brazil."[3] Some members of Mother's family had also dispersed to different cities and countries, but her three half-sisters, Schifra, Raizel and Rachael Leah, remained in Grodzisk.[4]

Chava and Mordechai's family continued to grow. In 1914, Mother gave birth to my sister, Channa. My brother Schloime was born in 1916. My parents supported their growing family by manufacturing hosiery in winter and practicing horticulture in summer. The endless upheavals and revolutions in Russia soon brought bad news. Mother learned that her half-brother, Milech Slak, who was living in Russia, had died during the turmoil. The fate of his wife and child were unknown. They, too, were believed lost. Mother later learned that Milech's wife and child had survived; however, Milech's widow had no desire to return to Poland and had stayed in Russia. Mother always mourned the death of her only brother.

During World War I Father was called back into the Russian Army, leaving Chava alone with their three children. Father was taken prisoner of war by the Germans and spent the rest of World War I interned in Germany. During this internment he worked in a kitchen and learned to speak impeccable German. Shortly after the Armistice of November 11, 1918, Father returned home to Grodzisk. He often spoke about his experiences as a prisoner. He had only praise for the German people. The only thing he had to say about the Russians was that they were 'brutes'.

Life had been hard for Mother while Mordechai had been gone. It had been a constant struggle to keep her children fed. But now that Mordechai was reunited with his wife and family, life returned to normal and the family continued to grow. My brother Moishe, whom everyone called Tusha, was born in 1922. Menashe was born in 1923. He was a precocious child. His dancing and laughter brought great joy to the family. Father, in particular, was spell-bound by the various talents displayed by this child at such an early age. When he was eighteen months old Menashe ate an unknown substance. It killed him. He died in his parents' arms. The family went into shock. Menashe's loss was unbearable, most of all to Father. His mourning developed into a deep depression. Father became suicidal. I was conceived to replace Menashe. I was conceived to console the family, to heal my Father.

I was born to them in March of 1926 and named Faiga Chaia. Faiga, to honor the memory of my paternal grandmother, and Chaia, in memory of my maternal grandmother, who had raised my mother and Chaia because it is the feminine form of the Hebrew word for life: to assure my survival.

My parents' love for each other was the bedrock of our family. Their understanding of one another created a very good marriage and a very good life together. We, their children, were brought up in this loving atmosphere. Mother was the family disciplinarian; she kept a sharp eye on us and was always teaching us to think right and do right. Father could find no fault with us that needed more than a few soft-spoken words and his smile. We loved our parents dearly. We were not a rich family, but neither were we poor. 'Poor' in pre-war Poland meant not being able to put food on the table. The Great Depression of 1929 was world-wide and poverty and hunger in Poland were widespread with the majority of the population living hand to mouth. But we were never hungry and we were always well dressed. We lived at number 19/21 on 11 Go Listopada Street in a wooden dwelling that Father had inherited from his parents. We were very fortunate; our lives were good.

Father had a gift for languages. In addition to Yiddish, he spoke Hebrew, German, and Russian, and unlike many Jews in small *schtetls*, he also spoke flawless Polish. Mother's Polish and Russian were not as good as her Yiddish and I would make fun of her accented Polish. She used to get angry with me and say, 'That's why we are sending you to school, so that you can speak Polish properly.'

My parents practiced a liberal Judaism. The high holidays and *kashrut* were strictly observed and enforced by the Bubbeh. At some point during my infancy she had left her flat to come and to live with us. She saw to it that there was no mixing of dishes and kitchen utensils, and that the Sabbath candles were always lit. On the Sabbath we rested. Father had inherited a seat in the synagogue. He attended the high holidays and on occasion the Sabbath services.

My parents' home was an open house. Our family always had visitors. Mother taught us that respect for others was first and foremost. She would tell me, 'When you see someone in the street always say 'hello'. Always say good day and you will be answered with 'have a good year'. People used to comment to Mother, 'What a nice child you have, she always says 'hello'.

My oldest brother, Chaim, was sixteen years older than me. He was tall, broad-shouldered, with a very slim body. His well-groomed brown hair, high cheek bones, smooth skin and brown eyes with their intriguing cast accentuated his aura of authority. He had a bobbing Adam's apple that as a child I was always trying to put my finger on. Chaim was a very elegant dresser. He wore the latest Paris fashions, which he made himself, copying them from the pictures in Paris Match magazine. Chaim was meticulous and thorough in everything that he did.

Chaim's schooling consisted of the obligatory *Chaider* education plus five years of public school, where he learned to speak Polish. As a teenager he decided to become a tailor so that he could make suits for Father and everyone else in the family. He apprenticed himself to Grodzisk's most reputable tailor. As in everything he did, Chaim excelled at tailoring. Once his apprenticeship was over, Chaim received many enticing job offers; one of them was to move to Paris and work as a designer. Despite these opportunities, he came home to work for Father. Chaim was very devoted to the family. He and Father ran the hosiery business together. He was Father's right hand.

When Chaim was eighteen he became engaged to a beautiful, sultry brunette. He was deeply in love with her. She, however, was in love with another who was away doing his military service. When her former suitor returned she called off their engagement. Chaim was heartbroken. He went out with other girls but would not make a commitment to marry because of the pain of his first rejection. Chaim did not have very many friends; he preferred the company of his family.

Being the first replacement child, Chaim held a special place in his mother's heart and he adored her in return. Mother could not bear to see him suffer the pain of rejection and her main goal in life became to see Chaim married. But Chaim was no longer interested in getting married. He knew how much Father depended on him and he wanted to continue working with the family. But

Mother persisted and relentlessly sought a 'match'.

Chaim was always concerned about my schooling. If I came home late he always asked where I had been. It was Chaim who disciplined me, not Father. Chaim being so much older than me, my friends naturally assumed he was my father. I would get mad and sternly say, 'No, he is not my Father, he is my brother.' And then I would point out Mordechai, with his bemused smile and twinkling eyes, and proclaim, 'He is my Father!'

Sometimes I was angry with Chaim for being too strict with me. He was always saying, 'You can't go out! You have to help your mother and the Bubbeh.' Instead of going out to play with my friends after school I would have to help around the house. As a child I considered this a terrible punishment.

One day, when I was eight years old, I asked for a snack of cheese and bread. Instead, I was given a slice of bread spread with chicken fat and *grieben*. In a tantrum I threw it away and ran down the stairs. Chaim chased after me. Fleeing out the gate I caught my finger in the latch, tearing it. It bled profusely. Chaim, seeing the blood, was beside himself with remorse. He cleaned up my cut and bound it with spider webbing. Then he gave me the bread and cheese that I had wanted.

On another occasion I decided that rather than going straight home from school to do my chores, I would play with my friends. Chaim came looking for me. When I saw him coming I feigned a headache. He picked me up, carried me home, put me in bed and sent out to the pharmacy for a headache pill. Now I could not refuse to take the pill. It caused me to perspire so much that everyone thought I was coming down with a fever. I never pulled a stunt like that again. Even though Chaim was strict with me, I knew that he loved me.

My sister Channa was a dark-haired, dark-eyed, beauty who danced with an effortless grace. Whenever she danced all eyes would be riveted on her. When Channa turned sixteen she began working for Father. She went to visit our cousins in Warsaw whenever she got the chance. She liked big city life and wanted the family to move there. She spent so much time in Warsaw, that as a child I did not know she was my sister. But whenever Mother took me to visit her, Channa would hold me on her knees, comb my hair, kiss me, and give me chocolates, money and all kinds of presents. I liked this. Whenever she came home to Grodzisk with a boy to introduce to our parents, the boy would be instructed to bring me chocolates.

By the time I was seven years old I understood that my sister was going to get married and freely gave my opinion of her suitors. 'I don't like him because he wears glasses,' or 'because he is fat.' I used to enjoy making fun of her boyfriends.

My brother Schloime was born in 1916. I was his little doll. He used to throw me in the air and kiss me and give me anything I wanted. Schloime was strongly built, with very dark hair and deep brown eyes. He was robust, outgoing and handsome. He was always smiling and laughing. His interests were girls, sports and clothes; he always wanted to have the same clothes as Chaim. School held no interest for him. He attended no more than four or five years of public school, where he barely made passing grades. He also had the obligatory *Chaider* education. He had to. Every day Mother would run to the *Chaider* to see if he was there. Too often, he was not. He was out playing soccer or roaming with his many friends and getting into trouble.

In general, Jews were not liked by Poles, but Schloime was an exception. Even though his Polish was not perfect, he had many Polish friends. He was so handsome and easy-going that everybody liked to be with him. He was always surrounded by Jewish and Polish friends. To Mother, of course, they were the wrong friends. She did not like most of them; she called them 'hooligans'.

One evening as Mother and I were walking home from the train station, one of the town's hooligans staggered drunkenly towards us. Mother held me close to her side. As he approached us we recognized him. It was the notorious Voiek, feared by everyone for his drunken rages which often resulted with Voiek stabbing someone in a brawl. When he saw us he halted abruptly and drew himself upright. He gallantly swept off his cap, stepped aside to let us pass, and said, 'A good evening to the mother of Schloime.' Mother nodded to him as we walked past him. A few steps later I heard Mother say to herself, 'Only this was missing to my problems.'

The problems resulting from Schloime's various circles of friends distressed Mother. She kept a close eye on whomever he associated with, but to no avail. Mother always reproached him with the same refrain; 'Why can't you be more like Chaim?' But Father always stood up for Schloime. Father was incapable of disciplining his children, especially Schloime. Mother would get exasperated and ask him, 'What kind of father are you that you never raise your hand to your children?' He would smile and reply, 'To me, my worst child is better than someone else's best.'

Schloime began to learn the hosiery trade when he was very young, and he also worked for Father. He was always asking Father for more money. He needed it because he often went to Warsaw to meet girls. More often than not, he would not be back on Sunday morning in time for work. He would come back a day later. Mother worried that he liked girls too much. He was the family Casanova.

At one point Mother forced Schloime to get engaged to a girl that she liked very much. Schloime, however, did not care for her. On weekends he would tell Mother that he was going to Warsaw to see his selected fiancée, but he visited other girls instead. Mother always found out that he had not seen his fiancée and would forbid him from going to Warsaw the next weekend. But he always had a good excuse for her and convinced her that next time he went to Warsaw he really was going to see the fiancée whom she had chosen for him. Of course, the next time he went to Warsaw he did not see her for one reason or another. And he kept getting away with it. He could get away with anything. Everybody loved him.

Occasionally, Schloime would bring his friends home, and if no one was around they would eat all the cookies the Bubbeh had baked, then raid Mother's alcohol preserved cherries. Schloime would refill the jars with water to cover up his pilfering. But Mother almost always caught him; the alcohol on his breath gave him away. His two most frequent accomplices were Uzeck Florenstein, whose family sold pianos, and a boy from the Pletman family.

Schloime also had a taste for the forbidden. He liked to indulge in a ham sandwich now and then. He bought them at Schneider's a *Volksdeutsch* shop, for twenty grosh. Mother once caught him coming out of there. Of course he denied that he had eaten anything, and as usual he got away with it.

Mother's problems with Schloime were endless. But to me he was the big brother that picked me up from school and always asked, 'How was school today?' 'Fine!' I would brag, and recite my daily academic accomplishments. Whenever I had a report card I would show it to him so that he could see how smart I was. Then he would buy me the biggest scoop of ice cream that could be put on a cone.

Tusha, the youngest of my three brothers, was a multi-talented, natural charmer with curly light brown hair, orange-flecked green eyes and an ever-present smile that showed his gaped front teeth. He was the cutest of them all. His real name was Moshe, after my paternal grandfather, but Tusha was the nickname everyone knew him as. Mother said that I had given him that name because as a child I could not pronounce Moishe. Father was crazy about him. I always wished that I had his talent to draw, sing and make things. When he was a very young boy he made his own wooden skates and taught himself to play the harmonica. He was only four years older than me.

Tusha, like his older brother Schloime, had problems at school, but unlike Schloime, Tusha's grades were excellent. Like Schloime, he, too, was a born leader. All the boys followed him no matter what he did. Even the Polish boys wanted to be his friend. Tusha's passion was soccer. One day, wearing a new pair of shoes that Mother had just bought for him, he organized a football game outside of town against some Polish boys. All the boys from the *Chaider* went with him. Not wanting to ruin his new shoes by playing soccer in them, he took them off. During the game his shoes were stolen and he had to come home barefoot.

Eventually he had to tell Mother what had happened to his new shoes. To my amazement Mother did not scream or punish him. She was just happy that the hooligans had not beaten him up, as well as stolen his shoes. She said, 'The hell with the shoes, don't lose them again.' My parents adored Tusha. He could never do anything wrong.

The school principal used to call on Mother regularly and tell her it was impossible to run the school with Tusha in it. Either Mother or the school principal decided that six years was enough schooling for him.

After his academic career was abruptly terminated, Tusha went to work for a tailor. He was so talented that every week he asked for a raise, and they gave it to him. In his free time he worked for Father. He did everything so well that Father was always asking him, 'Do this for me, do that for me.'

Tusha was crazy about films. He decided that he wanted to buy a film projector. The film projector cost forty slotyz, a considerable amount of money in those days. Tusha asked father to save his pay for him, because if he had it, he would spend it. But when Father was supposed to buy the film projector and he did not, Tusha was very upset and made his displeasure known.

Sure enough, the following week Tusha had his film projector and an assortment of films. He set up a white sheet in a shed and started to project Chaplin, Laurel and Hardy, and other comic reels. He charged children ten groshen admission. By the age of fourteen Tusha had become a movie mogul.

I used to bribe Tusha to draw for me so that I would have the best school projects. I would pass off his artwork as my own. The best artist in my class was Moniak Scheinfeld. His father was a well-known local artist. Moniak used to complain, 'That's not your drawing, your brother drew it.'

Tusha was always teasing me. Whenever he heard Mother mention how cute I was he would say, 'She's not cute, she looks like a monkey.' And then he'd rattle off all the names of the simian species, 'Chimpanzee, gorilla, orangutan, baboon .... ' Being a slender child I had a long neck and he used to say, 'How can she be pretty, she has a long neck like a giraffe!' I would run to look in the mirror and it was true. But I was very attached to him and always wanted to be around him and his friends, even to watch him play soccer. His friends used to take me along with them.

Whenever I saw Tusha buy girls ice cream, I would get jealous and ask him to buy me an ice cream too. He could not refuse me in front of the girls, so he would order me a five grosh cone. I would say, 'Why do you buy her one for ten and me one for five? I'm your sister.' Then he would buy me a bigger cone just to get rid of me.

In 1931, when I was five years old, we lost the house in which we lived. It had belonged to Father's parents and due to an inheritance dispute we were forced to give it up to Yosele Burman, one of my father's paternal uncles. It was emotionally difficult for us to leave our home and to live somewhere else in Grodzisk.

Channa's desire that we move to Warsaw was now considered. Mother reasoned that with three children working and the additional savings incurred by not having to transport our merchandise to Warsaw twice a week, we could afford an increase in rent. And perhaps we would be better off. Channa finally convinced my parents to move to Warsaw. The older children were happy to move to the big city, but I was devastated. I had to leave my cousins, my friends, my kindergarten and my beloved teacher Rachela.

Mother had one big problem; the Bubbeh, who had been living with us since her husband Menashe Slak had died, refused to move to Warsaw. The Bubbeh moved back into the flat she had given to Raizel and her husband, Lazar. There was nowhere else for her to go because by then Rachael Leah, Mother's favorite sister had died of tuberculosis at nineteen years old. And Mother's sister Schifra had married and moved away to Belgium. Only Mother and Raizel had remained in Grodzisk.

Raizel, my mother's sister, a sturdy attractive girl, had married the lean, redheaded Lazar 'Red' Srebrenik, who worked as a teamster for Mair Domb, Raizel and Mother's uncle. Mother did not approve of Lazar as he had left his wife of ten years, because she was barren, in order to marry Raizel. Raizel and Lazar had a tumultuous marriage. He was eight years older than her and prone to violent rages during which he beat her. Raizel's first child, a girl, Uteh, was born in the same year as I. Uteh was my only cousin from my mother's side of the family.

In Warsaw, we moved into a third floor walk-up on 18 Muranowska Street. I quickly began to hate living in Warsaw. I was a five-year old girl who had to sit at the window ledge looking out because I was not allowed to go outside alone. I longed for my backyard in Grodzisk where I used to build castles in the sand. Mother was not fond of living in Warsaw either. She was used to keeping her door open and having her neighbors come in at will. In Warsaw all doors were locked and you did not let anyone in. She missed the intimacy of living with her mother, who had remained in Grodzisk, and being close to her relatives, friends and neighbors.

Sitting at the window ledge of our third floor walk-up I could watch the tramways on the street below or look into neighboring windows. One of our neighboring families sold food from a cart in the market place. While the parents manned the cart, their two daughters spent the day in the kitchen preparing schnitzels and other foods. I could see directly into their busy kitchen and would spend hours watching the two girls work. There were also two boys in the family whom Schloime befriended. Mother got wind through the local grapevine that these two boys were thieves; she futilely tried to keep Schloime from associating with them. One day the girls had fried up a stack of schnitzels and had left them to cool near the open window. While the girls were pre-occupied with their endless cooking, I suddenly saw a long stick, with a nail protruding at a right angle from the end of it, being lowered to the open window. I looked up to see the girls' two brothers in the window above manipulating the stick. Within seconds they had managed to hook a schnitzel onto the nail and haul it up. I was dumbfounded. The girls never saw a thing.

Mother soon got homesick for her *schtetl*, Grodzisk. She was never comfortable with the fact that her mother, the Bubbeh, was living with Raizel and her husband, Lazar; Mother feared Lazar's violent temper. She frequently went back to Grodzisk to visit her mother and I always went with her. On one such trip to see the Bubbeh, we found her bed broken into pieces and Raizel crying. Lazar, during one of his rages, had destroyed the bed trying to find money he claimed the Bubbeh was concealing from him. Channa Kanterovitch, one of the Bubbeh's sisters living in England, had recently sent her some money. Mother brought the Bubbeh back to Warsaw with us that day.

Every time we returned to Warsaw from a visit to Grodzisk I used to cry and pray that one day we would move back to Grodzisk. In 1932 my prayers were answered. After almost two years Mother could no longer tolerate living in Warsaw. She decided that we would move back to Grodzisk. In Grodzisk my parents rented a nice, spacious, three-room apartment on Pilsudsklega Street from Mr Skoblewski. It was rare for a Polish landlord to rent to a Jew.

My sister Channa did not want to leave Warsaw. She went to live with one of our cousins, Yitzhak Slak, and his family. He, too, was in the hosiery business and Channa worked for him. Father visited her on his two weekly trips into Warsaw, and Mother went to see her at least once every week. I could never wait for Father to come back from his trips to Warsaw. He would always bring me some kind of treat, chalava or chocolate, and if he heard nice songs in the street, he would buy me the song book so that I could sing them.

Back in Grodzisk my parents resumed the myriad of family, social and political activities they had enjoyed before moving to Warsaw. In the winter they manufactured hosiery and in the summer they operated their leased orchards. Once again our home was filled with relatives visiting on Shabbat and the holidays. Shlomo Aleichem stories were recited and Pushkin's jokes elicited gales of laughter. My parents had a lot of Polish friends who visited with us frequently. They were good, decent people. Among them were Mr Swarcinski, the Szewczyk brothers, the Wawrzenczaks, the Fuchses and our landlord, Mr Skoblewski.

Mr Skoblewski was a tall, dark-haired, craggy-faced, handsome man, who loved *gefilte fish* and *challa*. On Friday when he smelled the fish baking he would knock on our door. When Mother answered, he would always say, 'I can smell the fish and *challa*. What a nice aroma.' And Mother would always invite him in for a plate of *gefilte fish* and *challa*. He and Father loved to discuss politics. He was known as a good man and it was rumoured that he had a Jewish mistress.

Mr Skoblewski used to make his own meat products, kilbasso, ham and other pork products. His wife sold them in a market stall near the church. She was a short, fat, unattractive woman with an acne-scarred face. I only saw her on Sundays, when she wore white gloves, a nice dress and hat and took her children to church. She was always distant with us.

When we moved back from Warsaw all my friends and cousins were now going to school, but I was still too young to enroll. I had nothing to do and no one to play with. I could not wait to go school. I cried and cried until Mother took me to speak to the principal, Mr Berel Kampelmacher. He put his hand on my head and said, 'Soon, soon. Soon you will start in the new school.' But I would have to wait until my seventh birthday.

Berel Kampelmacher was an innovative educator who had come from Galicia and had organized the funds from private and government sources to build a new Jewish school. The school had Jewish and Polish teachers. He pioneered an exchange program in which misbehaving boys from the Polish and Jewish schools were exchanged. There were some very hungry children in our school. Kampelmacher provided hot milk and a piece of bread for these children every day.

With all my friends now in school the only other children to play with at home were Mr Skoblewski's children. One of his daughters, Helena, a girl my age, was playing in the yard. Mother insisted that I stop clinging to her and go downstairs and play with Helena.

Helena was a freckle-faced, blue-eyed, red head. She had her mother's strange and distant look. I went downstairs and asked her if she would like to play with my ball. In an angry voice she replied, 'I don't play with Jews!' and, as she moved by me, she spit in my face. I froze in shock. Tears welled in my eyes. I stood rooted to the spot. It was a long moment before I could run up the stairs to tell Mother what had just happened.

Mother stood in disbelief, listening to me. She tried to comfort me. It was hard for her to believe the whole incident. Father got very angry. He took my arm and was ready to confront Mr Skoblewski, but Mother stopped him. The next Friday when Mr Skoblewski came in for his weekly fish and *challa*, Mother discussed the incident with him. It disturbed him. He was upset that his wife's anti-Semitism had infected his children. He assured Mother that it would never happen again. But I never looked at Helena again. At the age of seven I had learned about anti-Semitism from a child my own age.

By 1933 my parents' hosiery manufacture dominated our home. The machines were set up in the large main room which was divided into a living and a working area. Everything was stored in large stand-up wardrobes. Every day the goods were piled high on the Bubbeh's ornate iron bed in the living area, obscuring the angels flying across its burgundy and gold headboard. The hosiery machines were not big but they made an endless racket. Above the clattering of the machines could be heard the constant jokes, laughter and the singing of the girls at work. The endless comings and goings of all sorts of people added to the din. On the holidays Father would move things around and cover them up to make more room for the family. Our home was crowded, noisy, vibrant and joyous.

Both my parents, my three brothers, Chaim, Schloime, Tusha and my Aunt Raziel worked in the family hosiery business. Chaya Graiok, a Betty Grable look-alike, was our only year-round employee. Our other employees were seasonal and sub-contractors. The Bubbeh assisted in running the household.

Twice a week Father would take the train into Warsaw to sell his first- grade hosiery to retailers. Small merchants from Grodzisk bought small quantities of second-grade socks from Mother and merchants in the local markets were sold third-grade socks.

Summer was the off-season for hosiery and the hosiery operation was minimized. Father would store all but two of the machines. One was used to keep Chaya Graiok employed during the summer months and the second was for Schloime and for Esther Pasternak who worked only part time during the summer. Father would come in to make sure the stockings were pressed and Aunt Raizel would finish them. During the summer Father would bring his hosiery into Warsaw only once a month. The rest of the time he was occupied with the orchards which were our main source of income during the summer.

Our orchards were leased from various Polish farmers including the Szewczyks, Fuchses and Wawrzenczaks. They would not lease their orchards to anyone but Father. They wanted their property worked only by him. Father excelled in horticulture. He had a natural talent for it. He had never studied it, but he could look at a tree when it started to bloom and know how many kilos of fruit it would yield, or if it had been hurt by the winter and would not yield fruit. They had such faith in Father that when he proposed a lease price, based on his estimate of the crop yield, they never bargained with him. Never. Whatever price Father offered, it was accepted. It was like this year after year.

Many farmers came to seek Father's advice about their orchards.

During the spring Father would hire someone to sleep in the orchards to guard them. They were located four kilometers outside of town. Father also leased strawberry fields from both the Fuchse and the Wawrzenczak families. During the strawberry season, Mother and I stayed in town because I was still at school. Father tended the strawberry fields with hired help. Labor for picking and packing was very affordable.

After the strawberry season, we tended and harvested cherry and other fruit trees. As soon as school was over, Mother and I went out to the orchards for the whole summer. The Bubbeh never wanted to go. She preferred to stay in town to keep house and to help Raizel. It was also the time of year when she used the money her sister Channa Kanterovitch in London, England, sent her to make a pilgrimage to see the Piaseczne Rebbe, who gave her herbal medications for her ailments. When Channa came home for the weekends, she too stayed in town. She wanted to go to the movies with Raizel, not into the countryside. They were movie buffs.

Father's orchards yielded such beautiful fruit that he could never get to market to sell them. The buyers used to come out to the road to meet him and buy his crop on the spot. There were seasons when we did not make a lot of profit, but Mother would say, 'But we had fresh air, fresh eggs and butter and fresh fish.' She loved to be in the country. I did not. I wanted to be in the city and play with my friends, but I had no choice. I was always happiest when the orchard season was finished because I could go back to school.

Mother made whatever fruit was not sold into fruit jams and conserves. We had plum, strawberry, apple, cherry and raspberry jams for winter. She also pickled all kinds of vegetables and made sauerkraut. She made delicious apple cider and both blonde and black beer for the whole family. We all drank beer. Even I, as a child, drank beer. She had big pots in which she brewed the beer. It was quite a production. Bottles were closed with a special apparatus. In the summer she would store the beer in the cellar. She would bring up a couple of bottles and put it on ice for Shabbus. It was very good.

Finally the day came when I started my first grade of public school. I loved school and my first grade teacher, Miss Newhouse. My school years are amongst my happiest memories. I was a good student. Every night I slept with my school books under my pillow and the first thing I did every morning was review my homework. I always got the best parts in our school plays. My friends were from different backgrounds, but they were all good students. That was important to me.

I also attended a *Beis Yacov* twice weekly; the Bubbeh saw to it. Every morning as I rushed off to school the Bubbeh would ask me if I had said my morning prayers. I always nodded yes and in order not to have lied I would recite them as I walked to school. As I made my way I would wave off my friends who wanted to talk to me while I was busy saying my prayers.

During first grade, my maternal Aunt Schifra, who lived in Belgium, came to Grodzisk to visit us. She made an enormous fuss over me. She brought me delicious Belgian chocolates and everyday she sat me on her knees as she squeezed fresh orange juice for me.

My second-grade teacher was Ludwiga Boyarska. Her husband was the principal of the *gymnazium*. She was a very kind and attractive person, cute and petite, but she was very frail. This woman loved her students and we loved her. I was always privileged to be sent out to pick up her lunch. It was always two rolls and ham. When I went to purchase the ham I had to look around to make sure nobody saw me walking into the shop. They might think the ham was for me.

Mrs Boyarska was often sick, and some of the other girls and I would go visit her at her home. We were always warmly received. We always brought her cream-filled pastries, because we knew she liked them. She would lie in bed and we sat around her, proud to be with her, and we prayed that she would come back to school soon.

Due to the constant clatter of machines in our house I would frequently go to my friends' homes to do homework. I was always welcomed by their parents because I was always helping my friends with their homework. One of my friends, Madzia Wolonowski, lived in a large and spacious bungalow. The family had two maids. Madzia's father was a very successful tanner. I admired their lifestyle and often thought to myself how hard my parents worked to make a living. But as I would walk back home I would say to myself, 'Yes, my parents work hard but I would not change places with Madzia for anything in the world. How could I? I would have to give up my brothers, Chaim, Schloime and Tusha, and my sister Channa. I would not do that, they are my treasures. I would be so over-come with joy that I was going home to be with them, that I could not get home fast enough.

Every new school year we needed new books. Mother wanted me to buy the books from the children a year ahead of me. But I did not want to have used books. I wanted new books. By now I was making myself a few zlotys a week tutoring other children. I used this money to buy new books. I was always good at doing something to get what I wanted to have. Every school year ended with a class picnic in the Lesna Podkowa forest. All my classmates, among them Madzia, Chaya Lichtenstajyn, Regina Sierpska, Gutcha Liebhaber, Balcheh Frankel, Luzer Schulman, and I, looked forward to that event all year long.

On my way to school I always passed the Sendik home. Sendik was a shoemaker. He could make shoes and he could make children. Sendik's wife had eight children. The oldest was ten years old before the war. Mrs Sendik knew Mother and me. Her mother and my grandmother were friends. One day, on my way home from school with my friends, she called out to me. I went over and she said, 'Do me a favor, go to Krigsman's and buy me ten decca of butter.' I did not want to leave my friends so I asked her, 'Why don't you send your daughter?' She replied, 'My daughter will eat it up on the way home. That is why I cannot send her. Please get it for me.' I could not refuse. But from then on when I was with my friends, I would avert eye contact with her so that she would not send me for butter.

Shoemaker Sendik had an RCA Victor gramophone[5] and records of Tony Martin and other famous singers. He used to rent it out to people. Whenever Channa came home from Warsaw, she, Chaim, Schloime and their friends would rent it from him for five zloty and have a dance party at home. At one such dance party Chaim was dancing with Rifka, his girl friend at the time, a beautiful girl, and I separated them saying, 'No, no, you have to dance with me.' But I could not dance so I stood on Chaim's feet to tango with him. That is how I learned to dance when I was eight years old.

Both of my parents were social activists. Mother was involved with helping the city's orphans, the poor, and raising money for girls' dowries, and Father was always busy with numerous causes.

Father was a member of a loans committee. The Grodzisker Society in America sent the committee money to be loaned to the needy. After work he would wash up, change into a nice shirt and go to a committee meeting. When he returned home he would review all the details of the meeting with Mother. I was too young to understand what they were talking about. It was all discussed in secrecy. We children did not need to know about these things.

Of the children, only Tusha belonged to any organization, a Socialist youth group called Skifist.

Once, when I was searching for something in a wardrobe, I found a brown shirt wrapped in a little package. I asked Father, ‘What’s this? What’s this?’ He gently said, ‘Put it back, put it back.’

One day Father’s cousin came to the door and said, ‘Motta, tonight at eight o’clock.’ I did not know what he meant by eight o’clock. But when I saw Father go to the wardrobe and take out the brown shirt, I asked Mother about it. She did not want to talk about it and said, ‘Ah never mind.’

Incidents like this happened repeatedly. Another one of Father’s cousins often brought him messages. I finally learned that Father belonged to Ze’ev Jabotinsky’s Betar Organization.[6] He was a Revisionist.[7] It was Father’s dream to live in Israel. But Mother did not want to move anywhere. She just wanted to live with her mother in Grodzisk.

I always loved being with Father. Every Friday after work he would change into some fine clothes and then he and I would go out for a walk. Father loved to smoke cigarettes and whenever we walked he always smoked. Everyone we met showed him the utmost respect. I enjoyed how people treated him. I was so happy, so proud that everybody liked him. He was always smiling. The children of our relatives used to come over to say hello and he always gave them some change for an ice cream cone.

Father liked everyone and was thoughtful towards them. In return, he was liked by everyone. Our mailman, a young *Volksdeutsch*, was befriended by Father. Whenever he would deliver the mail Father would invite him in to have a coffee and a cigarette with him. Father knew that he was very poor and would always give him a little bit of money.

On Fridays we would always walk to Newman’s store, in the market square, where Father would buy his tobacco. The market square was dominated by a war memorial built of large, heavy stones. It honored the soldiers who fell in WWI and the War for Polish Independence. It stood right in the middle of the square. I used to read the monument’s dedication with pride.

From Newman’s, Father liked to go to Berle Bellmacher’s place. It was a small café off the market square, where members of the hosiery trade went to relax, gossip and discuss politics. There was a billiard table in the back and Berle Bellmacher sold beer and pastries. Whenever I wanted a snack, and I did not see Father around, I used to go and look for him there. Sure enough he would be sitting there having a beer or tea with his friends.

I used to come in and say, 'Daddy, buy me something.' The counter was so high that he would have to pick me up so that I could choose something. I liked that.

I also liked to listen to his conversations. He was well-read and knew what was going on in the world. He and his friends always discussed world affairs and their impact on Jewish issues. They were not overly concerned about Hitler; he was just one more German anti-Semite in politics. Anti-Semites in politics and in the church were very commonplace.[8] Nor were they worried about the many schemes to resettle Jews in Madagascar, or other places, as a solution to Europe's Jewish problem.[9] Even we children were aware of these resettlement schemes. One of these was a Jewish colony in Biro-bidjan that we sang ditties about.[10] When a movie about this colony was being shown in Grodzisk, I clamored that my parents take me to see it. As we watched the depiction of Jewish settlers clearing the swampy land and building log cabins Mother said, 'Who knows where our bones will end up-in swamps like that.' The ugly and brutal aspects of anti-Semitism, like pogroms, were kept from a young child like me.

Father's siblings were scattered. His older brother Yoska was in Brazil. David, one of Father's cousins, left his wife and children behind and also went to Brazil. When his visa ran out he went to Yoska and said, 'I'm going back to Poland. Your brother has grown-up children and if you would send him some money to buy machines, it would be a big help to him.' Yoska entrusted him with fifty dollars U.S. for Mordechai. This was a goodly sum in pre-war Poland.

David's family lived in the same building as we did. While he was in Brazil, his wife could not make ends meet. Mother fed her and her three children. After David came home his wife began baking and cooking up a storm. Mother speculated that he must have brought some money from Brazil.

After a while a letter came from Brazil. Yoska wrote, 'I sent you money with David, did you receive it? Why don't you write back if you got it?' When Mother read this she said, 'What a crook!' When David was asked, he claimed to know nothing about any money.

Father wrote to Yoska that David denied getting any money from him. Yoska wrote back detailing how David came into his shop with his story. Yoska never wrote again. He did not even reply to our later letters.

When spring came we went out to the Szewczyks' orchards to see how the trees had managed the winter. Mr Szewczyk, a strongly built man of mid-height, welcomed Father and then said, 'I have something to tell you. Two Jews came out here and begged me to lease them these orchards for the season. They wanted to give me a very good price. I presume that you know them and that they know you are always here with me.'

Mother asked what they looked like. 'One was a tall blond man and the other was a short, dark-haired, dark-eyed man.' Mother knew immediately who they were. The blond one was Moshe 'Whitey' Burman, a first cousin to Father. He was nick-named Whitey because of his white blonde hair. He was a very handsome man, who had served in the elite Polish cavalry. He wanted to marry my sister Channa, but Mother would not hear of it. The
other man was the husband of Mother's cousin, Esther. Mr Szewczyk said to Mother, 'They did not look honest.' Mother did not want to tell him that they were family. She did not want to be embarrassed.

When she came home she told the Bubbeh about the incident. We were not very close to these cousins. After all, Moshe 'Whitey' Burman was Yosele Burman's son and he now lived in the house from which we were evicted during the inheritance dispute. But I was very angry with them. I could not understand how they could do such a thing.

The Szewczyks had a big house. Its ground floor was used as a school room. In the summer it was empty and we used it as a kitchen. They treated us with a warmth and love that made us feel like members of the family. Mr Szewczyk's wife was a strong, healthy woman. They had eight children, and God forbid if one of them should ever be rude to us. Mr Szewczyk had a younger brother with whom he was not on speaking terms. The younger brother had married a woman whose father owned a very large amount of acreage. My parents, however, were friendly with both of them.

Mr Wawrzenczak was another Polish landowner with whom we had excellent relations. He was tall, slightly stooped and so thin that he looked ill. He was an educated man and his two children studied at the university in Warsaw. Father and Mr Wawrzenczak always discussed politics. We leased strawberries fields and pear and apple orchards from him. We often visited him on our Saturday outings. We were always warmly received. We would spend the day in the grass amid the orchards and after they milked their cows they always brought us fresh milk. The Wawrzenczaks lived next door to the Fuchses, with whom they did not get along.

The Fuchses were *Volksdeutsche* and they were my parents' best friends.

My parents attended all their Christmas parties, weddings and funerals. They had five children, four daughters and one son, Vladek. Their children were all well-educated. Their married daughters were teachers in various cities and Vladek worked in the P.K.O bank in Warsaw.

Many of my summer vacations were spent in the Fuchses' cottage. I was very attached to their youngest daughter, Basha. She was always giving me something to read or write and always had pencils and papers for me. She liked to have me working on a project at the kitchen table while she worked in the kitchen. I liked to be with her.

Vladek Fuchse was a tall, handsome and gracious young man. He was good friends with Chaim, Channa and Schloime. Whenever we came out for a weekend he would spend time with us and our visitors. In particular Chaya Graiok, the Betty Grable look-alike who worked for us. She had beautiful long legs, natural blond hair and a lovely round face. Everyone called her Betty Grable. Vladek, like any healthy male, was very attracted to her. We could see that he was falling in love with her. I overheard him tell Mother, 'Legs like hers are worth a fortune.' Mother repeated this to Chaya and added, 'Chaya, Vladek Fuchse is in love with you. You are so beautiful he would marry you right away.' But in those days, as poor as she was and as handsome and as well off as Vladek was, she would never consider marrying him. And it was not because she was religious; in fact, she was a member of the communist party. All her friends were communists. Marriage between Jews and Poles was a social taboo that was seldom broken, especially not in small towns.

Nor was Chaiah Graiok the only communist in Grodzisk. Many people thought my brother Chaim was a communist because his best friend, Akiva, was the most outspoken communist in Grodzisk. Akiva refused to work, claiming that he was not going to be exploited by the capitalists and that he was waiting for Stalin to liberate him. Mother detested Akiva because not only was he an old bachelor who did not work, but he let himself be supported by his widowed mother. Chaim, on the other hand, locked the door to the house every May 1st and everyone had to work.[11] 'Some communist!' Mother would say derisively.

Chaya Graiok was not the only one in Grodzisk who resembled a Hollywood personality. One of our cousins, Moshe Schgimek, who owned Grodzisk's most modern barber shop, where Mr Skoblewski, our landlord, used to get his hair cut, had an extremely pretty child. She had curly blond locks and blue eyes and was a Shirley Temple look-alike.

In 1935 Marshal Josef Pilsudski, the national hero, liberator and leader of Poland died.[12] Everyone mourned his passing. We were told of his death at school and we all wept. Pilsudski was a leader that Poland's Jewish citizens greatly admired for his fair treatment of them. He was succeeded by the overt anti-Semite, Smigly Rydz.[13]

One fateful day in 1935 my sister Channa met Max Szyldszrajber. They fell in love. Max was a trim man with a tough masculine appearance. He had a sharp, quick, practical mind, and except towards Channa, showed very little emotion. He was a resourceful young man with both feet on the ground. Max was from a prosperous family that owned a souvenir business in Chechochinek. He did not get along with his sisters and refused to work in the family business. He left home and moved to Warsaw where he found employment in a store that sold wood veneers.

Channa asked my parents to come to Warsaw to meet Max. Mother did not like him. 'A Jewish boy that leaves his parents? He's not working with his family? He's not a good boy, not good husband material.' Channa was in tears. She came home to discuss Max but Mother still said no. Channa returned to Warsaw, crying. But Max and Channa were truly in love and when my parents realized this, Max's father was invited to Grodzisk and a wedding was arranged.

The engagement party was held in Warsaw in the house of Mother's cousin, David Domb. David Domb was prosperous and lived in a beautiful apartment with red velvet sofas. The last thing I remember about the party was how beautiful my sister looked in a light blue dress with a white flower pinned on it, as she and Max were kissing. Then I fell asleep on the red velvet sofas and did not wake up until the next morning.

Channa's wedding was held at our home in Grodzisk. Not many people from Mother's side of the family were invited. Mother went to the *Beis Midrasch* and invited a few poor people to come to the wedding. She did not make a separate place for them but sat them at the table with everyone else.

Also sitting at the table was Father's rich uncle, Chaim Flint, and his wife, Nechah, my grandmother's sister. He was vehemently opposed to this egalitarian arrangement, saying, 'Those people shouldn't be at the same table.' A commotion ensued, and not to ruin Channa's wedding, we had to make a separate table for the poor. Having been poor and fatherless herself, Mother was very upset by this.

Only Max's father came to his wedding. His mother was paralyzed and in a wheelchair. She could not travel. None of his sisters came; they had not forgiven him for leaving home. Nor did his older brother Leon. Channa and Max lived in Warsaw on Novolipie Street. When their fortunes improved they moved to a bigger apartment on Leshno Street.

Shortly after Channa's wedding, Mother's unrelenting persistence finally resulted in a match for her first born son, Chaim. Arrangements were made. Chaim was to marry Surka Yabukofsky, a well-put-together, honey-blonde, brown-eyed girl from Lodz. Her family manufactured raincoats and he was to be taken into the family business. Mother was ecstatic that at twenty-six, Chaim would finally cease to be an old bachelor. Chaim traveled to Lodz to get acquainted with his fiancée and her family. He liked what he saw and her family was thrilled with him and his business talents.

In 1936 Channa gave birth to Felunia. Felunia did not resemble either of her parents; they were both brown-eyed and dark-haired. She looked like my father. She was a beautiful, blond, green-eyed girl. This infant transformed our lives; the entire family was overcome with joy. Every Saturday my sister brought the baby to Grodzisk. She had become the center of our family. Nothing was more important than this baby. By the age of ten I had become an auntie and I was very proud of it. I brought photos of Felunia to school to show her off to my classmates. I would be bursting with joy when my parents gave me some pocket money, put me on the train and sent me off by myself to Warsaw to visit Felunia.

No matter how far apart we lived, we all gathered to spend the holidays together. We were a very close family. Chaim and Channa were especially close. When Channa gave birth to Felunia, Chaim came home to take Mother to Warsaw. He had a box of presents for the baby with him. We were curious to see what he had bought. He opened the box and there lay three little cut velvet dresses, one in white, one in blue and one in pink. There was also a matching little striped pink velvet coat.

Mother asked why he had bought three identical dresses. He answered that they were so cute, he wanted Felunia to have one in each color.
Mother told him that one dress would have been enough. I was very angry with Mother for telling Chaim that he should have bought Felunia only one. Why should Felunia not have all three?

The Bubbeh's sister in England kept sending her money on a regular basis. These gifts financed her religious pilgrimages to the Piaseczne Rebbe and to venerated gravesites. She always kept her money in an inner pocket of one of the three petticoats she always wore. With her eyesight failing, she would fumble through the layers of petticoats to find the inner pocket. As often as not she would not quite get her money into that inner pocket, so that when she bustled around the house on her daily duties, the Zloty coins would invariably work themselves loose and fall down onto the floor in the corridor. We were always picking her money up after her.

One day I found a five zloty coin in the corridor. It was an enormous sum of money for a ten year old girl. A vision of countless ice creams and chocolates danced before my eyes. I knew that the money belonged to the Bubbeh and that I had to give it back to her. But, perhaps I could get a reward for finding it. This was definitely not an idea I could present to Mother. I had to take this scheme to Father. With him I could probably create a situation that would reward me.

When I found the right moment I said to him, 'Father, I found five zloty in the corridor.' He replied, 'It probably belongs to the Bubbeh, go give it back to her.' 'Father, why don't you give it to her and tell her that I found it and that she should give me a zloty reward?' He looked at me his eyes twinkling and smiled, 'Okay, we'll see.' I ended up getting only fifty grosh from the Bubbeh. I was disappointed, but it was more than I would have gotten had I gone to Mother with my little manipulation.

My summer as a ten-year old was spent at the Fuchses. My parents and I slept in the attic bedroom while my brothers slept in the barn on the hay. When my sister came with Max, Mother gave them the bedroom and we, too, went to sleep in the barn. Mother loved to sleep in the hay; she said it smelled so good.

On one of those summer days, while Mother was indoors with Mrs Fuchse, I was playing at the well. While looking at my reflection in the water something fell to the ground near my foot. My immediate thought was that someone had thrown a stone. I looked down and saw a little red bottle. I picked it up and read 'POISON' on the label. I looked around to see where it could have come from. I saw an open attic window, where a young Polish couple lived. She was a beautiful young woman with luxuriant long brown hair. I often saw her combing and coifing her hair. Her husband was a good- looking man who always wore a spotless white shirt. I reasoned that the little red bottle had been thrown from their window. I knew he was at work so I immediately thought, 'She swallowed poison!' I went running into the house. Basha was in the kitchen. I said, 'Look, this fell near me. I think it's from the upstairs window.' She took the bottle and ran upstairs. I ran up behind her.

The beautiful young woman with long brown hair was lying on the bed. She started to scream that she had swallowed poison. There was a commotion and she was rushed to hospital. I was startled and wondered what was going on. Mother told me that the woman wanted to commit suicide because her husband had a mistress and she could not bear the pain this caused her.

The whole neighborhood came to see Mother and to praise me for my quick-wittedness in saving the young woman's life. All the women patted and caressed me and said, 'Smart child! Smart child!'

After that I would often see the young woman's husband while I walked Felunia in her stroller. He was always on his way to the hospital to visit his wife. She had a very long convalescence.

Schmuelek Slak, a cousin of ours, was always running away from home. His mother, Yetta, and Mother were first cousins, and they were very close. After the death of her husband Yetta remarried a man with five children. Schmuelek deeply resented this man. He could not bear to share his mother with this man. Schmuelek was sent to live with his grandparents, Ettel and Mair Domb. Mair owned a successful transport company. He was brother to David Domb in whose home Channa got engaged.

Schmulek was close friends with Schloime. Too close. Mother did not like having him around the house. Schmulek, at sixteen, had already run away to Czechoslovakia and returned two years later. Mother knew he would run away again and that Schloime was a prime candidate for just such an adventure. She watched this relationship like a hawk.

Schmulek used to come to the house when Schloime was working. Schloime never needed much convincing to take a break and step out to talk with him. These conversations were overheard by Mother's network of spies; Schmulek was indeed trying to persuade the adventurous Schloime to run away with him. His plan was go to the free port of Gdansk and board a ship for foreign parts. The family went into an uproar at the revelation of this plan. Schmulek did not succeed in getting Schloime to go with him, but he did succeed in getting Handsome Yosel, the melamed's son, to travel with him.

Schmulek and Handsome Yosel set out to ride the rails to Gdansk. They were found by railroad bulls and had to jump off the moving train to escape them. Schmulek jumped first and rolled clear. Handsome Yosel did not make it. He lost both his legs above the knees. Handsome Yosel was brought home a cripple. Schmulek did not dare return to Grodzisk. He traveled on. The *schtetl* was scandalized by this tragedy. Mother cried and did not hesitate to point out to Schloime that it could have been him left without legs. Handsome Yosel was awarded a cigarette concession by the railroad, from which he could make a living. He even married.

That *Rosh Hashanah*, Chaim brought his fiancée, Surka, home from Lodz. Mother and I picked them up at the train station in a horse-drawn carriage. As we drove away Moshe 'Whitey' Burman stepped into the middle of the street and stopped the carriage. He came over to us and said, 'Chavcha, I hope that by now you are no longer so angry with me that we can't start off this New Year on good terms. Please, I invite Chaim and his fiancée and all your family to my house for dinner.' The whole family went.

Moshe 'Whitey' Burman had spared no expense in preparing a beautiful table for us. We finally became acquainted with his wife and their two children. Whenever Channa and her child came on weekend visits, Moshe 'Whitey' Burman always came to see her. He was still in love with her.

Early in the winter of 1937 Chaim got married and Schloime, now twenty-one, was drafted into the Polish Army. Only my parents, Channa and Schloime went to Chaim and Surka's marriage in Lodz. Schloime attended his brother's wedding in his military uniform. He was a handsome soldier and everyone was proud of him.

The day Chaim got married was the happiest day of Mother's life. I was happy, too. I could not wait for Chaim to get married, because then he would move away for good and not boss me around anymore. But as soon as he was gone, I missed him terribly. Everyone did. The house was in mourning. We all felt lost without him, except Mother. She was beside herself with joy that he had married so well, with a large dowry and an established business. She was ecstatic that he had finally started his own life with a wonderful girl like Surka. Whenever Mother missed him more than she could bear, she would get dressed up in her best and put on a nice little hat with a plume in it and go off to visit him.

Father missed Chaim the most. From the moment Chaim left, everything Chaim had done so efficiently fell upon Father's shoulders. Chaim had taken care of the daily administration, materials organization, the handling of sub-contractors and the management of employees. He repaired the machines himself and he made all the models. There was no part of the business Chaim could not do. And to make things even more difficult for Father, Schloime, who did not have Chaim's work ethic, nor his interest in the business, was now in the army.

Father was overwhelmed by it all. Perhaps he never realized just how reliant he had been on Chaim. He went through a very rough time before he adapted to Chaim's absence. But everybody helped out. Even the Bubbeh sewed some parts of the stockings. I was the courier.

My main job was to take the stockings to the sub-contractors, first the finisher and then the presser. I was always carrying big bundles of stockings. I worked hard. I had already started running various other errands the year before.

One of the sub-contractors I occasionally went to was Hirsh *'The Chish'* Opolion. Hirsh was an excellent spooler. He wound the thread onto the spools that we used. If the thread was not wound properly it would uncoil from its spool and be lost. Once I was sent to pick up an order from him. But Hirsh was in the process of preparing his breakfast and would not let the fire in his stove burn out just to take care of business. I had to wait. He said to me, 'Watch and see how I make an omelet.' I could not believe my eyes as he broke fifteen eggs into a skillet for his omelet. I went home and told Mother about it. She said, 'His wife and children barely have enough to eat and he indulges himself in a fifteen-egg omelet. Now you know why we call him Hirsh *'the Chish'*.

After my eleventh birthday, Mother started feeling ill. She could not keep her food down, nor could she eat. She started to weaken and to take to her bed. Channa and Chaim came home and took her to see a doctor in Warsaw. She was diagnosed by Dr Glaygewicht, a German Jew, as suffering from a stomach ulcer. Her weakness grew and Mother no longer had the strength to prepare for the Sabbath. I said, 'Mother I'll do it.' She protested, 'You cannot do it. There is a lot of shopping and cooking to do.' But I insisted that I could do it. I went to the market to buy and carry home the fish, the eggs, and everything else that was needed to make our own noodles. I had to make noodles for at least eight people. I used two kilos of flour and six eggs to make the dough. The table was too high for me so I stood on a stool to work. My grandmother poured the flour and I added the eggs and kneaded. I then flattened it out and cut fine thin noodles and farfel. Once Mother saw that I was indeed capable, it became my weekly task.

A neighbor came in one day and saw me standing on the little stool making the noodles. Her name was Channa, and she was a childless woman. She said, 'I can't believe that! How many eggs did you put in?' I said, 'Six eggs.' 'And you're doing it all by yourself?' She turned to Mother and said, 'You know Chavcha, when she does this, you better close the door so that nobody can see her and put a *nahora* on her.'

In addition to making the noodles I cleaned the carrots for the *tsimmis*, peeled the potatoes for the *chulent* and carried the *challas* back and forth to the bakers. It was a lot of work. From then on I could no longer go for a walk with Father on Friday afternoons. As soon as I came back from school my school bag was put away and I set to preparing for the Sabbath. I worked very hard as a child. I had no choice. I had to help out.

Mother's bouts of illness became more frequent. Chaim had a phone in Lodz and Channa could use the one at Max's workplace. Whenever Mother was not feeling well Channa would call him.

On one hot day that summer Mother and I were in the country, lying in the grass, when suddenly I saw a beautifully suited man coming towards us. I said, 'Mother, do you know who is coming? It is Chaim.' She said, 'Why do you joke like this? How could Chaim be coming now? It is impossible.' I said, 'Mother, I'm telling you this is Chaim! Come look, it is Chaim!'

As Chaim approached, he said, 'Mother, Channa told me you weren't feeling well; I want you to come see the doctor.' Mother replied, 'You have no right to come to me and to leave your pregnant wife. You don't leave a wife when she is pregnant; she needs you more than I do.'

I was furious with her. He had come to her as soon as he heard from Channa that she was not well and she rebuffed him with, 'You have to go back to your wife today.' Why was she saying this to her own son? But that is what she had him do. Later that day he had to take the train back to Lodz.

Not too long later Chaim's pregnant wife Surka went into labor. During the delivery a choice had to be made: either the mother or the child could live.

Surka had a still-born child. It was heartbreaking. Mother cried as she packed away a lace pillow that she had made for the baby.

The infant mortality rate was high in Poland. My Aunt Raizel had three sons, all of whom died in their infancy. Of the four children she had with Lazar only their first-born daughter, my cousin, Uteh, a pretty blue-eyed blonde, survived. Lazar was devastated by the death of all his infant sons. He went to consult a rabbi. The rabbi told him that he had been cursed by his barren first wife for divorcing her. He also told Lazar that to protect his daughter from the curse, he should wear only white socks. Fortunately for Uteh we were in the hosiery business and Lazar never lacked white socks.

Uteh was not a good student and Uncle Lazar hired me to tutor her at fifty groshen an hour. She was not my only student, but she was a difficult one. When she paid attention she was able to get passing grades. When she stopped listening to me and stared at the walls, she failed. It was very frustrating and I refused to tutor her anymore. Uncle Lazar begged me to continue. It was difficult to refuse him. After all, she was my first cousin and the only cousin I had from Mother's side. She was also the Bubbeh's favorite grandchild.

The Bubbeh would always give Uteh gifts and money. When Mother saw this overt favoritism she confronted her. 'Do you think Faiga doesn't see what you are doing? Do you think she isn't hurt by it?' The Bubbeh's reply was, 'Faiga already has everything.'

Early that year scandal struck the family. Lazar caught Raizel with her lover. He beat her. In the heat of the moment, they divorced. Lazar immediately married a woman in Grodzisk. Raizel moved to Warsaw. Uteh was shuttled back and forth between them and our house. A number of months passed and Lazar left the woman he had hurriedly married in Grodzisk. Raizel also had her regrets and it did not take long before they were reunited and had moved back to Grodzisk.

Schloime's military service was very difficult on Mother. Schloime disliked the army and whenever he got homesick he would grant himself leave. Every time he came home, Mother asked to see his leave papers. When he did not have any he tried to distract her or stall her with various unsuccessful tactics. Sure enough, when he would return to his base he was thrown into jail. The time he spent in jail was not counted as part of his service and had to be made up. He spent a lot of time in the stockade prolonging his service. It looked like he would never finish his army service.

While in the army Schloime would write Mother, asking to be sent non-*Kosher* foods, like spec and salami. Even though he ate these foods he never brought them into the house. Mother would not go into a Polish charcuterie to buy the foods my brother wanted. She asked a Polish woman, who did our laundry, to purchase the foods for her. She then packed them and sent them to him. All this had to be hidden from my very observant Bubbeh.

Somehow Schloime always managed to get furlough for the holidays and come home. I was always so proud and happy to see him. He was very handsome in his army uniform.

One day a soldier appeared at the house and asked to speak with Mother. He was a friend of Schloime's. He told Mother that Schloime was in the base hospital. She immediately left for the base to see him. When she returned home she told us what had happened to Schloime. Schloime was by now so desperate to get out of the army that he had eaten egg shells so that he would become sick enough for a medical discharge. He was hospitalized and operated on. What he did not realize was that he would have to make up his hospital time to the army. His plan had failed.

By 1938 I was in the fifth grade. My progress in school was excellent. Mrs Novak taught us geography. She was big and tall and always wore a black smock. One day, the school janitor found some buttered rolls in the waste basket. Many children in Poland did not have a piece of dry bread to eat every day, let alone buttered rolls. He showed this to Mrs Novak and she became very angry. In a rage, she said, 'Here you are throwing buttered rolls into the garbage! There will come a day when you will go through garbage looking for a piece of bread!' An inexplicable chill ran through me as she said these words. They proved to be prophetic and in later days her words would ring inside my head.

That year as I was walking down a street in Grodzisk, I saw members of a Polish fascist youth organization, called Andeckkes[14], standing in front of Jewish stores shouting, 'Do not buy in Jewish stores! Don't give them business! Down with them!' It felt like a knife was cutting through my heart. I panicked. Some Poles stood up to the Andekkes and refused to be intimidated by them. They yelled back at them and supported the Jews by going into their stores. This relieved my tension a bit. This incident was not isolated to our city; it was repeated all over Poland.

The significance of this event was argued to and fro by everyone. Most did not consider the Endeckkes a serious threat to the Jews of Poland. After all, fascism was the political trend of the era, and anti-Semitism was part of their platform. There were fascist parties and fascist youth groups in every country in Europe, even in North America.[15] Anti-Semitic outbursts were chronic, a fact of life, and we had coped with it for centuries. Those who insisted that these recent developments were serious, and not to be lightly dismissed, were labeled as over-reacting. It was far more comforting to believe that these events were of no great significance, that there was no point in being unduly paranoid, and to get on with our daily lives.

Then in October, 1938, the Polish government announced that the 15,000 Polish- born Jews who had lived outside of Poland for longer than five years would have their passports revoked and they would become '*Statenloss*',[16] Stateless. When the Nazis announced that there would be no place in Germany for 'Stateless Jews', we rationalized that we were in Poland and that there was nothing we could do. We did not know what implications all this had, and, like most Jews, we went on with our daily lives. We soon found out.

My Aunt Chaiah in Brandenburg, Germany, was affected by these developments. Father's now widowed sister was one of those who had become stateless. Chaiah's husband Godel had died in 1932. By 1938 Chaiah had no more illusions about her own and her children's future in Germany. Germany would not even recognize her German-born daughters as citizens. She tried to leave Germany but no country would give a widow with two children an entry visa. That year she succeeded in getting her eldest daughter, Friedel, rescued by the Jewish Youth Aliya[17] and taken to Palestine.

Several weeks later the Nazis ordered Chaiah and her two German-born daughters, Marga and Paula, to appear before them at the Brandenburg city hall. Assuming that they were being summoned for bureaucratic reasons, they went to city hall carrying only their handbags. Once there they learned that Chaiah's property in Brandenburg was being confiscated. They were being thrown out of their home. The Nazis ordered them to assemble at the synagogue for questioning. From the synagogue they were loaded onto trains, bereft of any possessions, and taken to Zbaszyn, a small town on the Polish-German border, where they were dumped and declared stateless. Chaiah and her daughters, Marga and Paula, were among thousands of such victims.

In Zbaszyn, Chaiah and her daughters, Paula and Marga, were housed in a stable and given straw to sleep on. Soon more transports arrived, carrying thousands of Jews who had been rounded up in Hamburg and Hanover. They too were dumped in Zbaszyn on the Polish-German border.

Among these arrivals was a very orthodox family, the Grynszpans. They slept in the stall opposite Chaiah and her daughters. When the Grynszpans heard that their son, Hershel Grynszpan, had shot and killed the Nazi diplomat Ernst Vom Rath in Paris, they wept and prayed ceaselessly. On November 9, 1938, the Nazis used the assassination of Vom Rath as a pretext to launch *Kristallnacht*.[18]

Father and the family did whatever they could to bring Chaiah and her daughters back into Poland. Aid from the Polish Jewish community arrived promptly. Field kitchens were opened, doctors and nurses came from the cities and opened clinics, a clothing and blanket depot was set up, and a special children's kitchen was set up in the home of Mr Leopold Cohen, an elderly accountant, who was probably Zbaszyn's only Jewish resident. Chaiah volunteered to cook for the children.

The Jewish Agency pleaded with the world community to take the children in. They begged England to give shelter to ten thousand Jewish children. By December, 1938, the British Jewish community had managed to obtain fifty six permits for children aged 13-15 who had only one parent. My cousin Marga, who was thirteen, was one of the fifty-six evacuated to England by the Jewish Agency. Paula left Zbaszyn a month later for a *kibbutz* near Cracow from where she was scheduled to leave for Palestine on September 1, 1939. Chaiah was finally allowed into Poland. She went to Warsaw and was looked after by her deceased brother David's ten children.

The prevailing opinion was that what was happening in Germany would not happen in Poland. Was not Poland protected from Germany by its alliance with France and England? That rationale was far too comforting and seductive to repudiate. Mother kept saying to me, 'Oh how I pray that what I went through when Father was in the army, the things that happened during the war, should never happen to my children.' And Mother was not a believer. Who could imagine what was awaiting us? Daily life went on.

In March of 1939 I turned thirteen years old. Mother continued to put her heart and energy into helping the poor and the orphans in our city, and I accompanied her everywhere. Mother always spoke with wisdom. Common sense was her virtue. People listened to her. At the time I could not comprehend many of the lessons I learned at her side.

That summer I received a parcel from my brother Chaim in Lodz. In it was a new navy blue coat, with blue trim, that he had made for me. There was also a matching beret with blue trim and a leather school bag. It was my new school outfit for my first year of *gymnazium*. I was thrilled.

It was also a happy summer for Mother. Schloime finally finished his army service. His military service had lasted far longer than the compulsory eighteen months he had been called up for. Our orchards were productive and we were looking forward to preparing for the high holidays and winter. Mother decided that it was time we moved, but finding a new apartment to live in was difficult. With help from one of her friends Mother found a new place for us. It was situated on the edge of town facing a field. It was well lit and very airy. I did not like it; it was too far from the market square. Mother came to an agreement with the Polish landlady and began to plan our move.

One summer morning Aunt Chaiah arrived from Warsaw to visit us. I had never seen her before, but since the events in Zbaszyn I had heard many things about her. She came with my sister and Felunia. She looked like my father's family. She had a pretty face, was in her forties and spoke German, which sounded funny to me. Father was out in his orchards when she arrived. Before going out to see him Chaiah decided to visit some friends she had not seen since leaving Grodzisk. I accompanied her on her rounds. When she was done it was time to go and see Father. My sister, Felunia, Chaiah, a friend of hers, and myself set out to the orchards. We stopped a farmer's wagon and paid him a few zloty to drive us out there. Before we got there I jumped off the wagon and ran ahead.

I knew that my father liked to take a nap in the afternoon. He liked to sleep in the fresh air. He would take off his shoes and make himself comfortable under his favorite tree. I did not want Aunt Chaiah to see her brother with his shoes off. I ran towards his tree and sure enough there he was fast asleep. I called to him, 'Papa! Papa! Wake up! You have a guest. Your sister is coming. Put on your shoes.' He stood up, his eyes twinkled as he smiled at me and said, 'Why do I have to put on my shoes? It's my sister.'

Mordechai and Chaiah had not seen each other for a long time. They embraced. I could feel their happiness at being together again.

By late summer the threat of war loomed. There was a general call-up. Schloime and Uncle Lazar were among those called up. We were not unduly worried; we believed that the gallant Polish army was more than a match for anything the Germans could muster.

Summer was coming to an end and I was running my Friday errands in preparation for the Sabbath. As I made my way home from the bakery carrying a heavy tray of six *challas* the heavens above me began to throb and rumble with the roar of rapidly approaching engines.

The noise stopped me in my tracks. I looked up towards the source of the ever-growing roar to see three heavy bombers cutting through the sky towards Grodzisk. Everyone around me had also stopped and stood looking up. Kampelmacher's son, Edek, and some others began arguing,
'Those planes must be ours. No! No! Look at how heavy they are! They must be Germans!' As they got closer and closer the throbbing and rumbling of the low-flying bombers became unbearable.

Terrified, I ran towards our house. I rushed through the gate, hurried up the stairs and as I put down the tray of *challas*, a horrendous blast rocked the house.

My parents circa 1908. Chava Domb Burman and Mordechai Burman.

My sister Channa 18 years old.

My brother Schloime circa 1937.

My Aunt Raizel Slak, her husband Lazar 'Red' Srebrenik, their daughter Uteh, and one of the baby boys that died in his infancy.

My first grade class on a picnic in the Lesna Podkowa forest. I am the first child seated on the left in the first row.

BOOK TWO

INTO THE GHETTO

September 1, 1939 – Autumn 1941

Another bomb exploded as everyone rushed down into the cellar. There was shock on every face. More bombs exploded. Some people running from the bombs ducked into our cellar and told us that the first German bomb had struck the war memorial in the middle of the market square. The large stones, with which the memorial had been constructed, had splattered in all directions killing many people.

Suddenly I realized Father was not home. It was Friday afternoon and he was buying tobacco at Newman's store on the market square. I became hysterical with the fear that Father might have been killed. I began screaming, 'Where is Father? Where is Father? Father is dead!' I went into shock and became feverish. I was burning up. As I screamed, 'Where is Father? Where is Father?' I was rushed into the cellar of another house where wet towels were put on my head.

A short while later Father arrived safely. The moment I saw him my fever disappeared and I was instantly better. All that mattered to me was that Father was safe and well. Father told us who had been killed. Most of the victims were Jews who lived around the market place. The other bombs dropped on Grodzisk blew up some train tracks and hit the local cemetery; one hit the local prison. All the prisoners were able to escape. It was Friday, September 1, 1939.

By the next day, Saturday, the entire population of Poland was in chaos. We were now at war with Germany. During the chaos, Schloime deserted his post and came home. His unit was stationed in Grochof, just outside of Warsaw, and therefore close to Grodzisk. He insisted it was too dangerous for us to stay in Grodzisk and that we leave with him at once for Warsaw where we would be safe. He assured us that the German Army could not take Warsaw.

Schloime's desertion of his post during war was an act punishable by death. My parents, fearing what would happen to him if he were caught, promised him that we would go to Warsaw if he returned to his post immediately. Mother trembled as she pleaded with him, 'Go back to your post, you are going to get killed like my Father did!' Schloime replied that he was not going back until Mother promised that she would bring the family into Warsaw. Mother in desperation said, 'We'll come as soon as we store all our valuables in Uncle Chaim Flint's house. I don't want to come back to an empty house like I did in the last war. Then I promise we will come to Warsaw.' Schloime then left us to return to his post.

The next day Mother started packing all our valuables and placing them with Uncle Chaim and those relatives who were not leaving Grodzisk. Uncle Chaim's daughter was about to be married and her entire dowry was in the house. Uncle Chaim had left his home during World War I and had come back to a ransacked house. This time he was not going to leave. All our hosiery machines were stored in the hope that one day we could use them again. Aunt Raizel refused to leave for Warsaw. She wanted the Bubbeh to stay with her, but Mother would not hear of it. The Bubbeh did not want to go to Warsaw; she pleaded, 'Where are you *schlepping* me? I'm old; leave me here.' Mother took the Bubbeh with us, despite her pleas to be left with Raizel. We joined the multitudes that fled to Warsaw for safety. In Warsaw we went to Channa's which was on the top floor of a fifth floor walk-up on Leshno Street.

For more than three weeks, waves of German planes flew over Warsaw unopposed, dropping their heavy bombs on us. We were afraid to sleep in Channa's apartment, directly under the roof, in case the building was hit during the night. Instead we slept in a friend's second-floor apartment located in the back of the building. Everyday we learned which of our relatives and Grodziskers had been killed in the latest bombardment.[1]

All services in Warsaw quickly broke down. There was no food to be bought or bartered for. There was nothing to eat. Hunger set in rapidly. Schloime became our source of food. At night he would desert his post and forage for us. One night he came back to the apartment carrying a bag and announcing that he had brought us potatoes. We hurriedly opened the bag to find it contained onions. In the dark he did not know the difference between a potato field and an onion field. But we were so hungry, anything was good. Schloime always managed to bring us something to eat, even if it was only carrots. On one occasion he and some other soldiers looted a liquor store. That night he brought us bottles of liquor and hard candies to go along with the onions we were having for dinner. It certainly put us all in a good mood. By deserting his post to bring us whatever he could forage, Schloime risked his life for us.

Whenever Schloime brought us food Father used to say to Mother, 'To you he was the worst child; what do you say now?'

By the end of September the bombing stopped. Poland had surrendered to Germany. The war was over.[2] The courtyard of Leshno 105 filled up with people, kissing and hugging each other, clapping their hands and thanking God that the war had ended. They believed that the worst was now over. People were so happy that the bombardment had stopped that they were not thinking about the fact that we were going to be under German occupation. As Mother and I walked among them she said, 'Look at them. Hitler is coming in and look at how happy they are. This is just the beginning of our problems. God knows what awaits us.'

As German troops occupied Warsaw we left for home, for Grodzisk. We and other Grodziskers were returning home in Uncle Maier Domb's transport wagons. All our family members rode in one wagon. The roads out of Warsaw were full of the people who had mistakenly believed that they would be safer in Warsaw. Those of us who had survived the German bombs were now going back to our home towns. When we reached the outskirts of Warsaw the horses turned onto Okopowa Street, which was the road leading to Grodzisk; the road was blocked. Directly in front of us we could see a large group of people crowding around several German Army trucks. German soldiers stood on the trucks distributing bread to the Polish population. The trucks were brimming with bread.

We had been deprived of bread for weeks. Everyone jumped off the wagons and ran towards the trucks to get a loaf of bread. Seeing us running towards them the Germans started shouting, 'Juden raus! Juden raus!' For Jews there was no bread. Many of the Poles were openly happy about this. Whenever they recognized a Jew standing in line for bread they began pointing at him and shouting, 'Jude! Jude!' German soldiers then marched over to the betrayed Jew and beat him severely. If he had any bread they took it away from him. Father did not look Jewish. He went and stood in line. He did this several times and brought back enough loaves for the entire family.

We arrived in Grodzisk without further incident, but we had come back to a Grodzisk that was already occupied by the Germans. We went straight to our house and found the door broken down. Everything that could be looted had been carried away. Only the heaviest furniture remained. Mother said, 'Again the same story. A good thing we stored a lot away.' I cried when I found out that even the new school bag that Chaim had sent me had been stolen. In our haste to get away to Warsaw, I had forgotten to take it to Uncle Flint's for safe-keeping. Mother decided that since the house had been looted and everything else was packed, it was the time to move into the new apartment she had rented just before the war. I went with her to see if the place was ready for us.

When we arrived at the apartment, the Polish landlady stopped us and said, 'I'm sorry, Mrs Burman, I cannot give you the apartment. The Germans are here and I do not want to let in Jewish people.' Mother stood still and just looked at the woman. Not a word came out of her. Finally she turned and we walked back home. We fixed up our home and moved back in.

We quickly learned that not one bomb had fallen on Grodzisk during the entire siege and bombardment we had endured in Warsaw. Fortunately our family had all survived, but many other Grodziskers who had fled to Warsaw for safety had been killed. While we were gone the Germans had entered Grodzisk during broad daylight on September 8, 1939, and that very night the most important and influential Poles and Jews were taken out of their beds and shot. They also replaced the entire city hall bureaucracy with *Volksdeutsche*.

All *Volksdeutsche* now wore the Swastika arm band and collaborated with the Germans. There were many *Volksdeutsche* who collaborated willingly and there were those who were unwilling but had no choice. Pawel Fobe, a *Volksdeutsch* who owned a local garden nursery, became mayor and his son took over the administration of city hall. Some Poles, with German sanction, simply took over Jewish businesses and homes. The Germans made it clear to the Poles that they could do whatever they wanted with us.

The Germans immediately began passing laws against us.[3] Now all Jews had to wear an arm band with a yellow Star of David on it. We had to form Jewish Committees answerable to the Germans. The first task of every local Jewish Committee was to register all Jews in their community.

Poland was now partitioned between the Germans and the Russians. Western Poland was annexed outright by Germany and eastern Poland became a Russian territory.[4] Only the central part of Poland, which was German occupied, was still Poland. It was officially referred to as the Government General of Poland and Grodzisk was located in it. Numerous Jews in central Poland began leaving for the new Russian territory.[5] There was no knowing how long the new border would be open or how long one would have to wait before one would be allowed to cross it. Waiting meant living out in the open, without any shelter, during the cold autumn weather. Despite those factors, entire families, with small children and infants, left with whatever possessions they could carry for the eastern part of Poland that was now Russian territory. Some of Mother's cousins and friends were among those who left their homes and all their possessions and fled to Russia.

One night as I was sleeping with Mother, there was a knock on the door. It was Chaiah Korcarz, one of our neighbors. She came into our home carrying her youngest daughter. She had come to say goodbye. She and her husband were taking their four daughters, leaving their prosperous business and heading for the Russian border. She said to Mother, 'Chavcha, don't you see what is going on? Don't you realize the situation we are in? You have grown-up children. Why don't you pack? Why don't you go? You see I have four small children; this one is only eighteen months old. I bought them each a pair of warm shoes. I'm leaving every-thing behind. Do the same.' Mother replied, 'It is very hard for me to leave. I cannot take my old mother. Who knows how long we will have to camp at the border before they let us in? She will freeze to death there. I cannot leave her here; who will take care of her? Secondly my married daughter lives in Warsaw. I will have to convince her to leave as well. Also my health is not so good. I need my bed. You see, it is not so simple for me.' Chaiah Korcarz bid us farewell and left. Other families that we were close to also left for Russia. Among them were Ben Zion Becker and Yudel Goldfarb, their wives and their children.[6]

Some of the Jewish men who had been called up at the beginning of the war began returning to Grodzisk. Uncle Lazar was not among those who returned. Had he been killed like many that we heard about, or taken prisoner?[7] His fate was unknown.

With the war over, I eagerly anticipated returning to school. Father gently told me that the Germans had put up large posters proclaiming that Jewish children were forbidden to attend school. I was devastated. I could not understand why. I cried and screamed, 'Why? Why? I want to finish school!' Mother, trying to reassure me, said in a low voice, 'My child, if you live, there will one day exist a free world for us. You will catch up.'

Even though I was denied the right to go to school, I began wearing the new navy blue school coat that my brother Chaim had sent me that summer.

One day as I was walking down the street on an errand, a German soldier suddenly appeared in front of me, pointing his finger directly at me. I froze to the spot, petrified. I did not know what to do. He came up to me in a rage and ripped the buttons off my coat, saying, ‘Now go home and put on different buttons.’ I ran home terrified. I took a circuitous route home so that he could not see in which direction I lived.

I arrived home extremely distressed and told my parents what had happened. I could not understand why the German soldier had torn the buttons off my coat. Father calmed me down and explained, ‘Of course, those buttons had the Polish white eagle on them; that’s why he tore them off.’ Mother soothed me by immediately sewing new buttons onto my coat.

Things got worse and worse for us. Every day the Germans imposed a new restriction or hardship on Jews. The beatings and killings of Jews increased daily. Every day German soldiers forced Jewish men into labor. The Germans would arrest Jewish men on the streets or pick a Jewish home at random, kick down the door and drag the Jewish men out. Young or old, abled or disabled, it did not matter. It was terrifying. The most menial and laborious work was reserved for Jews. They were used to unload coal cars, clean latrines and sweep streets, all while being physically beaten and verbally abused. The Germans made Jews sing this ditty on work details:

‘Long live the golden Hitler
who taught us Jews to work
while our Rydz Smigly,
taught us Jews naught.’

My brothers managed to avoid the Germans. They would hide in the attic or run when they saw the Germans rounding up Jews. Schloime got caught several times. Each time he came home from forced labor he would say to Mother, ‘Mother I will leave. If you will not decide I will decide and one day I will leave for Russia.’

Father, due to his impeccable German, was usually able to talk the Germans out of taking him. The older German soldiers were not so easily swayed. Father was forced into labor several times. On one occasion Father was arrested in the streets. Because of his German fluency and kitchen experience he was assigned to work in a kitchen. The German chef became very friendly with Father during the short time he worked there. He always gave Father cheeses, sardines and salamis to take home.

Arguments about leaving for Russia were endless. Mother said, 'Motta, take the boys and go to Russia. They will do nothing to the women and the children. You see that they are only after the men.' Father would not go anywhere without her. Mother would not go without the Bubbeh, Chaim and Channa. Max, Channa's husband, would hear nothing of leaving. The discussion was ceaseless and no one knew where Chaim stood on the issue.

Mother had not received a word of news from Chaim since the war broke out. She insisted that Schloime take the train to Lodz and find out what had happened to him. Schloime put on his best Sabbath clothes and left for the train station. On his way there, several young Poles who knew Schloime began pointing at him and screaming, 'Jude! Jude!' Two German soldiers quickly appeared. They seized him and began ridiculing him, 'Good! Good! You are perfectly dressed. Just right for cleaning latrines.' They marched him away. When they got to the corner Schloime pointed to a locked liquor store and asked, 'Gentlemen would you like to have some vodka?' 'Jawohl, sure, go in and get us a couple of bottles.' 'You can't send me in, the Pole won't give me any alcohol. But if you go in he will be afraid and give you some.' The German soldiers knocked on the door and the Pole refused to open it. Schloime suggested that since they were German soldiers they could knock the door down. Who would oppose them? Schloime helped them break down the door. The moment the door gave in and the two German soldiers followed its momentum into the store, Schloime took to his heels and escaped. He hid in cousin Yeta's house. Towards evening Yeta came to our house and told Mother what had happened to Schloime and that he was waiting for nightfall to come home. After that incident he swore that he would leave for Russian territory at the first opportunity.

One day Father came home carrying a sack of coal. Coal was now very hard to come by, and with winter quickly approaching, a sack of it was a rare and valuable commodity. Father told us that German soldiers had seized him on the street and had pressed him into labor unloading coal from the trains. This was a particularly hard job and the Jewish men forced to do it were brutally beaten to make them work more quickly. Jews could never work quick enough for the Germans.

Fortunately for Father, the *kapo* in charge at this work site was none other than our mailman, the young *Volksdeutsch* whom Father had befriended and always treated kindly. When our former postman saw Father among the unloading gang he took him out and assigned him to a much easier job. He also told Father, 'Work slowly and take coal home; prepare yourself for winter.' Father said, 'I didn't know whether to trust him or not, he was being so nice to me while beating everyone else. I was worried he might accuse me of stealing the coal.' But it was not so. For several days Father came home with sacks of coal.

Despite the rapid degradation of our rights and liberties we did not flee to Russia. Instead we hoped that conditions would not get worse. We accepted our plight and attempted to get on with our lives.

One day in November, Father came home very disturbed. He had seen Vladek Fuchs in a Volkswagen with a Swastika on it. The Fuchs family were my parents' best friends. Mother had such great trust in these people that she simply answered, 'Swastika or no swastika, Vladek is a good man. He cannot harm anyone.'

The next day there was a knock on the door. It was Vladek Fuchs wearing a Swastika armband. He asked that the door be closed. He took off his Swastika armband and sat down on a low stool stretching out his long legs. In a low voice he said, 'I want you all, the entire Burman family, around me. Look, you are my dear friends. Listen to me. I know the Germans plan even greater difficulties for the Jews. I have come to warn you and to ask you to leave here. Sell what you can, store the rest and leave. I will help you. I will take you, one by one, in my car to the Russian border.' Mother began to cry, 'How can I leave my old mother, my married children and go?' Vladek insisted that we leave and promised to take all of them.

Schloime decided immediately. 'Vladek, I am the first to go. If my parents don't listen to you, I will. Take me.' 'My car can carry two others besides Schloime.' Vladek said to us. Since no one else in the family was prepared to leave right away, Schloime took two others with him. His friend, Beryl Goldfarb, and a first cousin of ours from Warsaw, Faige Burman. She was a pretty young girl and it came as a surprise to us that he was in love with her. Moments before they were to drive off, one of our neighbors realized where they were going. She came into our home and begged Vladek to take her nine month pregnant daughter to her husband on the Russian side. Vladek agreed to take her. In moments she was in the car with them. Vladek drove them in his

Volkswagen to the border. They were lucky; the border was open and they crossed to the Russian side.

Vladek came back with a letter from Schloime stating that he was safely on the Russian side. Vladek said to us, 'Everything is in good order. Now go to Warsaw and convince Channa and Max to leave. I will come back and take you one by one.

My parents made plans for all of us, all the children and the Bubbeh, to leave. Mother went into Warsaw to tell Max and Channa what Vladek had said and done. But it was to no avail. Max would not hear of leaving. He argued that the Germans were just after the wealthy Jews. The Germans did not mean him. He had neither properties nor valuable possessions; therefore, no harm would come to him or his family. In addition he had skills that the Germans needed. No matter how hard she tried, Mother could not convince Max to leave. Nor had we any news from Chaim and his family in Lodz. There was no question of us leaving for Russia without Chaim having the choice of coming with us. Mother also refused to leave her aged mother behind; she did not trust Raizel to take care of her. Mother knew that at her age the Bubbeh could not survive living in the open at the border and the rigors of being a refugee.

A few days later Vladek came back to us and asked who else was ready to go. Mother told him what Max had said and how she could not abandon her married children nor her mother. Vladek could do no more for us. He left.

There was no end to the rumors about our fate at the hands of the Germans. No one knew what to believe. However, we did fear for the lives of our men; we did not consider the women to be in mortal danger. As the situation for Jewish men worsened daily, Mother finally convinced Father to leave with Tusha for the Russian side. She gave him all the jewelry which she had inherited from his mother and said, 'This is the jewelry from your mother and this is your father's gold watch and chain. Take it. Take a little bit of money, take your youngest son and go.' This time Father could not refuse to go. Father and Tusha left for Bialystock.

With Father and Tusha now on the Russian side, Mother and I now had to earn a living. *Kosher* meat was now very hard to get in Warsaw. The Germans had made the practice of Jewish ritual slaughter punishable by death. Our religious relatives and many of my sister's neighbors were desperate for *kosher* meat.

The Willing brothers were *kosher* butchers who lived in Grodzisk. They risked their lives by ignoring the German edict and continuing to make *kosher* meat available to their fellow Jews. They worked in a secluded shed at night. Mother and I would go there at night and buy *kosher* meat from them. During the day I strapped the meat to my body and carried it into Warsaw. There I resold it to our religious relatives and my sister's neighbors.

If I were caught carrying *kosher* meat it would be the death penalty for the Willing brothers. Not to arouse any suspicion as to why a thirteen-year old was traveling back and forth to Warsaw empty-handed, I would also buy and bring in other provisions to sell in Warsaw. Sometimes I teamed up and traveled with Chaya Lichtenstajyn, a classmate of mine for six years, who was doing the same thing. While Chaya and I went into Warsaw, our mothers would keep each other company.

One day after concluding our business, Chaya and I were leaving Warsaw to return to Grodzisk when a young Polish boy, of about eleven, went over to a Polish policeman and said, 'Look! Those are Jewish girls!' The policeman, a mean-looking older man, grabbed the two of us, saying, 'Come with me.' We did not know where he was taking us until we arrived at the gate of a prison.

We were put into a room that had only one small window and another closed door in it. The room was crammed with thirty to forty other men and women. Among them I recognized a woman I knew from Grodzisk. As we sat there I said to Chaya, 'If we don't get back home tonight my mother will die of worry and so will yours. We have to get out of here.' She asked, 'How can we get out? What can we do?'

I started to cry and scream, 'Let me out! Let me out! I have to go back to my parents! Let me out!' I did not stop screaming and crying until the other closed door in the room opened. Behind the door was a gigantic desk and sitting behind it was the Police Chief, a huge good-looking man. He asked me, 'Why are you screaming and crying like this?' I answered, 'You locked me up in jail and I live in Grodzisk. I'm not from here. I'm not from Warsaw. I live in Grodzisk. I was bringing things to my sister. She lives here. Now I have to get to the train and get back to Mother. She is very sick. If I do not get back today she will die. I have to go back today.' He looked at his watch and asked, 'Are you sure you will get back today?' I replied, 'If not by train, then I will run on foot, but you have to let us out.' He had us released immediately. Chaya and I ran for the last train to Grodzisk. We caught it and returned home late that night.

There were the rare times when I did not get home to Mother for the night. On those nights I slept at my sister's and made my way home after I had concluded my business in Warsaw the next day. On one of those occasions I arrived home to learn that Mother had been robbed the night before by a beggar woman.

The beggar woman was from the town of Blonie some eight kilometers from Grodzisk. She was a regular at our door. The Bubbeh always fed her soup and bread. On the night I was not home, and the Bubbeh was fast asleep, Mother was preparing to go to bed when she heard moaning outside the door. She went to see who it was. Huddling on our stoop was the beggar women sheltering herself from the cold night. Mother feeling sorry for her, invited her in. She gave her a blanket and a place to sleep, then went to sleep herself. Mother kept what little money we had in a small purse that she always put under her pillow. When she woke up the next morning the beggar woman was gone and so was Mother's purse. Mother was shocked; the means to secure our livelihood was all gone, and she was too ill to chase after the beggar woman. Just at that moment my Aunt Raizel came in. She was on her early morning rounds during which she always looked in on the Bubbeh. When she heard what had happened she immediately set out after the beggar woman.

Raizel caught up with her at the cemetery two kilometers from Blonie. She confronted her. The beggar woman denied having stolen Mother's purse. Raizel did not believe her and insisted on searching her. The beggar woman refused. Raizel being a strong young woman searched her anyway and found Mother's purse with the money still in it. She then gave her a few blows, warned her never to come near our door again and sent her on her way. Raizel brought the purse home and we could continue to support ourselves. Raizel had saved the day.

Mother and I did not hear from Chaim until December when his wife, Surka, suddenly appeared in Grodzisk. Chaim had sent her to stay with us. She was pregnant and had taken a great risk in traveling to Grodzisk. By now if a person traveling on public transport was recognized as a Jew, they were beaten up and thrown off the moving vehicle. Surka told us that Chaim and her family had fled Lodz to Zyrardow, a town not far from Grodzisk, where she had family. But Chaim could not find a way to make a living there. Somehow Chaim heard that his father and brothers were now on the Russian side, in the city of

Bialystock. Surka insisted that he, too, leave. He listened to her and went to Bialystock hoping to find his father and brothers. Surka stayed with us for only two weeks before she was overcome by homesickness and returned to her family in Zyrardow. Once on the Russian side, Father and Tusha could not find Schloime and Chaim could not find any of them. All the refugees in Bialystock were waiting to be transported to the Russian interior by the Russian government. It was a long slow process. While their money lasted, Father and Tusha could afford to board with families in Bialystock. But when their money ran out they had to take refuge in a synagogue. Refugees sleeping in synagogues were plagued by lice, mice and contagious diseases. After several weeks as penniless refugees, Father and Tusha came home.

Mother was furious when Father returned from the Russian side. She said, 'Why did you come home? I gave you everything we had to keep you away from here. The worst of what awaits us here will befall the men.' Father replied, 'I cannot stand to live with my son on a lice-and rodent-infested floor when I still have a clean home and can be together with my family.'

Once again Mother gave him what money we had accumulated and sent him and Tusha back to the Russian side. By the end of March they returned home again and this time Father would not hear of going back. They had learned that Schloime had been lucky enough to be able to join one of the many groups that had been transported into the Russian interior.

By now, Chaim had also returned home from the Russian side. He had not been able to find his father nor his brothers while he was there. Over-come with guilt for leaving his pregnant wife behind, he came home. That March, Surka gave birth to a beautiful baby girl named Sheva. This time the celebration was different than the one for Felunia. Sheva had been born into a different world.

Every day it became harder and harder to make a living. Father and his good friend Swarcinski started buying bread from the local bakeries and reselling it in Warsaw, where everything was much more expensive. Father was able to earn a living this way. Mother asked Chaim to come and join Father and Mr Swarcinski in their bread enterprise. Chaim, Surka and the baby stayed with us in Grodzisk during the time it was possible to conduct the bread business.

During April of 1940, the Bubbeh died. She was 78 years old. Mother was devastated. She cried constantly. It unnerved me. I wanted her to stop crying. Instead of consoling her, I added to her suffering by saying, 'Why are you crying? Your mother was already an old woman.' Mother looked at me as she pointed her finger and said, 'Never say that. Remember a mother is never old.'

In May, the Jews of Lodz were enclosed in a ghetto. We now knew that rumors that a ghetto was going to be built in Warsaw were true. Mother panicked, 'Oh my God, they're going to close us up! We have to do something.' Mother started to buy all kinds of provisions for us to stockpile at my sister's in Warsaw against the day we would all be locked up in the Ghetto. I carried the food to my sister's by train. The trip into Warsaw took a half-hour. Once there I would store half the food and sell the other half. I would take the profit and go back to Grodzisk to buy more food. I often made two trips a day into Warsaw. I was thirteen years old and had become a smuggler.

One day, returning home from a trip to my sister's, I found a beautiful lady visiting with Mother. Her pitch-black hair was drawn back. She wore a black tailored suit over a white blouse pinned close at the neck by a big cameo brooch and high-heeled black patent leather shoes. I could not take my eyes off her. Mother introduced me to her, as she always introduced me, as her little girl. The woman's name was Regina Cukier; I was star-struck. Mother called her Rifkaleh. I knew who she was because Mother had told me about her many times. They used to be friends and neighbors. Regina Cukier had been a poor, uneducated girl with a great talent. She had become a popular stage actress in Poland's Jewish theater, and later on, in the world. Mother always talked about how Regina could sing and dance. When Regina performed in Warsaw Mother never missed a performance. Mother loved the theater.

Regina sized me up and asked me to come close to her. When I did she pulled up my skirt saying, 'I want to see if you have nice legs, so that when the war ends I will take you to America. I hear that you can dance.' I realized that Mother had been bragging about my school play performances.

By the time Regina came to visit Mother in Grodzisk, they were related by marriage. In London, Regina had married Mother's first cousin Karl Cimbalist who was an actor, producer and impresario. Mother was offended that her cousin Karl had not come with her. Regina defended him by saying, 'You must forgive him; he is very busy preparing our show in Warsaw.'

Regina Cukier and Karl Cimbalist were trapped in Poland by the war. They had come from London, England, to perform in Warsaw. Their misfortune was that they had never obtained the foreign citizenship which they now needed to leave Poland.

By the summer of 1940 the Germans issued orders to all the Jewish Committees throughout occupied Poland: every Jewish male between the ages of sixteen and twenty one had to register with their local committee for three months of work in a labor camp. Tusha, now seventeen years old, and all his friends were on the list. Two groups were going to be sent, one group now in summer and the second group in autumn.

Reinberg, a close friend of my parents, worked on the committee. Mother went to him for advice. He would not give her any. But Raizel gave Mother the best advice. She said, 'Wait. Let him go with the second group. Wait for the first group to come back as promised.' Mother did not heed her advice. She reasoned that Tusha would be better off working outside during the summer rather than later on in the cold of winter. She sent Tusha off with the first group.

During the summer Uncle Lazar returned to Grodzisk. He had been among a Polish group of prisoners of war finally released by the Germans. When he had been taken prisoner he feared that the Germans would immediately kill all the Jewish soldiers. Since he was red-headed and had a Polish sounding surname, he had passed himself off as a Pole.

The summer months passed and we did not receive any letters nor any sort of news from Tusha. We were now certain that we would never see him again. Mother was beside herself; she could not stop crying. She blamed Father for coming back from Russia, 'If you would have stayed there with him we would have been spared all this.' She got sicker and sicker with grief. She was unable to walk and took to her bed. Mother lay in bed crying, blaming herself for this catastrophe. 'It's all my fault, if I had listened to my sister ... and I say my sister is not smart ... if only I would have listened to her.'

By fall, we learned that Mother's worst fears were being realized. Our boys had been sent to Belzec[8], a labor camp on the new border with Russia run by the brutal SS. Some of our boys, those from the well-to-do families, started coming back from Belzec. Exorbitant amounts of money had been extorted from their parents to pay to have them sent home. They all arrived home on the brink of death due to the beatings that had been inflicted on them.

The boys who were able to talk described the horrors they had endured. The SS made them dig graves under trees. Other boys were forced to climb up into the trees. The SS then shot them out of the trees so that they fell into the graves their friends had dug. Then the boys had to bury their dead friends. We now knew that the purpose of the labor camps was to kill all the young Jewish males. Mother despaired of ever seeing her youngest son come home alive. The Germans knew which boys came from well-to-do families and let their parents know that if they wanted to give their sons a Jewish burial they would have to pay, and pay dearly, to have the bodies of their sons sent home.

When we heard that Berek Gothelf, a close friend of my brother's, had just returned home, Mother and I ran to see him. His family refused to let us in to see him. As we stood in their doorway they explained why; Berek was about to die. He had been beaten until his lungs had collapsed. But when Berek heard Mother's voice at the door he asked to see her. With his last breath he whispered Mother's name and assured her that my brother, Tusha, was still alive.

A few days later a letter arrived. It had been mailed from Kolopilzno, a town near Belzec. The name of the sender was a Polish female. My brother, Tusha, wrote: 'Dear parents. Don't worry, I am well and I am working. Soon, I will write another letter.' Our spirits soared when we read his letter. We waited and prayed every single day to get another letter with more news from Tusha.

One day the Germans announced that they were going to burn down Grodzisk's main synagogue. They informed the local population that they were free to carry away as much wood as they could from the building. With the weather growing colder and the need for firewood great, the Poles began tearing apart the synagogue. The Germans burnt the remains of the ravaged synagogue to the ground.

Now the rumors circulating that we would soon be evacuated into the Warsaw Ghetto were taken seriously.[9] I started carrying provisions to my sister's twice a day. My parents were now desperately selling off their possessions to obtain cash for the inevitable day when we would be confined in the Ghetto.

We were still in Grodzisk in early December when a second letter from Tusha finally arrived. He wrote that he would be coming home during the Christmas holidays for a visit. We could not understand this. Furlough from a death camp? How was this possible? We could not believe the letter. And then we wondered if we would still be here for him to find us.

Several days later I returned home from one of my daily runs to Channa's in Warsaw to find my brother Tusha lying in bed. I immediately feared that he was sick or crippled. He quickly assured me that he was well, but that Mother insisted that he lie in bed and rest. He had already told his story to my parents, but I had to hear it for myself and made him tell me the whole story again.

When Tusha got to the Belzec work camp he had the good luck to run into a friend of Schloime's who had arrived there in a previous group. Schloime's friend arranged for Tusha to work in the kitchen with him. This was one of the safer jobs and they had access to food.

After seeing most of the boys with whom they had arrived killed off, Tusha and the other boys working in the kitchen knew they were going to be killed next. They decided that they must escape the camp if they were to have any chance of saving their lives. Their plan was simple: as soon as it got dark enough they would all make a run for it. The SS could not catch them all. And they had their lives to gain if they made it.

When it got dark enough they all started running from the camp. The SS pursued. With the SS in pursuit Tusha jumped over a fence. In mid-air a bullet hit him in the thigh. He fell over the fence and found himself in a lumber yard. He hid himself in one of the lumber stacks. Once hidden he managed to take off his underwear and used it to staunch the blood flowing from his wound. Fortunately the bullet had just cut his leg and not lodged in it. He then fell asleep until early morning.

When Tusha awoke he crawled out from his hiding place. His leg was very stiff and painful as he limped away. He didn't have any idea of where he was or where he was going. He didn't go very far before he came to a house surrounded by a gated fence. Inside the gate was a well with a water pump. He was terribly thirsty and needed to wash his wound. He pumped up some water, drank and started washing himself.

As Tusha was cleaning his wound a little boy of about five years old appeared from inside the house. He was wearing the typical Nazi schoolboy uniform. The boy came close to Tusha and greeted him with a Heil Hitler salute. Tusha saluted back. Not wanting the boy to run off and raise an alarm he took out the harmonica he always carried and began to play it. The child was so happy that he begged him, 'Play more, play more!' Then Tusha heard the boy's father calling him from inside the house. However, the boy did not answer his father's call; he wanted to stay and listen to the harmonica.

Tusha could hear the footsteps of the boy's father approaching as he came looking for his son. He looked at the doorway and saw the boy's father dressed in the uniform of a high-ranking German Army officer. His heart sank. He stopped playing. Tusha could see that the boy's father knew immediately that he was one of the boys who had escaped the Belzec Camp. But for his own reasons he said to Tusha, 'Keep playing.' Tusha played on. 'Nice ... nice. You must be hungry,' and he sent the boy into the house for a sandwich. Tusha could see he was trying to decide what to do with him. He then said to Tusha, 'Wash up some more. Wash up. Now what is your profession? Can you sew?' Tusha replied, 'Yes I can sew.' 'Good. Finish up and I'll take you somewhere.' As Tusha ate the sandwich the officer studied him. He did not ask Tusha any further questions.

Tusha followed the officer deep into a forested area. Tusha was now afraid. He was thinking, 'Maybe he's just taking me here to kill me where nobody will see us.' But they soon came to a factory hidden deep in the forest and the officer led Tusha into an adjacent workshop run by a German SS foreman. Tusha noticed that all the workers there were interned Jewish tailors. The officer handed my brother over to the SS foreman and said, 'I'm placing this boy in your charge. Take care of him and give him work.' My brother could not believe his ears. The SS foreman sized him up and said, 'You are going to work for me. Not in the factory but in here. You will be in charge of looking after my uniforms. See that they are cleaned and pressed and that my shoes are polished.' Tusha could not believe his luck.

The work was easy, the food was good and the SS foreman took a liking to him. Tusha got to know a young Polish girl working in the kitchen of the sewing factory. She was from Kolopilzno. It was she who had risked mailing his letters to us.

With Christmas approaching, the SS foreman began preparing to visit his family in Germany. He told Tusha, 'While I'm away you will go and see your family.' He gave Tusha a three-week leave, coupons for the canteen and loaned him an aluminum valise for the trip home. Tusha used the coupons to buy cigarettes for Father and chocolate, sardines and Swiss cheese for the rest of us. With his papers stamped with the swastika, Tusha was free to ride the trains wherever they went.

Tusha had brought home his bloodied underwear. His thigh had healed, leaving just a small scar. He told us how each one of the boys from Grodzisk had perished in the Belzec work camp and described the macabre joy the SS got from shooting boys out of trees. Tusha was planning to go back to work for the SS foreman once his leave was up. But one week before his leave was over we were informed by the Jewish Committee that all Jews were being expelled from Grodzisk. We could take whatever we could carry and go into the Ghetto. They did not care where we went in the Ghetto, whether we had family or a place to go to or whether we were in the streets. We had to go. Many Poles welcomed this development. Now they could take over empty Jewish homes and buy our possessions for next to nothing.

Mother still had furniture, portraits, and other items of sentimental value. A Polish friend of hers offered to buy her bedroom set, but Mother could not part with it. Mother's friend said, 'Well if you don't want to sell it I can keep it for you.' Mother thought that this was a better option; maybe one day she would return for it. Her friend also said, 'I'll also store your pictures for you, those of your grandfather and those religious things and when the war is over you will have them back.' Mother entrusted her with everything. Mother's favorite credenza went to a farmer in Chrzanow. We sold our remaining household goods for whatever we could get.

Our hearts were heavy as we left our beloved Grodzisk carrying our pillows, blankets and a few items of clothing. We were being up-rooted from the place where we had been born and had lived for generations and we were being thrown into a ghetto. Our good fortune was that my sister's apartment was within the Ghetto walls. We had a place to go. The four of us moved in with Channa, Max and five-year old Felunia. We were now six adults and a child in a one-room apartment at 43 Ogrodowa Street. Channa and Max had been forced to leave their three-room apartment on Leshno because it was outside the Ghetto walls. They had been lucky to find this place. Many others were not so fortunate. They arrived in the Ghetto stripped of possessions, without any money, without the means of earning a living, and with nowhere but the streets to live in.

Once we were in the Ghetto, Tusha's leave was up. He asked our advice. Should he go back or stay? We debated, but we had no answer. My brother packed his little valise and again asked us for advice. No one said a word. Father finally said, 'My son, do what your heart tells you to do.' Tusha kissed us all goodbye, closed his valise and left.

The tension was unbearable and we all broke down crying. Not a minute passed before the door opened. It was Tusha. He could not leave. He put down the valise and said, 'Whatever will happen with you will happen to me. As long we are all together, that is all that matters to me.'

During this early period in the Ghetto I learned from my Aunt Chaiah, from Brandenburg, of the fate of her daughter, Paula. The war broke out the day Paula was to leave the *kibbutz* for Palestine. The children on the *kibbutz* were dispersed among the Jewish community and Paula was taken in by a Jewish doctor and his family in Lemberg. Chaiah was able to visit her there once before we were imprisoned in the Ghetto. In the subsequent chaos Chaiah never saw or heard from Paula again.

By January, 1941, Chaim and his wife's family had also been forced into the Warsaw Ghetto. They rented an apartment on Nalevkey Street. Chaim came to see us every day. One day he came to bid us goodbye. He and his father-in-law were going to buy their way out of the Ghetto. They were going to a city called Wegrow where Jews were still relatively free. Wegrow was very close to a place called Treblinka. My Aunt Raizel, her husband Lazar and my cousin Uteh also fled the Ghetto. They went to the city of Rawa. We had heard rumors that in Rawa, despite Jews being restricted to certain parts of the city, there was more freedom than in the Warsaw Ghetto and even more important, food was easier to come by. Raizel promised to write and let us know what the situation was really like there.

No one could survive on the rations[10] which we were given in the Ghetto. The rations consisted of 250 grams of bread and nothing else. It was not long before people were starving and dying in the streets. Because Mother had the foresight to store provisions, we did not go hungry. Mother was always giving some of our provisions to our relatives who were already starving. She would wrap some of the barley, or peas, or flour, in a piece of newspaper for them. Max, my brother-in -law, tried to stop her. He said to her, 'You cannot keep doing that. I have a small child.' Mother rebuked him by asking, 'How can you eat knowing that the other is hungry?' She kept giving out our food and our supply dwindled rapidly. Mother did whatever she could to keep her relatives alive.

There were only two ways to get food in the Ghetto; one either had to purchase it at inflated prices from those who smuggled it in, or to smuggle it in oneself. Smuggling food into the Ghetto became the only way to avert death by starvation. Buying smuggled food required a lot of money, which we did not have. We had no choice but to smuggle. And smuggling was dangerous.

To smuggle one had to first get outside the Ghetto walls. To do so you had to get past the Jewish Police[11], the Polish Police and the German Gendarmes. Once outside the Ghetto there were Poles who preyed on Jews. They hunted for Jews whom they could rob. The worst of these Poles not only robbed Jews but then betrayed them to the Germans for the reward offered for turning in Jews.[12] In addition many Polish vendors were unwilling to sell to Jews because if they were caught they would be sentenced to three months of hard labor. Finally, one had to get back into the Ghetto with the purchased goods. You had to get past all three police groups again to get back inside the Ghetto walls.

If adults were caught smuggling, they would be killed. Young teens like myself were more likely to be severely beaten than killed, but it could go either way. It depended on which police caught you. If the Jewish Police caught you and there were no German Gendarmes around for them to answer to, then a bribe could get you free. If the Polish Police caught you and there were no German Gendarmes around, you lost your goods, your money and you could get a beating as well. If you were caught by the Germans, or by one of the other groups in the presence of Germans, you could expect only the worst.

By the time I was thirteen years old I had become my family's lifeline. I was the one who smuggled. No one in the family was better suited for the task than I. I was a young female, agile as a cat.[13] Once or twice a day I made a run out of the Ghetto by any means possible to buy provisions. If I could not get out at a checkpoint I climbed over the Ghetto walls and through the barbed wire when the Jewish Police were not watching or when they were distracted with someone or something else. Once on the other side, I had to evade the Polish Police and German motorcycle patrols. It was the same coming back in. First I had to dodge the Polish Police while they were catching someone else or bringing the poor children they had already caught over to the German Gendarmes. And then I had to get past the Jewish Police. I always had money on me to bribe the Jewish Police, who shared the money with the Polish Police, so that everyone would look the other way. Sometimes these methods failed and I had no choice but to run past the German Gendarmes controlling the Ghetto gates.

My best route out and back into the Ghetto was the check point on Zelazna-Grzybowska. It was also close to where we lived on Ogrodowa. When I returned into the Ghetto with the goods I had purchased, usually a few kilograms of barley, flour and peas, Father would take them from me and give me money to go back out for another run. He resold part of what I brought in and kept the rest for us.

We young smugglers studied and knew each and every German Gendarme. We gave them nicknames. One extremely skinny Gendarme we called the Dead One. A big fat Gendarme we nicknamed Balvan, the snow-man. Another extremely mean and dangerous one we labeled Ivan the Terrible. There was also one German officer who was known to us as Frankenstein. He was not a Gendarme but he came to the Ghetto to kill Jews, in particular those who were smugglers.[14]

In February, Father heard a rumor that there were many Jews staying at Reinberg's in Grodzisk. Reinberg was his friend who had been on the Jewish Committee. He was a carpenter by trade. The Germans needed furniture and had given Reinberg a workshop, near where the synagogue had been, and permission to employ approximately fifty workers. Those fifty carpenters brought their families to Grodzisk and the total number of Jews at Reinberg's swelled to a few hundred people. Father suggested that the next time I was outside the Ghetto on a smuggling run, I should go to Grodzisk and see if this rumor about Reinberg's carpentry shop was true.

The next time I left the Ghetto I took the electric train into Grodzisk and walked past the charred ruins of the synagogue to Reinberg's. I could not believe my eyes at the sight of so many Grodzisker Jews employed in his workshop. They did not want to attract any attention to themselves and did not go into the town's streets. However, there were many other Grodzisker Jews roaming around town. They had managed to get out of the Ghetto and return to Grodzisk where they worked on the surrounding farms in exchange for food. When I returned to the Ghetto I told Father that what he had heard was true, but more important was the presence of those working for the local farmers.

We decided that instead of sitting around and eating up our food supply, Father should come back to Grodzisk with me and ask his good friend Szewczyk if he could stay on his farm and work for him. The next day we bribed our way out of the Ghetto and set out for Grodzisk. We went directly to the Szewczyk farm in Chrzanow four kilometers from Grodzisk. When we got there Mr. Szewczyk's reply to Father's proposal was, 'Of course! You can stay here as long as you want. And you can work in the fields only if you want something to do. But I'm going to keep you here.' I left Father with the

Szewczyks that very day. I bought a few kilograms of provisions and smuggled them back into the Ghetto.

I reported to Mother that, 'Father is fine. He is with the Szewczyk family and he is going to have good food and everything he needs.' Then I said, 'You know what Mother? It would be a good idea to bring you to Grodzisk, too. You'll see all your people there. Reinberg is a good friend of yours. You can stay with father's cousin, Sarah Burman Dancyger. She has a big house. I've already spoken to her and she said that, 'I always have place for your mother.' Of course this action had been planned beforehand by my sister and I. We knew that Mother would not pass up an opportunity to see her beloved Grodzisk again. And she did not.

I dressed Mother like a peasant to hide her Jewish features. Again I bribed the police to leave the Ghetto. I brought Mother to Sarah Burman Dancyger's house. It was packed with people taking refuge there. Mother said to me, 'How can I stay here? They are sitting on the floor and cannot even stretch their legs out.' Sarah replied, 'What can I say? Whoever comes I let in.'

Mother asked me to take her to see a Polish friend of hers, a widowed woman with three children. This woman used to clean our curtains and finer household goods. Mother used to give her stockings. They had become very good friends. She lived right across from the police station on Kilinskego. I walked with Mother to her house. Our hearts were pounding as we passed the police station.

I could not believe how happy this woman was to see Mother and how warmly she received us. She immediately sat us down and began to prepare a good meal. Without any hesitation she said to Mother, 'Mrs. Burman, stay here with me for a while, it will do you good. I know what is happening in the Ghetto. Why don't you stay? You are going to eat well. I will take care of you.'

As we sat at the table looking out the window, we saw her daughter, a beautiful blond girl, coming into the yard with two men wearing German pilot uniforms. Mother became frightened. The Germans needed only to take one look at her dark hair and black eyes to know she was Jewish. The woman said to her, 'Mrs Burman, don't be afraid. When you are in my house there is nothing to fear. Those are nice Polish boys, *Volksdeutsche*; they are pilots. One of them is my daughter's fiancée. Please relax.' They came in and greeted us very politely. The pilots spoke perfect Polish. The daughter was very happy to see Mother and greeted her by name. Then she and her two friends went to another part of the house.

When it was time to leave I pleaded with Mother, 'What do you say? Give her a chance. She is begging you to stay with her.' Mother replied, 'All right, but come and see me in a day or two.' I promised that I would return. I said goodbye to Mother outside the house. With tears in her eyes, she said, 'You see, my child, when you do good in your life, it will come back to you.' I left her there and returned to the Ghetto that same day. I told Channa how well Mother had been received. She replied, 'Mother deserves that because she always goes out of her way to help others.'

Several days passed and Channa asked me if I had been back to Grodzisk to visit Mother. 'No.' 'Why not?' 'Because the minute she sees me she will want to come back to the Ghetto and she has it good there with this woman.' 'You cannot do that. She may be homesick. You better go and see her.'

Mother was waiting for me. She was sad and depressed. She was homesick and could not understand why I had left her there for so long without coming to seeing her. I told her, because the minute I came back she would want to leave, and I wanted her to be warm, well fed and well taken care of. She said, 'It's enough. Now take me back.' I argued with her and convinced her to wait for me to come back because I had to go see how Father was doing. Outside the house her friend told me that Mother could not eat and that she had tried everything to make her feel comfortable.

I ran the four kilometers from Grodzisk to the Szewczyk farm. When I got to the farm Father was at work in a field. He had gained weight, had a nice tan, looked healthy and was in good spirits. I was very happy to see him like this. He told me not to worry about him, that he was being very well taken care of by the Szewczyks.

I returned to Mother in Grodzisk and told her that Father was well and that she should stay with this woman for as long as Father was on the farm. She agreed, but asked me to come back to see her in a day or two.

When I got back to the Ghetto I told Channa about Mother. She ordered me to go back to Grodzisk and bring mother home at once. By the time I got back to Grodzisk, Mother was gone. Her friend told me, 'Your mother left earlier today to visit her friends at the carpentry. It was raining and I asked her not to go, that she might catch cold. She told me she would come back. But she hasn't.'

I went to Reinberg's looking for her. People there told me that she had gone out with a friend and rumor had it that a young Pole had denounced them to the Germans as being Jewish women. They had been arrested and put on a train back to the Ghetto. I rushed back to the Ghetto. The rumor was true. Mother was back at Channa's before I was. Mother confirmed that a young Pole had pointed at them and started screaming, 'Jude! Jude!' The Germans arrested her and her friend and put them on the train. I asked her why she did not get off the train two stations further and go back to her friend's house. She answered that she had not thought of it.

A week or so later, I went to visit Father again. I spotted him working in a field. He saw me and waved for me to wait. With a sad face, he told me that he was returning with me to the Ghetto. I refused to listen and said, 'Look Tata, you look good, you are in the open air, you have plenty of food, the Szewczyk brothers treat you so well.' 'Yes, it is true,' he replied, 'but signs are being posted everywhere announcing that whoever harbors a Jew, will have his home burnt down. You must understand that I cannot subject these good people to such a tragedy. They have families; it is not fair on my part.'

The older Mr Szewczyk arrived and remarked to me how good Father looked. Father turned to him and said, 'Mr Szewczyk, I am leaving you; I am going back with my daughter to the Ghetto.' Mr Szewczyk was taken aback to hear that and asked, 'Did someone say something bad about your being here; is my family at fault?' 'No! No!' Father replied, 'You and your family are the kindest people. You are my good friends; one can see that when one is in need. I have to leave in order not to put you and your family in any danger.' Mr Szewczyk stood there speechless. Then he said, 'Mr. Burman, I want you to know that you are leaving of your own will.' Father and Mr Szewczyk embraced and then we left.

There was now no longer any reason for me to go back to Grodzisk. Every time I went back it was harder for me to leave. I could not accept the fact that we did not belong there any more. Yet I went back again.

Our money was dwindling. Mother decided that I should go into Grodzisk to see her Polish friend with whom she had stored her bedroom set and some sentimental items for safekeeping and ask her to buy them from us. She instructed me to take any amount the woman offered. The next time I was outside the Ghetto, I went to this woman's house. Her dog was in the yard and he started barking when he saw me. I was afraid to go into the gate. I called out the woman's name. There was no answer from the house. I spotted a movement among the curtains; it was her standing behind a curtain looking at me. She quickly moved away from the window. When I got back to Mother

I told her that her friend did not even want to talk to me. Mother was sure that I was wrong. Maybe it was not her at the window. She asked me to go again.

Once again I found myself in front of the Polish woman's house. Once again the dog kept me at bay. This time I went to a neighbor's door. Mrs Swarcinski, the wife of my father's good friend, was home. I told her that I was trying to see her neighbor, but the woman would not answer my calls. Mrs Swarcinski told me not to go back there; the woman had told her that she would turn me over to the Germans if she saw me again. Again I had to return to Mother empty-handed; I did not know what to tell her. I said, 'She is your friend, we trusted her.' She replied, 'What can we do?' Mother was very hurt. She had considered this woman a very good friend.

Our daily news consisted of the endless rumors circulating in the Ghetto, but from time to time we would get a letter from Chaim in Wegrow telling us that he was earning a living by traveling into the surrounding countryside and sewing for the local farmers. He was still free and alive.

I continued to smuggle. I bought provisions at Warsaw's Hala Kazimierza Wielkiego market, where I had developed a network of vendors. One woman, who really liked me, rapidly prepared anything I ordered so I could get back to the Ghetto before the guards changed. A grocer on Ogrodowa Street, Mr Freedman, bought anything I had to sell and always paid me a good price.

I had met Mr Freedman during one of my runs. On that day I was sneaking back into the Ghetto through a barbed wire fence, when a Polish policeman spotted me. He shouted for me to come back. Knowing that the Polish Police would not shoot, I did not stop. When I was halfway through the barbed wire a Jewish policeman caught me around the middle, tearing my jacket. By then I was on the Jewish side. Mr Freedman grabbed my parcel and helped me through, scolding the Jewish policeman, 'Leave that child alone! Can't you see she is risking her life to bring in some food.' Mr Freedman walked me to his store on Ogrodowa St. He was unaware that I lived on that street too. Mr Freedman was a fine man. He never put my products on the scale, he always took my word for their weight. He was also a religious man, and would always put his hand on my head and bless me: 'God be with you'.

One day Mr Freedman said, 'I have a favor to ask of you. Will you please take this letter to this address on Wronia Street? When you ring the bell, someone will open the gate. Just give them this letter.' I agreed to do it for him. Twice I delivered a letter to his Polish friends outside the Ghetto.

By now I was an established smuggler. I put my life on the line day in and day out, often twice a day. I had to do it, or my family would starve. I never listened to Mother as she tried to dissuade me from going on my runs with reasons like, 'It's cold today, or it's raining today. Don't go, we won't starve, we have enough food to last for a while.' I knew that every day conditions in the Ghetto were getting harsher and harsher. And it was only going to get worse. I had to prepare us. I began carrying a big hand muff in which I could hide things, like cigarettes, a piece of salami or the biscuits which I bought for Felunia. I also carried it for protection. I could cover my face with it when I was being beaten. The muff, once trimmed with fur, had belonged to Channa. Its fur trim was now gone. The Nazis had ordered the Ghetto to surrender all furs.[15]

One spring day in 1941 I had made two good runs and was feeling lucky. I decided to go for a third run. Mother begged me, 'Don't go. Don't be greedy. You went twice, you made your money today. Please don't go.' I did not listen. I went.

I bought my supplies and came back to the check point on Zelazna Street and Grzybowska. My luck had turned. The German guards had changed. The Deadman was on duty. He was dangerous. The guard would change again in two hours, but by then it would be curfew in the Ghetto and the streets would be empty. One hour after that and it would be curfew on the Polish side too. I had no choice but to take the tramway that ran through the Ghetto on Zelazna Street. My plan was to ride it into the Ghetto where I would jump off and run into any building I could. With luck I'd be safe.

While I stood at the tramway stop, waiting for the next tram, it started to rain. I was the only one standing there with a parcel. It was filled with barley. I started to regret my greed and not having listened to Mother's warning. I could not help myself and started crying. I did not want my crying to attract anyone's attention and stepped back against a wall to wipe my tears. My dirty hands streaked my face.

As I leaned against the wall, a kind-faced young woman in her thirties came to the tram stop. I debated with myself whether I should talk to her. She kept looking at her watch and then came over to me and said, 'I know you are from the Ghetto and it is curfew there. It is ten to eight and in a few minutes it will be curfew here too and no one will be allowed in the streets. 'Do you have a place to go?'

I began crying again and said, 'No, I don't.' She said, 'Come with me.' I did not know what to do. Should I go with her? Was she going to turn me in to the police or was she an angel sent from heaven? I had no choice but to follow her. We walked over to a building on Wronia Street. As we climbed the stairs to the first floor, she said, 'You will sleep here tonight and go back to the Ghetto in the morning.' She knocked on a door. It was opened by a good-looking young man in a stark-white shirt. We went in. It was a two-room apartment. I was introduced in a low voice, 'This child will stay here over night.' I could not hear what else this woman said to the young man. He turned to me and said, 'I will warm up some water for you to wash up with.' I realized that she did not live here. How could she leave me with this young man? I had mixed feelings. As the woman started to leave I went over and said, 'You cannot leave me here.' She replied, 'I have no choice. Don't worry, you are in good hands. This man will take good care of you.' Suddenly I remembered that the people to whom I had delivered letters for Mr Freedman were also on Wronia Street. But I knew that if I showed up there with someone else they would not even answer the door. I said, 'Could you take me to a place I know and stay a distance away while I go and see if these people will let me in?' She agreed. I was kicking myself that this idea had not entered my mind earlier. I always suspected that Mr Freedman had some kind of underground business with these people.

She walked me to within a few buildings of the address I wanted and then waited for me as I went up to the gate and rang the bell. While I was trying to open the latch of the gate, a man came out with his dogs and asked what I wanted. I said, 'Don't you recognize me? I bring you letters from Mr Freidman.' He said, 'Do you have a letter?' 'Yes, I have a letter,' I lied, 'Let me in.' As he turned to lead me into the house I waved to the woman that all was well. The man asked if anyone knew about my coming here. Not to lie again, I did not answer.

The aroma of a soup cooking filled the house. There were a number of people inside the house. I was asked for the letter. I confessed that I had no letter from Mr Freedman this time, but that they must surely remember me as having delivered letters from Mr Freedman to them before. I started crying as I told them my story and said I needed their help to get back into the Ghetto. 'I know you have the means to get into the Ghetto.' 'We won't discuss that,' one man said. 'You have to take me in tonight. My mother is a sick woman. If she doesn't see me tonight she will be sure that I am dead.' 'Don't worry,' he reassured me, 'stop crying now, wash up and have something to eat. You will be back in the Ghetto shortly.' I was given a towel to freshen up with and then a bowl of hot barley soup. 'Eat and go to sleep. We'll wake you up when we are ready.' Tired and half asleep, I did not comprehend what this all meant. How would I get back into the Ghetto during the night? I was thinking of my poor parents, my sister, my brother, my Felunia, Max, all sitting there crying and fearing that the worst had happened to me because I had not returned. I fell asleep near the stove.

During the night I was awakened, handed a blanket and told to put it over my head. 'Don't worry,' a voice said, 'you will be home soon. Now bend your head.' I do not know where they took me. I kept my head down and crawled. The voice was continuously telling me to keep my head down. Before I knew it I was in Mr Freedman's house. Mr Freedman said, 'Now go home, your parents must be awake waiting for you. I always knew that you were smart.'

It was three a.m. and still curfew as I walked the three blocks to where we lived. I rang the bell for the concierge. He came out cursing a blue streak, 'Who the hell is bothering me in the middle of the night!' When he saw me his whole demeanor brightened. He said, 'I'm so glad to see you. Your father was worried about you. Run. Run up fast to your apartment.' Father was always good to him and always shared his cigarettes with him.

When I opened the door they were all sitting there waiting for me. They looked at me as if I had risen from the dead. I told them how I had managed to get home. When I finished they looked at each other and did not say a word. I was glad they did not say anything. In the morning, Mother said, 'You are not to go out of the house, not today, not tomorrow. Never again will you put us in such agony.' I stayed home for one day and then started smuggling again.

I had one smuggling routine in which Father would help me. After buying my provisions on the Polish side I went to the tramway terminus on Narutowicza Street. A tram ran from here through a part of the Ghetto. I could not simply board the tram with my package, I would instantly be recognized as a Jewish smuggler and the tram conductor would refuse to let me aboard. If I got by him, a Polish passenger might turn me in for the reward. I had to be invisible and not attract any attention. I watched the conductors. When one of them left his tram unattended, to go for a coffee or on a break, I would sneak aboard and hide under a seat. The space under the seat was very small, just big enough for a small girl like me and my package. Sometimes a German gendarme would board the tram to make sure it was empty. I would hear his voice and see his boots. When the conductor got back on and started to board the new passengers I would slide out from under the seat and sit down again unseen, so that it looked like I had been among the first to board. When the tram crossed through the Ghetto, I would look for Father at a pre-arranged point. When I saw him I would throw him my package, then jump off and run into the crowd. We would do this a couple of times a day.

My success as a smuggler did not go unnoticed by the rest of the family. One day my Aunt Chaiah came to me and asked me if I would take my cousin Basha with me so that she, too, could learn to smuggle and help keep her family alive. I agreed. Basha was a small blue-eyed, blond of my age; she could easily pass for a Pole. The next day I took her on her first smuggling run. She was in a state of complete dread. I tried to reassure her that everything would be fine. I began to worry about how we were going to pass as Poles with her so visibly afraid. I did not know what to do. I began to laugh. The more she was afraid, the more I laughed.

My laughing worked. She pulled herself together. I told her not to walk next to me. 'Walk either in front of me or behind me.' We went over the wall to get out of the Ghetto and took the train to Grodzisk. I took her to my vendors where we bought supplies. We then went back to the Narutowicza tramway terminus. There we snuck aboard an empty tram and hid under the seats. When the tram went through the Ghetto we jumped off. I took Basha with me a couple of times more and then she struck off on her own.

During my dealings with Mr Freedman I realized that he was quite wealthy. His dealings with many small-time smugglers like myself was nothing in comparison with the trade he carried on with the Poles through the sewer system. He even sold fresh milk in the Ghetto. I learned that he had several cows stabled inside the Ghetto. I also got to know his daughter, Eva, and his ailing wife. Eva was about twenty years old, and as befitted a rich man's daughter, she dyed her hair, wore make-up, red lipstick and red nail polish. I thought she would be a great girl friend for my brother Tusha, and knew that she would fall for him immediately. But Tusha refused to come with me to meet her. He was shy. He was not the Casanova that Schloime was.

With his wife ailing, it occurred to me that Mr Freedman could use a woman around the house. I blurted out, 'Mr Freedman, don't you need a woman to cook and clean for you? I know of a very good woman.' He looked at me surprised and said, 'Yes, yes! Send her in.' The next day Chaya Lichtenstajyn's mother began working for Mr Freedman. She now had food and a good place to stay. Mother was so proud of me for helping her.

By now the Ghetto was overflowing with people. Every day more and more Jews were brought in from the towns and small cities surrounding Warsaw. Thousands of people with no shelter were living in the streets. Men, women and children were sprawled on the sidewalks, dying of hunger and disease. I saw the faces of people I knew, lying dead in the street. Nobody could stop me from going out to bring in food. Everyone in the family depended on me. No matter how hard my brother-in-law Max tried, there was no work to be found. Max would have done any kind of work so as not to depend on me. I even supplied him with cigarettes. I continued to smuggle.

Bad luck caught up with me once again. That day I had been lucky to find good provisions and I bought a lot. When I returned to the Zelazna and Grzybowska check point, I was surprised to see that the German Gendarmes had changed. Nor was I the only one affected by the change. A few other teens assessing the situation knew that we were going to have a hard time getting through and if these gendarmes caught you, you would be lucky to get away with only a severe beating. I waited for an opportunity to run through the check point. Using an oncoming tramway as a cover I started running. The German Gendarme saw me, shot at me and missed. In a rage he ordered a Jewish policeman to run after me. The shot attracted a crowd.

A woman I knew was standing among the crowd watching my dilemma. Her children were also smugglers. I ran towards the crowd. As I passed her, I threw her my parcel, ducked into the closest building and ran up some stairs. The Jewish policeman caught up to me and grabbed me by the neck. He hauled me down into the street and dragged me by the neck towards the German Gendarme. Jews in the street began yelling at the Jewish policeman to let me go. He shouted back, 'I will not give up my neck for hers.' He brought me back to the German Gendarme at the check point. The German Gendarme was busy checking people in and out of the Ghetto. The Jewish policeman stood me up against a wall to await my sentence.

While I waited I looked over the pile of packages which had been taken away from people. I noticed a parcel containing three kilograms of butter. Each kilogram was packed separately in heavy green leaves. I could not pass up this opportunity. Things were not going to get any worse for me no matter what I did now. I bent down pretending to place my parcel with the other confiscated packages and quickly stuffed the three kilograms of butter into my hand muff. I straightened up and waited for the worst.

The German Gendarme turned suddenly, grabbed me, slapped and then backhanded me in the face. I heard my teeth breaking. I broke free and turned to run. He grabbed me again and spun me back towards him. He let go of me to kick me in the torso. I pivoted to avoid his kick. His foot struck my rear, instead of my midriff. He kicked me so hard it propelled me out of his reach. I used the momentum created by the force of his kick to continue running despite the pain. I ran towards the crowd, rubbing my behind as it went numb. I could not feel my legs, but they kept running. I expected to hear another shot, but the German Gendarme was not shooting. I made it into the crowd. Now I started to hurt, but at the same time I was very happy that I still had the three kilograms of butter safely in my muff. I found the woman to whom I'd thrown my parcel. She had already given it to Father. I met Father as he was coming back to see what had happened to me. I was glad that he had not been present to witness the beating I had received. Father had had enough for that day. He said, 'I would rather endure hunger than have you go through what you went through today.'

Miraculously, a postcard arrived from Raizel in Rawa. It read that they were free and had plenty of food and that we should do everything possible to join them there. We started making plans to leave for Rawa. My parents, Tusha and I would go. My sister Channa, Max, and little Felunia would stay. We were glad that we could leave them with all the provisions that we had accumulated.

Leaving the Ghetto to travel to Rawa, about 100 km from Warsaw, during the summer of 1941, was not an easy task. My parents were now in their fifties, Tusha was nineteen years old and I had recently turned fifteen. I arranged everything. I bribed the Jewish Police with enough money so that they could pay off the Polish Police. The route out of the Ghetto was over a high brick wall. This was not easy for my parents. The Jewish Police arranged for some strong men to help carry my parents over. On the other side of the wall the Polish Police were on the lookout for German motorcycle patrols.

I had told Father, 'When you get over the wall walk to the restaurant you will see on the corner. Go inside and wait until you see Mother. Then come out and walk slowly toward the train station.' Father went over first, then Mother. We put a flowered scarf over her head to hide her Jewish features.

Tusha went next and I went last. As soon as Father saw Mother he started walking towards Novogrodzka Street where we could take the electric train to Grodzisk. We walked a good distance from one other so that we would not appear to be together. We were afraid of attracting the attention of Polish hooligans looking for Jews they could extort money from and then turn in to the Germans for a reward. Slowly we walked the distance towards the electric train.

We arrived in Grodzisk without incident and went straight to the house of Father's good friend, Mr Swarcinski. Unfortunately he was not home. His wife was not very sympathetic and flatly stated that we could not stay in her house overnight. Mother's friend, the woman with whom she had stored her bedroom set and some items of sentimental value for safekeeping, lived nearby. Mother asked Mrs Swarcinska about her, saying that she would sell those things she had stored with her for whatever she would offer. Mrs. Swarcinska told Mother what she had already told me: 'Do not go there because she has told me that if you ever showed up she would report you to the Germans.' Mrs Swarcinska gave us some bread and said, 'You cannot stay the night. I will not risk my life. You must leave.'

It was our bad luck that Mr Swarcinski was not home; he would have let us in. Father said that he was probably out at his mistress's or playing cards. Night was falling and we had no place to go. It was too risky to go out to the Fuchses and stay with them overnight. They were *Volksdeutsche* and some Germans might be visiting them. We decided to set out for Rawa in the dark. It was seventy-two kilometers from Grodzisk, but Father knew all the side roads.

When it was dark we put our shoes over our shoulders, Mother's scarf back over her head and started to walk. When we tired, Father knocked on a farmer's door and offered to pay him to let us sleep in the barn for the night. The farmer refused our money and told us to go into the barn. He brought us bread and warm milk and asked us to please leave before dawn so that his neighbors would not see us.

We started walking before dawn. Anyone seeing us would think that we were going off to work. A farmer driving his horse and wagon overtook us. Father stopped him and offered him money to take us to Rawa. He knew we were Jews and refused. The next farmer driving his horse and wagon hesitated before accepting Father's offer. He told us that not only was he afraid of the Germans but that other Poles might denounce us. He gave each of us a tool to hold. Clutching shovels and rakes we looked like peasants going to work and did not arouse the suspicion of the many Germans and Poles who passed us on the road. Within two kilometers of Rawa, the farmer stopped his wagon and said he was not going any further. We walked the last two kilometers into Rawa, which was overflowing with people who had fled the Warsaw Ghetto and other cities and towns.

Our Rawa relatives were the children of the Bubbeh's sister Mindel. They received us warmly and accommodated us as best as they could. Mindel herself was in her eighties and bedridden. My parents stayed with one cousin and I was sent to sleep at another cousin's house. I slept on the floor with nine other people in one room. Among them was my Aunt Raizel, her husband Lazar, and my cousin Uteh. Lazar was working on farms in exchange for food. There was plenty of food in Rawa. We were not hungry and I did not have to risk my life. Now Mother's main concern became how Channa was doing in the Ghetto.

Father immediately bought needles, thread and zippers. Every day he and Tusha went out to trade their supplies and services to the local farmers. Father could never ask for food and give nothing in return. While the men were out working and bartering for food, we women spent our days cooking, cleaning and laundering. In our spare time we visited Mother's family and friends. As always, Mother took me with her everywhere. I saw that we were the lucky ones. We had relatives who had taken us in. Hundreds of other people who had fled the Ghetto and other cities were sleeping in the park and streets of Rawa.

Raizel welcomed us to Rawa by inviting us to a meal of meat and vegetables at a Polish family's house. She explained that since our Rawa relatives were very religious, she could not cook the non-*kosher* meat there and had arranged to cook it elsewhere. When we got there she took out a huge pot of meat and potatoes from the oven. It was delicious. We had not eaten meat in ages. But Mother became suspicious and asked Raizel, 'Is this horse meat?' 'Yes, what else did you expect?' When Mother heard that she had eaten horse meat she began to vomit. I had never seen Mother that sick in her life. It took a long time before Mother would talk to Raizel again. Father found a Polish farm family willing to keep my brother. Tusha agreed to stay and work for them. The farmer was a tall, husky, middle-aged man and his wife was a robust woman. They had a prosperous farm and a solid stone farm house in which Tusha had his own room. They were delighted to have Tusha with them and he was treated very well. They explained to Mother that they had lost a son and now God had sent them another one. Whenever we visited Tusha the farm couple gave us food to take home. We had plenty of food and, as always, shared it with those less fortunate. I wrote to my sister Channa about our good fortune. Her letters were very sad. She informed us about everything going on in the Ghetto. We knew that the mail might be censored and always wrote with that in mind.

On our way home from the last visit to see Tusha on the farm, Mother suggested that we should take a short cut through the Jewish cemetery because it was getting late. Since Mother was not feeling well I was carrying the more than ten kilos parcel of food we had been given. The package consisted of potatoes, eggs, barley and cherries. I followed her into the cemetery. Because of the war the cemetery had been neglected this year. There was no one to look after it. Everything was overgrown with weeds and grasses. As I followed Mother I stepped into a hole and fell down wrenching my ankle. I could not stand up. The pain was excruciating. My ankle and leg began to swell immediately. Mother was too weak to help me. She took some of the contents of the food package and went for Father. I waited alone in the cemetery, afraid that Father would not get there before dark. The entire time my leg was throbbing. It was almost dark when he arrived. Father had to carry me and the rest of the food package back into Rawa. I was put into a bed with one of my Rawa cousins. She wasn't thrilled with my company, especially since I spent the entire night writhing in pain.

The next day my leg was even worse. The swelling had grown and the discoloration had spread up my leg. Some of the local women came over and placed a plant poultice on my leg. The drawing action of the poultice caused the pain to increase. To let my cousin sleep undisturbed I dealt with the pain by tearing at the walls with my nails. Finally the swelling suppurated releasing an incredible amount of pus from the broken skin. After that the swelling went down and my ankle healed quickly.

Mother was always on the look out for people from Grodzisk. One day she was looking out the window and saw someone she knew. She went running out and came back with Cyma Hirsh and her two children. Cyma was the wife of Opolion Hirsh *'The Chish'*, our spooler, who had shown me how he could devour a fifteen-egg omelet. Cyma told us that he had died of hunger in the Warsaw Ghetto. Cyma had managed to escape from the Ghetto with her two children, a ten-year-old girl and a six-year-old boy. They had been sleeping in the woods and were very dirty.

Mother brought them water to wash with and prepared something to eat. The boy started crying that he wanted to eat first. When Cyma took off her blouse to wash up, Mother noticed bruises on her body and asked her, 'Cyma, what is that?' Cyma replied, 'I don't know if I should tell you.' Then to Mother's surprise Cyma showed her other parts of her body where pieces of flesh had been bitten out of her. Pointing to her six- year old son, she said, 'See this boy? This child is a monster. He is just like his father. When he is hungry he bites me and eats my flesh. If I had the strength and the will-power to kill him, I would. But I cannot. He is my child. Now my daughter is doing it, too.' Cyma broke down and cried, 'This child is not human; I gave birth to a monster!' Neither Mother nor I could believe what we were hearing. After Mother did what she could for them, Cyma and her children left to look for shelter. We never saw them again.

By late summer of 1941 Mother's health took a turn for the worse. She got weaker every day. She now told Father that she wanted to be taken back to Warsaw. 'Bring me back into the Ghetto. There I have Channa to take care of me. I have my bed to sleep in. I don't have to lie on a floor. Please Motta, take me to Channa's. When I heard this I went into a panic. I pleaded with her not to go back into the Ghetto: 'Ma, how can you do that? We left Channa what little food we had. We know there is nothing to eat in the Ghetto. We have heard that so many people from our city have died there already. Why do you want to go back to the Ghetto; Channa herself has nothing?' 'I don't want to know anything. If I die, I'll die there. On my bed. With my daughter.' I could not change her mind. I feared that she would die of hunger without me there to bring her food. I immediately wrote to my sister telling her about the situation and asked her what we should do.

Mother made her plans. Father was to accompany her back to the Ghetto and then he would return to Rawa to stay with me. My brother was in good hands. I was to stay with the sister of the farmer whom Tusha was with and baby sit her young children until Father came back.

On the day my parents left for the Ghetto my Aunt Raizel, Uteh and I walked with them the three kilometers to where the woods began. There we said goodbye. I could not bear parting with them. I was filled with dread that I would never see them again. I was afraid that Father would not return to be with me. I cried and begged Mother, 'Please wait until Channa answers my letter before you go back!' She refused to wait and they left. As soon as I returned to the house in Rawa one of my cousins waved a post card at me. I grabbed the card. It was from my sister. She wrote, 'I beg you not to come. The hunger here is acute. Max can't do anything. He is unable to find any work. He is desperate and afraid that our food supply will run out. Everyday I take Felunia to his sister Franka's house for a meal. The situation in the Ghetto is very bad and getting worse every day. We are happy for your good fortune. You are free and not hungry. Do whatever you can to convince Mother and Father to stay in Rawa.'

Showing her the postcard, I asked Raizel to run after my parents with me. She refused, saying we would never catch up with them. I was furious with her. I ran by myself, clutching my shoes in my hands. When I approached the forest I hesitated. The road through the forest was four kilometers long and I was terrified of being alone in the woods. I feared that I would never reach the city of Biala, another five kilometers beyond the forest, before sundown.

My parents planned to stop in Biala for the night. From there they were to continue the following day to Grodzisk and then into Warsaw. They would have no problem entering the Ghetto. Every Jew was allowed in. The problem was getting out. Overcoming my fear and rising panic I began to run. I ran with all my might. My heart pounded in my chest. I ran to save my parents. I ran to keep them from returning to the Ghetto.

I arrived in the city of Biala after curfew. I had never been there before. I saw a horse-drawn wagon pull into a large yard filled with other horse-drawn vehicles. I followed the wagon into the yard and ran into the house it fronted. I knew that Father would be looking to hire someone with a horse and wagon to take them to Grodzisk. Distraught, I ran through the house asking everyone if they had seen a man and a woman with black hair. They all looked at me as if I were insane and pointed out that a lot of women have black hair. Running out of the house, an elderly man caught me, 'Don't you know there is a curfew in the city? Nobody should be in the street.' I screamed at him, 'I have to find my parents! To stop them from going to the Ghetto!' He let me go. As soon as I ran out of the yard I was stopped by two Jewish policemen. They asked me where I lived, who I was and did I not know there was a curfew? I started to cry and said, 'Look, I have to find my parents here; they are on their way into the Warsaw Ghetto. Here, look! Read this card my sister sent. I must find them and stop them.' They asked me, 'So where are you running to?' I replied,

'There is a family somewhere here in Biala where my parents might be! I must find them!' They replied, 'No! No! No! If the Germans catch you, they will kill you.' They took me to the police station.

The police station was only a dingy room with a bench in it. They ordered me to sleep on the bench saying that tomorrow I would be free to go out and look for my parents. I started to cry and pleaded with them to take me to the family I knew was here somewhere in Biala. 'They are my parents' friends. They could be staying there overnight.' They realized that I would scream all night so they asked me to described this family to them. My parents' friends had fled the Ghetto and lived in a barn in Biala. The policemen knew every newcomer in Biala and from my brief description of them took me directly to their barn and handed me over to them.

To my dismay, these people told me that my parents had been there earlier but were determined to go on to Grodzisk that day if they could find transportation. If they could not, they would return and spend the night there. My parents had not come back. The woman invited me to sleep over and suggested that in the morning I go out to the main road and watch for them. It was possible that my parents had not found transportation to Grodzisk that day and had slept somewhere else, in which case I could spot them leaving Biala. I had no choice but to spend the rest of the night there.

It was raining as I set out in the early dawn for the main road to Grodzisk. Shivering and hungry I stood in the rain scrutinizing every passing horse and wagon that drove by, hoping to see my parents. Luck was not with me. Aunt Raizel had been right; I could not catch up with them.

It was almost noon and I was still standing there hoping to see my parents, not knowing what to do, when I saw Channa Grzymek, a girl I knew from Grodzisk. It felt good to meet someone I knew. Her sister had married Handsome Yosel after his accident. She told me that the Buldock family from Grodzisk was also in Biala. They, too, had escaped the Warsaw Ghetto and now lived in a barn. Their son Berel Buldock was one of Tusha's friends. She took me to see them. Mrs Buldock was happy to see me. She comforted me and asked me not to cry. It was noon by then and she shared her soup with me. She also gave me water to wash with and said she would convince her husband and son to accompany me back to Rawa. I thought to myself, maybe I was being repaid for the good Mother always did for others.

Two days after I returned to Rawa, the woman for whom I was to baby-sit came, as she had promised my parents, to take me to her farm. I was not willing to go. She began speaking to me in a soft voice; somehow her kind words convinced me to go with her. I was astonished to see what a fine house she lived in. They were very prosperous farmers. She and her husband had two sons. Jurek was eleven years old, and Tadek was three years old. Her husband's brother, a mute, lived with them. I had never met such gentle people. The food was delicious and there was plenty of it. They treated me like their own daughter, just like Tusha was treated at her brother's farm. While they worked in the fields, I played with the little, chubby, red-cheeked Tadek. He was so cute, I adored him. Jurek was very polite and I always helped him with his school work.

Soon after my arrival I overheard a neighboring woman who was visiting my hostess say to her, 'Why do you do that for them? They aren't worth it.' She did not reply. Later in the day I mentioned the incident to her. She said, 'Don't mind her. I do what I feel I have to do.'

Whenever I became sick with worry about my parents' arrival in the Ghetto, I ran the four kilometers to Rawa to see if any mail had arrived for me. There was none. A few days later I was preparing to go to Rawa a second time. The good, gentle woman tried to talk me out of going, saying that there was a terrible typhus epidemic in the city. 'You may catch it and bring it here to my children.' But I refused to listen.

Walking into the house where Raizel lived, I found my cousin Uteh in bed sick. She was eating potato dumplings. I had some from her plate. There were no letters from my parents. I kissed my aunt goodbye and quickly ran back to the farm. Little Tadek, always so happy to see me, ran toward me. I grabbed him and kissed his cute round face.

Two days later, after helping Jurek with his homework, I began to feel sick. I started shivering. My body had never felt so cold. As soon as everyone left for work, I started a fire, hoping it would warm me up. Nothing helped. I was trembling. I felt that the only way to stop freezing was to put myself into the flames along with the wood I kept putting onto the coals. Now I began to feel guilty about not having listened to this good-hearted woman and was also worried about infecting the children.

When the couple came back from their day's work in the fields I tried to pretend I was fine, but she immediately saw that I was sick with typhus. She said, 'I see that you have fever. I asked you not to go to the city. I must protect my children and I don't want anybody to see you. The neighbors could inform on you and where would you go?' She moved me into her brother-in-law's room, which was still under construction, in the back of the house. He was moved into the barn. She nursed me. I could not believe that there were still such generous people in this world.

Two days later Tadek came running in, yelling, 'Your father is here! Your father is here!' Father came into the room, his shoes hanging over his shoulder. Father had had typhus fever during WWI. He took one look at me and muttered to me, 'I don't know how these people kept you here.' My fever was getting worse. He asked the farmer to bring us into Rawa. I was placed on a wagon wrapped in a blanket and covered with straw so that no one could see me.

The kindly farmer let us off in front of the Jewish Committee office in the center of the city. Father knew that one of Mother's childhood friends worked there. Father was sure this man would help get me admitted into the local hospital. Knowing that he would not be allowed to carry me into the Jewish Committee offices, Father took off his jacket, spread it on the sidewalk and put me on it. He told me to wait for him while he went to get me admitted to the hospital. By the time he returned my raging fever had caused me to move a few meters away and his jacket was gone. He hoisted me onto his back, and with the hospital admission papers in hand, he carried me to the hospital gate. The hospital itself was no more than a small bungalow.

At the gate I was taken away from him by two women. They took me into a small hut adjacent to the hospital and sat me down on a table. One held me while the other, scissors in hand, took hold of my braids to cut them off. As sick as I was, I grabbed her hand to stop her, but I had no strength. I said, You cannot do that to me! You cannot cut my hair!' The one holding me gently said, 'My dear child, if you survive your hair will grow again. We have to cut your hair. It will fall out. Let us cut your hair.' They cut my long braids off.

I was placed into a bed which already held another woman. We were lying head to foot. Even though I was sick and burning with fever, when my foot touched her body, I was aware that she was as cold as ice. I knew that this woman was dead. I had always heard that a dead person is as cold as ice. When the nurse came by to check on her, she just pulled the blanket over her head. Despite my fever I was horrified to be lying in bed with a dead person, but I was too weak to move.

Early the next morning I was placed in a bed near a window by myself. This luxury did not last long. The hospital was overcrowded. Within a few hours another woman was placed in the bed with me. She was a large, tall woman whom I knew. She, her husband and her children had visited my family here in Rawa. The typhus she had was of a different sort than mine. She was crazed and wildly violent from the fever. She would pull the blanket off me and cover herself as she cursed her husband and children. I was sure that at any moment she was going to jump on top of me and kill me. I was drifting in and out of consciousness and helpless to protect myself against her. During the day the nurses were around, but at night I was afraid to drift off. I started to cry, saying to the nurses, 'Please take her out! She is going to kill me!' After what may have been a couple of days, she was removed from my bed.

By now the continuous burning fever had me hallucinating. I was flying to heaven. I saw Tusha, wearing his olive green blazer, which suited him so well because of his big green eyes, standing on the hospital fence holding apples in his hands and looking in at me. I believed that he had come to fly with me. I remember thinking, 'This can't be real, I'm dreaming that my brother is here.'

When my fever broke there were apples on the table next to my bed. I asked the nurse about them. She told me that they were mine, that my brother had brought them for me when he had come to see me. 'We could not let him in but told him to look at you through the window. He was very concerned. I took the apples from him and promised to give them to you.' That was the last time I saw Tusha's beautiful face.

It was autumn when Father came to take me home from the hospital. I could not stand on my own two feet, let alone walk. Again, Father carried me on his back. I felt so sorry for him. He took me back to our relative's home, the small single room I had been in before. Now there were fewer people and I was given a bed. Aunt Raizel, Lazar and Uteh were still there. Uteh had already recovered from her bout with typhus. Father cooked for me. He prepared meals that I liked so that I would eat, gain weight and recover my strength.

I noticed that people who knew me did not recognize me when they saw me. I did not have a mirror and asked Father for one. He refused and would not give in to my pleas for one. Later that day, someone came in and told us that Rosa Frankel had died. She was the mother of my best friend Balcha and she had loved me like one of her own. I started to cry hysterically and screamed, 'Give me a mirror!' I was given one to calm me down. When I looked into it, I did not recognize myself. I was skinny and hairless. I looked like a boy.

After a while I started to feel better and I wanted Father to go see Tusha and tell him that I was well. He promised to go soon. But he would not leave my side. I also tried to convince him to go to the farmers and to accumulate some provisions in case we were forced back into the Ghetto. He said, 'When you are stronger I will go.'

Father continued nursing me into the autumn and I was starting to get stronger. It was already very cold and Father had still not collected any provisions. Again I pleaded with him. He finally agreed to do so the next day. I was relieved that I had convinced Father to begin gathering supplies and fell into a deep sleep.

A hand was gently rocking me awake. The murmur of my Father's voice calling my name penetrated my sleep. I became conscious of shouting and throbbing of truck engines outside. As I awoke Father told me that the Polish police had ordered all newcomers to leave the city. The Jewish citizens of Rawa could stay, but the rest of us were being rounded up and loaded into trucks waiting in front of the house. We were not told where we were being taken to. Father put a blanket around me and carried me out to the truck. Uncle Lazar had accumulated some provisions and carried them onto the truck. We had nothing.

BOOK THREE

TO THE GATES OF HELL

November 1941 – May 8, 1943

Father knew that we were traveling in the direction of Warsaw. We sat in silence as the trucks rumbled into the empty streets of Warsaw in the dead of the night. We finally stopped at the Zelazna and Grzybowska check point leading into the Ghetto. As soon as the trucks stopped, the German SS guards and Polish police began screaming and yelling as they hurried us off the trucks. 'Off! Off! All packages against the wall! Everyone goes through the checkpoint empty-handed!'

Checkpoint procedures were well known to me and this was my favorite checkpoint. In the midst of all the disorienting commotion I beckoned to Father to follow me. I pointed to a large sack of provisions among the packages stacked against the wall and told him to put it on his back. I then threw my blanket over it. It looked as if he were carrying a child. I guided him to a place from where we could watch for a moment when all the German guards and Polish police would be busy searching the others. When it came, I prodded Father to go. 'Fast!' I urged him. He quickly walked through the check point undetected. Once I saw him safely inside the Ghetto, I grabbed two more bags of provisions, one in each hand, and also positioned myself for a chance to get through the checkpoint unobserved. The instant it came I slipped past the busy SS guards and Polish police. Father and I then marched to Ogrodowa Street where Mother, Channa, Max and Felunia were sleeping. Our arrival in the middle of the night caught them by surprise. They were all shocked by the way I looked. I did not know that they had not been informed about my being in the hospital.

We were all happy to be together once again. Mother was glad that we had had the foresight to have brought provisions in with us. Father then told her what had happened and how very fortunate we had been to bring in these three bags of provisions. They consisted of flour, barley, peas and other foodstuffs. We now had the means to extend our survival by a few more months, if we were careful.

The next day I noticed that Felunia, who was now five years old, was not getting out of bed. I asked Channa, 'Why is she still in bed?' Channa answered, 'She's not feeling well.' However, Felunia did not look sick and whenever I came near her she pulled her blanket up to cover herself. I became suspicious and pulled the blanket off her to see what she was hiding. I was shocked to see that her legs were bandaged from the top of her thighs down to her knees. I demanded to know what had happened to my precious Felunia. Channa told me that Felunia had turned over a big pot of hot soup onto herself. Her burns were so severe that she was unable to walk. She had to lie in bed while healing.

A few days later when Felunia's bandages were changed I saw how severe the burn wounds on her thighs really were. I began crying inconsolably, 'She is a girl. She will want to be able to wear short dresses.'

That very same day Aunt Raizel came to see us. She wept as she told Mother how all the provisions she and Lazar had collected had been taken away from them at the check point. Mother immediately shared everything we had with her.

By mid-November I was fully recovered from the typhus and feeling strong once again. By now our food supply was dangerously low. I planned to resume smuggling once my hair grew back. My family protested. They pointed out to me that many of the Jews leaving the Ghetto were either disappearing or getting killed. My sister informed me that my best friend, Chaya Lichtenstajyn, had never returned home to her mother and sister from a run. Chaya and I had been friends from the time we started school and had smuggled *kosher* meat together; I took this news very hard. I went to see Chaya's mother and found her swollen from starvation. I came home very depressed. My sister then recited to me the name of every Grodzisker she knew who had died. But I was not deterred and planned to continue smuggling. We had no other option if we were to survive.

The next day I went out to the checkpoints to evaluate them and plan my smuggling strategies; I was unaware that my sister was following me. When she saw me heading towards a checkpoint she caught up with me. For the first time in my life Channa was prepared to strike me if I did not return home with her immediately. She insisted that I did not have to risk my life at this time, because Max had figured out a way to provide for all of us.

Max's best friend had been one of the many Jews killed while serving in the Polish army as it resisted the German invasion of September, 1939. Mother had always admired what a handsome soldier Max's friend had been. He had married well and had prospered in his in-laws' business. They had sold wood veneer to cabinet makers. Now his widow controlled their large warehouse on Novolipie Street, which was still full of valuable wood veneer. Max was going to make the widow a proposal to which he expected a favorable reply; he would sell off her inventory on a commission basis. I went home with Channa.

Max approached his deceased friend's widow and begged her to help him keep his family alive by letting him earn a commission selling the wood veneer. She refused. She replied that she had enough money to see her through the war, which was going to be over soon, and that she wanted to keep her inventory for when she could return to business as usual. Max quietly left. With his family's life at stake Max put his scruples aside. He knew that the guard at the warehouse was a very poor man with a large and hungry family. Max approached him with an offer the warehouse guard could not refuse. The warehouse guard began providing Max with as much wood veneer as Max could sell to the Poles.

By the end of November we received orders that everyone had to move from Ogrodowa Street. The Ghetto was to become smaller and we were part of the populace that had to squeeze into its reduced confines. With great difficulty Max managed to get a one-room apartment at the top of a fifth floor walk-up at 63 Dzielna Street. But this was impossible for Mother. By now she was too weak to climb five flights of steps. Fortunately, Mother ran into Yitzhak Slak, a cousin with whom she had always maintained a good relationship. He invited us to share his first-floor, one-room apartment on Dzielna Street until we could find a place for ourselves. Yitzhak's apartment was right across the street from where my sister and Max lived. We spread our bedrolls on the floor of their bright and sunny apartment. It was good. Yitzhak was glad to have us. We fed him.

A few days later Father came in with good news. He had met his old Aunt Devora, his father's sister. She and her husband Josef, both in their eighties, were childless and living in a large one-room apartment also on Dzielna Street, just a few blocks away. Father had described our situation to them and she had invited my parents and me to come and live with them. We left Yitzhak Slak's and moved into Devora's. We shared our dwindling provisions with them and their hunger was temporarily abated.

Several days after we began living with Aunt Devora and Uncle Josef, Max came to see us. He looked around the apartment and decided that he had to have this place for Channa and Felunia. He made Uncle Josef a cash offer to trade apartments with him. The terms of the deal were that Mother stayed with my sister, Max and Felunia in this first-floor apartment, while Father, Aunt Devora, Uncle Josef and I were to go live in the fifth-floor apartment. Uncle Joseph had no choice but to accept the money. Now he could buy something to eat.

With every passing day, food in the Ghetto became scarcer and more expensive. Only the very rich or the very resourceful could obtain enough food to keep hunger at bay. Blood pudding was being sold in the streets. Rumor had it that it was made of human blood. While the majority of people were starving to death in the streets, the Germans saw to it that the shops on Smocza Street were brimming with produce and goods of every kind. The Germans filmed and photographed these shops for propaganda purposes.

Every street was teeming with people. Running errands would often take me along Smocza Street where I would frequently see a crowd gathered around a man in his early thirties, whose name was Rubenstein. He was always running and jumping along the streets, singing and joking. He pretended to be, or was, deranged. He would make jokes about the misery of our daily existence and say things like, 'Don't worry, schmaltz will soon be cheap, the rich people are melting.' Or when he saw corpses being put on a stretcher he would go up to them and say, 'Move over boy. Make room for another.' Everyone would stop to listen to his street theatre. People would laugh and give him money. He was the talk of the Ghetto.

As the autumn cold deepened, Mother's health took a turn for the worse. She deteriorated a little bit more each day. Father found work with Max's older brother, Leon Szyldszrajber. Leon, his wife Sara and their two children had been driven into the Ghetto from the city of Torun where he had been a prosperous merchant. Leon now owned machinery that made wood chips used for heating. Father's job was to deliver the chips to customers. The pay was extremely low, but being occupied and able to contribute to our well-being made him feel better. He also spent time collecting food from our other relatives to keep Aunt Devora and Uncle Joseph alive. My sister shared every scrap of food she could spare with Aunt Devora and Uncle Josef. However, it was not long before Uncle Josef could no longer walk and became bedridden. Aunt Devora catered to his needs.

Late one night while we were all sleeping, Uncle Josef woke us all up with his urgent cries of, 'Devora! Devora!' She was not answering. Nor would she answer anymore. She had died of hunger in her sleep. Father arranged for men to take her body away. She was buried in one of the innumerable mass graves.

Uncle Josef wept and begged, 'Have me taken away. I have no reason to live, I've lost my Devora.' We felt great pity for him. A few days later Father came back from the carpentry shop and found the apartment door locked. He knocked, but Uncle Joseph did not answer. Father and a neighbor broke the door down and found Uncle Joseph dead. Father arranged his burial, too.

When Aunt Raizel heard that Father and I were now alone in the fifth-floor apartment she went directly to Mother and said, 'You have to let us into that apartment. We are being thrown out of where we are now and we don't have any other place to live.' She, Uncle Lazar and Uteh came to live with us.

Every day when I came back to the apartment I noticed that another article that had belonged to Aunt Devora and Uncle Joseph was missing. Uncle Lazar was selling off everything in the apartment, piece by piece. It did not disturb me until he started to sell off our things as well. I was angry and went to my sister and cried, 'He's selling all our belongings!' Channa replied, 'Why are you crying? He's hungry. He has no choice. He's hungry!' I stopped crying and said no more.

After Lazar had sold everything of value in the apartment he announced to Raizel, 'I will not stay in the Ghetto! I am getting out and I want to take Uteh with me.' With his red hair and excellent Polish he could easily pass for a Pole. Raizel answered, 'Go. Save yourself. It's all right. You can find work with a farmer, but Uteh will not go with you.' Lazar left alone. He was never heard from again.

Despite the difficulty and danger in leaving the Ghetto[1], Raizel asked me to go to Grodzisk to see a Mrs Kolska. Mrs Kolska was a *Volksdeutsch* married to a Pole. Mrs Kolska and her husband had no children of their own. They had been Raizel's neighbors and good friends and they adored my cousin Uteh. Raizel wanted me to describe our situation to Mrs Kolska. I was to ask Mrs Kolska if she was willing to keep Uteh. My parents left the decision on taking the risk or not up to me.

Once again I went back to Grodzisk. I left the Ghetto by brazenly mingling with a group of Poles as they walked out through a check point. Mrs Kolska was happy to see me. She was concerned and told me to bring Uteh to her.

It was difficult to get Uteh out of the Ghetto. Uteh was a pretty, blue-eyed, blond, whose looks did not betray her, but she was scared to death. It was not possible to bluff our way through a checkpoint with her. I had to bribe our way out over the barb-wired Ghetto walls. We jumped from the wall and took the electric train into Grodzisk. Throughout the entire journey, I had to keep her from panicking. I did this with promises of all the good food and things she was going to have once we arrived at Mrs Kolska's.

Standing outside Mrs Kolska's two-room apartment, I told Uteh to wait while I went inside to make sure everything was all right. As I entered Mrs Kolska's home, I was shocked to hear voices singing in German. I looked into the second room and saw a table full of Germans drinking and eating. I wanted to leave immediately but Mrs Kolska told me not to be afraid and explained that she ran a private restaurant for Germans. She insisted that Uteh stay with her. Before I left I counseled Uteh to do whatever Mrs Kolska asked of her, and because Uteh's Polish was not very good, to speak as little as possible. I went back to the Ghetto. It was never a problem getting into the Ghetto. Once back in the Ghetto I assured Raizel that Uteh was in good hands.

Not too many days went by before Raizel came to me in tears. She was not sure that Uteh was happy at Mrs Kolska's; she missed her, and wanted me to go to Grodzisk and check on her one more time. Would I do it for her? Uteh was my only cousin on my Mother's side and she had been practically brought up in our house by our grandmother. Despite the risk Mother and Channa could not forbid me from going. Again I went back to Grodzisk and returned to Mrs Kolska's. Uteh was fine but she wanted to return to the Ghetto with me. I persuaded her to stay with Mrs Kolska, where she was comfortable, and went back to the Ghetto alone.

Another week passed and again Raizel asked me to go check on Uteh. Again I went. This time Uteh was not at Mrs Kolska's. I was terribly upset. Mrs Kolska told me that Uteh had been very homesick. Uteh had stopped eating and spoke Yiddish in her sleep. Uteh had left to return to the Ghetto. Mrs Kolska had tried to convince her to stay but Uteh would not listen to her. I went back to the Ghetto alone.

When I got home Uteh had not yet arrived. Curfew time came and still Uteh had not arrived. We began to fear the worst. A few days went by and there was no sign of her. Nobody knew what had become of her. Raizel was in agony. I now had to promise Mother and Channa that I would not dare leave the Ghetto again. Another few days went by and we finally received a message from Uteh. She had been caught and taken to the Gesia Street jail. She had somehow managed to send a note out to us. Raizel and Mother had a cousin, a son of David Domb, who ran a restaurant opposite the Gesia Street jail. Its police officers were his daily customers. Through his contacts Raizel and Mother were able to send Uteh food in jail. We had no way of knowing whether she ever received any of it, but we sent the packages anyway. We even entertained the hope that we might be able to buy her way out through our cousin's contacts.

The winter that started in December, 1941 was a cold one. For those in the Ghetto it was critical. The men, women and children in the streets froze to death. Their frozen bodies, their faces covered with ice, looked like statues. The dead children usually froze sitting up. Their bodies would stay in the street for days before they were taken away. During the second month of that winter, in January, 1942, Regina Cukier performed at the El Dorado.[2] Max took Channa to see her show. I never tired of Channa's description of Regina starring in 'The Rabbi's Daughter'.

One day my sister asked me if I would be willing to baby-sit for Franka Mihalska, one of Max's sisters. Franka was an intelligent, soft-spoken and wealthy woman. She had a four-year-old son, Leonek, who needed looking after while she conducted her business of smuggling shoes out of the Ghetto. Franka would not trust her child and the possessions she had in her one-room apartment to a stranger. Channa told me that I would be fed by Franka, and then she could use my food to help others. I did not like to be separated from Mother all day long, but I could not refuse.

Several mornings a week I ran through the cold to Franka's fifth-floor walk-up at 27 Leshno Street to baby sit Leonek. Franka was grateful for my help and rewarded me with a pair of new shoes. While working for her I made friends with Sabina, the girl next door. Sabina was eighteen years old. She and her parents lived with her sister, Mrs Grief, and her ten-year- old son, Heniek. Sabina's father was already bed-ridden from hunger. Franka helped them out with a little bit of food. The husbands of both Mrs Grief and Franka had escaped to Russia. Their conversations were always filled with the hope that their husbands would one day return to them and their children.

In addition to babysitting for Franka I cleaned and washed for my parents at home. Every night I went from Franka's to my sister's and waited for Father to come back from work. I would be with Mother, and my only pleasure was to spend every spare moment with my beloved five-year-old niece, Felunia. My sister had the biggest burden, she took care of our ailing mother. We shared every bit of our food with Raizel and we sent whatever food we could to Uteh in jail. Every night before curfew, Father, Raizel and I would go back to our fifth-floor walk-up.

One February night while waiting for Father to come back from his job, I heard a moaning in the corridor. By now the starving had started going from door to door in the hallways of buildings hoping their moans would open a door and they would be given some bread. It was impossible to help them. It took all our resources just to keep ourselves alive. But that particular moaning disturbed me. I said to my sister, 'That is our father's voice!' She replied, 'No. It's the moans of those begging for bread.' But the moaning disturbed me. When I heard the sound come closer, I opened the door. There was my poor father, crawling on his belly, his face as white as snow, in terrible pain. He could barely tell us what had happened to him. He had slipped on some ice in front of the house and fallen onto a cast iron street ornament. He struck it with his back. Max, Channa and I carried him up to our fifth-floor walk-up. Max went out and immediately returned with a doctor who lived on the second floor. I was not told how grave Father's injury was. Only Channa and Max knew that the fall had broken his spinal cord.

I stayed home and attended to Father's needs. In the evening I would go to my sister's to fetch a thermos of hot tea and a roll for his supper. Four days after his accident I was so busy washing the laundry that I almost forgot to go to Channa's for Father's tea and roll. I quickly ran to Channa's and hurried to prepare the tea so that I could bring it back before curfew. Mother rushed me along.

When I got back up to the flat Father was snoring heavily. As I poured the tea into a cup I said, 'Pa, prepare yourself, I want you to eat before the tea gets cold.' He did not answer. He just snored. I did not want to wake him up and decided to wait for him to wake up by himself. But the longer I waited, the heavier he snored. I put his meal on the bedside table and again tried to wake him. Raizel, lying in a nearby bed, called out to me, 'Can't you see he is sleeping soundly. Let him sleep.' I replied, 'No, I don't like this sleeping.' I could not wake him up. Father's silver cigarette container lay on a small night stand beside his bed. I opened it. It was full. He had not smoked one. I now realized how ill Father was. Cigarettes were more important to him than food. He used to wake up during the night to smoke. Again I tried to wake him up. I could not. I said to Raizel, 'Can't you see that something is wrong?' I panicked and ran out the door to get my sister. It was after curfew and the gate to the building was locked. I ran to get the janitor to open it for me. He refused, yelling, 'Don't you know that it's curfew and that the German patrol is always at the tobacco monopoly across the street at this time? Do you want to get killed?' I cried and yelled, 'Father is dying, I need my sister to come!' He opened the gate saying, 'Okay, you want to get killed, go ahead!' What the janitor said was true. There were always two German SS men on patrol in front of the tobacco monopoly across the street. I ran as fast as I could. The German SS men saw me but did not shoot at me.

I burst through the door of my sister's apartment screaming, 'Channa come fast. Something is wrong with Father. He doesn't want to wake up ... I'm afraid, come!' She ran back with me. Max ran with us as well. Max stopped at the second floor to call the doctor. The doctor's brother was there when Max called. The brother was a doctor as well. They both came up with Max. One of the brothers gave Father an injection. It stopped his heavy breathing. As he was preparing another injection his brother stopped him with a hand signal. He turned to us and said, 'Your father is in a coma.' After four days in bed, Father died, on Tuesday, February 10, 1942.

I wanted Father to have a normal burial, but I did not have the money to pay for it. Max refused to pay for it saying, 'I would rather spend the money on the living than on the dead.' Two men came to carry Father down. We kissed him goodbye. My sister and I held each other and cried. Father was buried in one of the mass graves in the Gesia cemetery.

I wrote letters to my brothers, one to Chaim and his family in Wegrow and another to Tusha in Rawa, where he was still working for the farmer. I wanted them to know that our father had died so that they could say *Kaddish*. Letters arrived from both my brothers saying that they were reciting *Kaddish* for their father.

Once Father was gone, Mother did not want me to live alone with Aunt Raizel on the fifth floor. Even though she was very sick, Mother insisted that she come and live with me. She had to be near me. Raizel and Channa looked after Mother on the days I went to baby sit for Franka. Every night Mother cried, 'Motta take me to you ... take me away ... take me away.'

That Friday night I awoke from a nightmare. I had dreamt that the Bubbeh, Father and all the dead people that I knew were dancing around Mother. The next day, Saturday, Franka came up to Channa's and asked her to send me over to baby sit for a few hours, because she had an appointment she could not miss. Channa came up to our place and told me, 'Go, do Franka this favor. Leave everything. We'll be okay.'

When I got to Franka's she sent me out on an errand. When I returned to her apartment, Max was sitting there. I found this strange because Max never visited his sister. I also did not like the way he was looking at me. I knew something was wrong. I asked Max, 'What happened? What happened?' He could not speak. Franka told me, 'Fela, go home, your mother wants you to come home.'

I ran home wondering if I would find Mother still alive. As I came into the apartment Mother gave me a big smile. She had been waiting for me. Raizel told me, 'She doesn't want to eat or drink.' 'Did you try?' I asked. 'Yes, I tried.' Raizel replied. I embraced Mother and then gave her some valerian drops. 'Ma I'm going to run down to Channa's and have her make you some kliskalech. You'll eat them, right?' Potato dumplings were her favorite food. She nodded, yes. I ran to Channa's and while she prepared the kliskalech I went out to the nearest bread distribution shop for more valerian drops. In the brief time it took me to return with the valerian, Channa had prepared the kliskalech. I carried them up to Mother.

When I got there Mother was drifting in and out of consciousness. I quickly gave her some valerian drops to revive her. I stroked her pitch black hair. I tried to feed her. She ate a bit just to please me. But she kept closing her eyes and then opening them again to look at me. I said, 'Ma, I think Schloime will be here soon.' She opened her eyes and replied, 'How will he come? He's in Russia.' Her eyes closed again and I said, 'Ma, soon we will see Chaim.' She just opened her eyes and looked at me. I knew what she was thinking. A few minutes later Channa and Max arrived. Mother opened her eyes and asked them to come closer to her. She said, 'Channa, Max, I want you to listen to me. Please take care of her; she is so young. She needs you. Please take care of her.' Channa could not hold back her tears. Neither could Max. But I did not cry. I refused to accept that Mother was leaving me. I sat on the bed holding her, stroking her black hair, thinking to myself how she did not have one gray hair. Her eyes opened and closed. I heard a neighbor say to my sister, 'Take her away for a bit.' I wondered, 'Why is she saying that?' Channa came, took me by my arm, and gently pulled me away from Mother's bed. Mother opened her eyes once more and looked around the room until she saw me. She then closed her eyes and died peacefully. It was Saturday, February 21, 1942. She died twelve days after her husband.

I did not want Mother to be buried in a mass grave. I asked Channa if we could provide for a proper burial. Max refused, 'It's no use. We need the money for food.' The cost of a funeral was prohibitively high. I held Mother's body, her arms hanging limp against me, until they came to take her body away. Again I wrote letters to my brothers.

I now lived alone with Aunt Raizel. Channa asked me to baby sit for Franka every day. She said, 'The food I have for you I can give to Raizel; otherwise she will die of hunger. I know that Franka is stingy, but I'll come up there every day to check on you.' I could not refuse. My Aunt Chaiah also asked me to cook for my Uncle Aaron, who was now alone with his two youngest children. His wife had left the Ghetto with the older children in order to leave them their ration coupons. Again I could not refuse.

In March my brothers wrote back. Tusha wrote that he had to leave the farm that he had been on all this time. He never gave us a reason why. His letter told us that he was now wandering from one village to another looking for work, but not to worry because he always managed well. Chaim wrote that he was reciting *Kaddish* for his parents and that their situation was now very dangerous. They were in hiding. We never heard from Chaim again.

I now babysat for Franka every day and Sabina often kept me company. Franka did not object to Sabina being in her apartment with me, but warned me about our other neighbors, two couples and a woman who lived at the end of the corridor near the bathrooms. Two of the women were sisters and one of the men was their brother. The second man was the husband of one of the sisters and the third woman was the brother's girlfriend. Franka told me, 'Never let them into the apartment, especially if you are alone.' I could not understand why she feared them so much; they were always so well dressed. The three women were very attractive and pleasant, especially the brother's girlfriend.

She was so beautiful people could not keep their eyes off her. On occasion one of them would come to the door asking to borrow some hot water or some other small item. I would pass it out to them but I would never let them in.

Despite the fact that I was almost sixteen, I was still very naïve. One Sunday on my way to the bathroom at the end of the corridor I had to walk past several men standing in the hall. I could tell from their Polish that they were not Jews. I wondered what they were doing there. When I returned to the apartment I asked Sabina what those men were doing out there. She looked at me and said, 'In case nobody told you, our neighbors are professional thieves and their women are prostitutes. Those men out there are their clients.' Now I knew why I was not to permit them to enter Franka's apartment.

Channa came by Franka's every day to ask what I had been fed and to bring me more food. She would ask, 'What did Franka give you today?' 'Three thin slices of bread with some jam and the same thing for herself.' My sister replied, 'She eats plenty when you don't see. That's why I'm here.'

One morning after Leonek went next door to play with Heniek, there was a knock at the door. I opened it. A woman, a short brunette I had never seen before, asked me, 'Is your name Fela?' 'Yes.' 'Max is your brother-in-law?' 'Yes. Who are you?' In a nervous voice she told me, 'A woman by the name of Franka Michalska has been captured by the police and taken to the police station. She gave me this address and asked me to come here and send you for your brother-in-law.' Franka had left only a half an hour ago and the story sounded suspicious. Seeing that I was unsure, the woman said, 'You have to rush. Tell Max about it. He will know what to do.' I was confused. I did not know what to do. I went into Mrs Grief's and asked her to keep Leonek for a half hour because I had to run an errand. I did not tell her what this woman had told me because I thought that Franka's smuggling business was a secret.

Despite my mixed feelings about the story I ran with all my might to find Max. It was a fifteen-minute run. When I opened the door to my sister's and blurted out the story, she screamed, 'Oh my God! They got you! Run back fast! Those thieves have played a trick on you. They had it all planned.' I ran back like a torpedo. When I reached the yard, a man, his face streaming blood, was running away from Max. The stairs to the apartment were splattered with spilt flour, rice and sugar, and the neighbors were scooping it up as fast as they could. I was shaken and very ashamed. I could not forgive myself for being so stupid and naïve. The only thing Franka said was, 'I should have prepared you better.'

Franka conducted her smuggling business from the Palace of Justice Sadgrodzki. Leshno Street ran through the building housing the Palace of Justice, dividing it in two. One half was in the Ghetto, the other outside of it. There Franka was able to conduct her business with people from outside the Ghetto. Her business was not the secret I thought it was. Everyone knew about it.

When the summer of 1942 finally came I was still babysitting for Franka and cooking for Uncle Aaron and his two little boys. When Uncle Aaron came home from work and smelled the aroma of the meager potato and barley soup I was making, he would bless me, saying, 'My child, I wish you eternal life. You are saving my children and myself.' I also helped Aunt Raizel put together some food to send to Uteh who was still languishing in jail. A day did not pass without my seeing my precious Felunia. The way she greeted me, the way she felt in my arms when she embraced me, made life bearable.

Another letter from Tusha arrived. In it was a small picture. It was of Tusha wearing a white windbreaker with zippered pockets. He looked so handsome, and I missed him so much, I kissed his picture. He wrote that he had been making money sewing for the farmers but that the situation was constantly worsening. Jews were being assembled and sent away. It was now impossible to hide. He and his friend Beryl Goldfarb were on their way back into the Ghetto. Tusha wanted to be with us, no matter what would become of us, and of him. I could not wait to see him again. With every passing day I anticipated his arrival. He never arrived.

On July 18 I came home hoping that Tusha had finally arrived. Instead I found my sister in a state I had never seen her in before. She was wringing her hands and crying, 'We are doomed. Now it is the end of us. Did you hear that Czerniakow[3] committed suicide by taking poison? The Germans demanded that he sign a declaration that the Ghetto be liquidated and that we all be transported to God knows where. The Jewish Committee has to help collect the people for transport.'[4] Just looking at my sister caused me to panic. I ran down to the yard to where Felunia was playing. Every face I passed was filled with despair. I found Felunia, grabbed her and held her close. I did not know what to say. How could I explain the fear we felt to a six-year-old? I held her tight, as if that could prevent what was to come, and prayed that we would never be parted.

I decided to run over to Franka's for more information. Because of her contacts she was always knowledgeable about every situation. When I reached Franka's, she asked why I was crying. I began to wonder if she was aware of our predicament. How could she be so calm while my sister was so distraught? From Franka I learned that with money, a lot of money, you could buy a work permit from the Germans. With a work permit you could work at the Schultz factory or for the German SS industrialist Walter Toebbens, repairing German army uniforms. A work permit was an insurance policy against deportation. Working meant being safe from raids. Capture meant being sent away to Treblinka[5] or Poniatow.[6] But Max did not have enough money to buy a work permit.

The next day Franka told me, 'I've covered you. I bought papers to work at the Toebbens factory and registered you as my daughter. You will stay home with Leonek while I go to work.' I did not like this development. I went back to Channa and told her about it. She said, 'I'm happy about it. At least you will be covered, and we'll see; in time, we, too, might find a cover.' I did not want to leave Channa and Felunia alone to run and hide during the raids. I told her, 'I want to be with you. If you get caught I want to go with you. I don't want to be left all alone. What will I do by myself?' Channa insisted, 'No. Not until I am covered.' The next morning I went back to Franka's to take advantage of her offer. She gave me the papers necessary to protect little Leonek and myself in case of a raid and left for work.

On July 22 the deportation of Jews from the Ghetto went into full swing. German, Ukrainian, and Lithuanian soldiers[7] surrounded the buildings and rounded up six thousand Jews. This was their daily quota and the raids, or actions as they called them, were carried out every day until the quota was met. The people caught were marched to the *Umschlagplatz*, loaded into cattle cars and transported to Treblinka.

During the first two raids I did as Franka had instructed me. I presented the swastika-stamped papers to the German soldiers. Those with papers were spared. Channa, Max and Felunia had no papers. They had to hide. I was terrified that my sister would be found and taken away. Hundreds were taken away from our building block alone. After each raid my sister came running to see if I was still alive. She was happy that at least I had a cover. Again I begged her to take me with her into hiding, but again she refused. During the next raid, the Germans, Ukrainians and Lithuanians began shouting that everyone had to come down into the courtyard, including those with papers. I began making my way down to the courtyard with Leonek as slowly as I could. Everyone around me was in an absolute panic, screaming and shouting as they ran desperately in all directions. I realized that the Germans were taking everyone away, even those with work permits. I held onto Leonek and ran back up the stairs to the roof. Many others were also running along the rooftops to escape capture. Suddenly everything became very quiet. The Germans had captured their daily quota of Jews and were now marching them off. Everyone who escaped the raid went down into the court yard. After four o'clock, Franka came running back from work. She was aware of what had happened that day and she could not believe her luck that Leonek and I were still there.

Now that the Germans were no longer honoring work permits I told Channa that I was not going to work for Franka and that from now on I was going to stay with her. 'Whatever happens to you will happen to me as well.' She could not argue with my decision. When I told Franka, 'You have to take responsibility for your child. I am not going into hiding with you. I will be staying with my sister,' Franka said that she understood my decision but begged me to stay with her until she could find a solution to her problem. In the meantime we would hide with her friends in the attic of their furniture factory. We survived a number of raids there. After one raid Franka learned that her brother Leon and his family had been taken. Franka broke down.

One day, after the German raids had caught their daily quota of Jews, Channa and I were walking in a passageway through the deserted market on Novolipie and Leshno when my sister said, 'Look. There is Regina.' I ran over to her and said, 'Regina, it's me, Chavcha's daughter.' 'Oh yes!' She grabbed me and held me tight and said, 'I heard that both Mother and Father have died.' I started to cry. She was crying too. I told her that Channa and Max had seen her perform in 'The Rabbi's Daughter' at the El Dorado and how surprised they had been to see the theater packed to capacity for her performance. When we parted she said, 'Our future is uncertain, who knows what will befall us? Who will cry for us?' I never saw her again.

Once the raids had started, the Germans announced that those who would come along voluntarily would get bread and jam.[8] Thousands overcome by hunger gave themselves up. After one of the raids Raizel came to find Channa and me. It was evening when she found us in a courtyard. Raizel had been hiding with our cousins, Yitzhak and Elka. She told us she could not endure anymore. With the loss of her husband and her daughter, she no longer had any reason to suffer hunger and fear. She had no reason to live anymore. She was going to give herself up. Channa pleaded with her to stay and hide with us. She refused, "No, no. Yitzhak and Elka have gone and I will join them.' We cried as we kissed each other goodbye. I never saw my Aunt Raizel again.

Before long a few people had escaped from the transports and we heard about the fate of those captured in the raids. They were loaded into cattle wagons at the *Umschlagplatz* for the two-hour ride to Treblinka and its ovens. The rumors that we could not believe, that we had rationalized as not being possible, were true. Treblinka was a death camp.

Once the raids started it became more difficult than ever to get food in the Ghetto. We were now constantly hungry. We went for days without food. But as long as there were still Jews who had gold, diamonds and money to exchange for food, there were Poles who brought food into the Ghetto.

After every raid Channa came running to find me. Whenever possible she brought me a morsel of food. Channa promised that as soon as Max could arrange a cover in some factory she would come and take me with her. Max was always changing hiding places. I never knew where they were. On one of those days when I did not know where my sister was hiding, Franka informed me that she had bought into a better *hiding* for her and Leonek, and that she could not take me with her. I asked her for the keys to her apartment at 27 Leshno Street so that I would at least have a place to sleep.

I returned to 27 Leshno to find it almost deserted. Sabina, her parents, her sister and Mrs Grief were all gone. Miraculously ten-year old Heniek Grief had survived. He was so happy to see me that he ran into my arms. He told me that his mother had hidden him under the bed before she and the others had been taken away. As he clung to me he said, 'Fela, I want to live, I do not want to die, what shall I do, tell me?' My heart was breaking as I looked at his beautiful face and blond hair. He was so young, so innocent. I found it so strange that he did not mention his mother or anybody else. He was just thinking of himself, of how he could survive. What could I tell him? I said, 'Run where the people are running. That is what I do. If they run onto the roof, I run onto the roof.' A day or two later, Heniek, the beautiful little boy, just disappeared. I never saw him again.

There were raids almost every single day. To escape I ran along the rooftops with others who were still free. We jumped from one roof to the next, fleeing from the pursuing Germans, Ukrainians and Jewish Police. After several close calls I realized that I needed a better way to avoid capture than to just run along the rooftops. I had to create a hiding place for myself. I went back to my room, opened the window, tore the curtains, left the door open, and messed up the room and bed to make it appear as if it had already been searched. The open window and door created a draft that caused the torn curtains to blow in the wind.

During the next raid I hid myself under the bed, covered myself with big lumps of coal and lay as quiet as a mouse. I could hear the Germans and Ukrainians shouting, 'Everyone rauss!' as they came crashing into the room. Lying under the bed I could see their boots and hear them say, 'Nobody is here anymore!' I prayed that if I were caught it would be by the Germans and not the Ukrainians. I hid there for several raids.

One morning just after I had left my *hiding* and went down into the street I met a girl I knew from Grodzisk, named Sylbernadel. As we stood there talking a raid started. We began to run. We ran through a courtyard where Jewish Police were assembling the people they had captured. We veered into a building and started up the stairs to get to the roof. As we ran up the stairs we were caught from behind by a Jewish Policeman. But fortune was with us. We recognized him. He, too, was from Grodzisk. His name was Karvasser. He came from a family that had owned a lumber yard. We called him by name. He recognized us as two girls from home. He took a quick look around, saw that we were unobserved, and said, 'I'm not going to take you in. Run that way. The raid has already passed there.'

Max was captured during one raid. The Germans caught him in the street. Channa came to say goodbye to me. She was taking Felunia and going to join Max. I was furious with her, 'Don't be stupid! Max is so smart, he will find a way to come back. You will not go! You will stay here with me!' As we stood arguing I saw Max enter the courtyard of 27 Leshno. 'Look! Here he is!' I said. At the *Umschlagplatz* Max had been put to work loading confiscated clothing into a rail car. He managed to hide himself among the clothes and jumped off the train once it was in motion.

A few days later Channa came looking for me. She took me to the one-room apartment on 63 Mila Street where she now lived. There was a *hiding* in the attic of 63 Mila which sheltered over two hundred people, but Max did not like it and we did not use it. The raids did not stop. It was very easy for the Germans to locate us. We had to eat whatever we could find and prepare it whenever we could. Our cooking smoke was easy to see. It showed the Germans where we were. But our luck held and we were not detected.

By the autumn of 1942 the Ghetto had shrunk drastically. The majority of Jews that had been in the Ghetto had been captured and deported to Treblinka, Uncle Aaron and his children among them. Leshno Street was almost empty. All the surrounding streets had been depopulated as well.

Most of the remnants of the Ghetto's population were now on Mila and the surrounding streets. Two to three families lived in one room. I had not seen Franka and Leonek in some time and knew nothing of their whereabouts. Not many of us were left.

Max managed to buy his way into a protected job at the *Deustche Tishlerei Verkstaten,* German Carpentry Works, on Gesia Street making furniture for the Germans. He received work papers that allowed his wife and child to be with him at the factory while he worked. I was not covered by his papers. Every morning when Max took Channa and Felunia with him to the assembly point from which they were escorted to work by Jewish policemen, I hid.

Max did not like the *hiding* in the attic of 63 Mila. It was too big, and too dangerous. The father-in- law of the man who ran it was an older man who was always coughing. Max said, 'One cough and they're all finished.' I, too, preferred to hide on my own. I re-created the same *hiding* for myself on 63 Mila as I had made at 27 Leshno. Again I chose an empty room, opened the window, tore the curtain, made myself a place under the bed and covered myself with coal. When the hallway was deserted I took the door off one hinge and let it hang open at an angle. With the draft flapping the curtains, the room looked deserted. I survived many raids hidden that way. Every time Channa came back from work she was sure she would not find me.

The Germans running the *Deustche Tishlerei Verkstaten* told Max and the others working there to search the deserted buildings and bring them gold, silver, carpets, paintings, anything of value. They would be given food in return. Sometimes Max came home with a piece of herring or bread.

Until January, 1943, Max, Channa and Felunia followed the same routine; they went to work together and came back at night. But one morning Max returned with Channa and Felunia shortly after leaving the apartment. Max, always alert and perceptive, had noticed a change in the daily procedure that disturbed him. He was very nervous as he told me, 'While we were waiting our turn to enter the factory yard I saw them separating the women and children from the men as they counted them. They don't have to do that. I don't like it. And yesterday there were too many Germans around. What are they up to? Maybe you can convince Channa not to come back with me today.' Channa said, 'I have to go with you. If they take us, they take us.' I screamed at her, 'Don't be stupid. You know his intuition is always good. Listen to him. Listen to me. Stay here with the child. We'll hide, the three of us. Let him go back to work.' She listened to me and we hid in the attic on 63 Mila Street.

It was the first time any of us had gone to this attic *hiding*. We stood in line as two men carefully screened the people they allowed in. They ordered everyone to remain calm. Standing in line ahead of us was a man known by everyone. Everyone liked and respected him for his character and intelligence. He was with his wife, two children and a blanketed infant whom he carried in his arms. The two men would not let him enter the *hiding* with the infant. One of the men said, 'Sorry, I can't let you in with an infant. It is too dangerous. The infant might cry. I cannot risk the lives of two hundred for your baby.' The father of the infant stood there and looked at the man denying him entry to the *hiding* and pleaded, 'You want me to abandon my baby? I can not do that, but I give you my word that if some-thing happens I will know what to do.' The two men let him in.

It was a terrible raid that day. The Germans knew we were there, some-where. They sensed us. They just did not know exactly where we were. But they had to proceed carefully. The stairs and floors surrounding the attic *hiding* had been weakened so that when the Germans ran over them they would cave in and the soldiers would fall to the floor below. They stood on the roof above us yelling, 'Raus! Raus!' There was a lot of shouting and shooting. I heard a small noise from the baby but it quieted down. The raid lasted for hours. We just lay in the attic silently. Fortunately we were not detected. It was late in the day when the Germans finally left.

We filed out of the attic one by one. I watched the man holding his infant go to the two men who had admitted us and hand them the blanketed infant. 'Here,' he said. The baby was dead. It had been suffocated by its own father. We all cried as we looked at this man standing there with his head bowed. Night was falling as we all stood in the backyard of 63 Mila and buried the eight-week-old infant and recited *Kaddish*.

When Max got back from the *Deustche Tishlerei Verkstaten* that night, he told us what had happened there. All the women and children had been separated from their men and kept that way after the count. People panicked. They paid the Jewish Police with gold and diamonds to put their children in knapsacks and hide them from the Germans. It was to no avail. When the Germans came they found all the children. All the women and children who were at the *Deustche Tishlerei Verkstaten* that day were taken away to Treblinka.

Every day after the men left for work the German raids started. During every raid, Channa, Felunia and I ran up to the attic *hiding*. By February 1943 Channa insisted on taking Felunia back to the *Deustche Tishlerei Verkstaten* on Gesia Street where Max worked. Other women whose husbands worked there had already returned with their children. The Germans had not been there for a while and the men had arranged hiding places for their families nearby. Whenever the Germans arrived the women and children ran to these hiding places.

One day several truck-loads of Germans carried out a surprise raid on the factory. There was not enough time for Channa to get to her hiding place with Felunia. Max ordered Channa to run by herself. He grabbed Felunia, who was now almost seven years old, and told her not to utter a word. He laid her down on the cement floor near the machine he was operating. He placed bricks on each side of her and a piece of plywood on top of them. He then stood on the plywood working as the Germans approached him. They paused to watch him work and then left. When Max uncovered the child, she said, 'I was quiet, wasn't I, Daddy?'

Max no longer trusted the Germans to honor the work permits. It was only a matter of time before the Germans would come to the work place and take everyone, men included. Max stopped going to work. Now that he was no longer protected by his work permit, he came into hiding with us during the raids. Max still did not like the *hiding* on 63 Mila Street. The constant coughing of the father-in- law of the man who ran it made Max very nervous. 'One cough and we're all finished. I have to find a better place.' Max began to prepare a *hiding* for Channa and Felunia.

One day Max came home and said to my sister, 'You still have that nice navy dress? Put it on. We have to go out right away. I met this friend of mine from before the war, Yakov Brezinski ... it's a long story; I'll tell you all about it on the way.' I also had a navy dress that my sister had given me. As usual she had given me the nicer one. I gave Channa my dress and baby-sat Felunia while they went out. When they came back I heard the whole story.

That day Max had met an old school friend, Yakov Brezinski, walking on Mila Street. Yakov Brezinski had worked for the Dikty furniture factories and had bought plywood and finishing from Max before the war. They were happy to see each other. Max and Yakov had gone to school with Sala, a petite, pretty brunette who had been Yakov's sweetheart during their school days. Sala was a fatherless child and her mother had eked out a living running a small grocery store in Warsaw Solec. Yakov's family would not accept his choice of Sala as a bride. They did not find her suitable. She was too poor. Yakov was forbidden to marry her and obliged to marry a girl from a more prosperous family. Yakov was heart-broken.

During one of the recent raids, as Yakov was running to hide, Sala fell into his arms. Fate had reunited them. Yakov's first wife had already been captured in a raid and sent to Treblinka. Madly in love with each other, Yakov and Sala decided to get married. Regardless of the times and circumstances Sala insisted they get married under a *chuppah*, adhering to Jewish tradition. She would now have the wedding she was once denied. Yakov asked Max and my sister to be among the witnesses. Max and Channa had the honor and mitzvah of escorting the couple under the *chuppah*. From that day on we were all very close friends.

The Germans raids continued. They were furious that so many of us were still eluding them and roaming around the streets of the Ghetto. Poles continued to smuggle food into the Ghetto and sold it to us for whatever jewelry, clothing and money we had left or could scavenge from the debris left behind by those who had been taken away. During this period of raids there was a bakery operating somewhere in 69 Mila Street. How they got the flour and how they baked bread without being detected baffled me. We bought a few loaves whenever they were available. Max always managed to find some additional food. My sister shared what little she had with the less fortunate.

One evening just after we had started eating a thin soup that we had scraped together, there was a knock on our door. Channa opened it to find a woman begging food. Without hesitation, and before I could say a word in protest, Channa took her soup bowl and poured its contents into the woman's bowl. I became furious with her and screamed, 'How could you give away the food from your mouth! We have nothing! Have you no consideration for your child?' Max said nothing; he would never berate her, but he was glad that I had. Her only reply was, 'Don't you remember, Mother always said that you should never eat until you are full when you see another human being who is hungry.' I remembered and said no more.

Yakov Brezinski and Mr Greenberg, an acquaintance of Max's, both lived in a five-storey building at 58 Mila Street. They, too, wanted a better *hiding* but did not have the construction expertise that Max had. Yakov and Mr Greenberg invited Max to design and build a *hiding* with them. Max accepted, provided that we move into 58 Mila Street while the new *hiding* was being built. Mr Greenberg and his wife and son, Mietek, lived on the second floor. Mrs Greenberg had taken sick after their other son had been captured in a raid and taken to Treblinka. Yakov and Sala Brezinski lived on the fourth floor. We moved onto the third floor.

The building at 58 Mila already had two *hidings* in it. Many people had survived numerous raids undetected in these *hidings*. One *hiding* was in the attic and the other one was in the basement. We preferred the basement *hiding* to the one in the attic. The basement *hiding* was located beneath the floor of what used to be a ground-level store. The store's interior was piled with debris and broken shelves. Part of it had been made to look like horses had been stabled in it. Horse manure was spread over the trap door leading down into the basement *hiding*. In the basement *hiding* were wooden beds, a store of dried foods and most of the belongings we still possessed. We survived many raids in this basement *hiding* while our own *hiding* was being completed.

By March, 1943, the Germans had still not gotten rid of us. The smoke from our cooking fires told the Germans that we still existed. Their raids continued. While the women and children slept in the basement the men hid on the roof watching for the Germans. On days when there was no sign of immediate German activity we scavenged for goods, left behind by the people who had been killed or captured in the endless raids, to exchange for food with those

Poles who dared come into the Ghetto. When we had food we had to cook it outdoors. Most of the time it was a thin soup of potatoes and carrots. We were so hungry that it tasted unbelievably good. We always asked each other, 'How come we never made this before the war?'

Max and a few others decided that because the raids were getting worse all the men would spend the night on the roof as lookouts. While the men were on the roof, the women and children slept in the basement. In the middle of the night we were awakened by six Polish men shining their flashlights on us. They demanded money and jewelry. They took all our valises and pulled one of the girls upstairs and raped her.

As I lay in our bunk with my sister and Felunia, a young Pole about eighteen years old, pulled our blanket off of us and said to me, 'You! Come upstairs with me and show me which belongings are yours and I will give them back to you.' I was so naïve, I believed him. Channa had to restrain me from getting up. 'Don't be stupid! Just sit here with me! Don't move!' She pulled me close and said, 'Never! Go away, you've robbed us enough.' The young Pole became angry. He held out his hand. In it was a grenade. He said to Channa, 'If you don't let your sister come upstairs I'll throw this grenade at you and blow you all up'. At that very moment the other Poles, wanting to get away, saw that he was missing. They called, 'Josef! Come! Come!' Josef threw the grenade at us as he left. It landed on our bunk. We were paralyzed with fear as we stared at the grenade, anticipating its explosion and our deaths. Seconds, each the length of eternity, passed. The grenade did not explode. It was a dud. I will never forget the faces of those six Poles. In particular, the face of Josef.

When the men came down from the roof top they were beside themselves with self-recrimination. They couldn't believe that they had been on the roof looking out and had not seen anyone come into the *hiding*. How could it possibly have happened? Had someone given us away? Were those the same Poles who had come during the day to exchange food for all kinds of valuables? How did they discover us when the Germans could not?

A few days later, after we had scavenged more goods to exchange for food, the same six Poles came back into our *hiding*. Once again the men were on the roof top and did not see them. Once again the Poles robbed us. This time they even stole my shoes. Our men were totally at a loss as to how this had happened again.

During the final phases of the construction of our *hiding* Max met an acquaintance of his, an electrician. The electrician told Max, that he, his wife and mother-in-law were members of a *hiding* at 69 Mila Street that was so well-constructed it had food stored for two years and an opening to the canal which led to the Polish side. The price to get into that *hiding* was very high, 150,000 zlotys. Channa argued with Max that we should buy into that *hiding*, saying that our new *hiding*, 'Is standing on chicken legs.'

A few days later news reached us that the electrician's elaborate *hiding* had been discovered. All the people in it had been taken out and shot on the spot. We heard that the very same electrician who had told Max about the *hiding* had led the Germans to it. The Germans had captured him and offered to spare his life if he showed them where his *hiding* was. When he took them to the *hiding* the Germans could not see it even though they were right on top of it. They were sure that he was trying to deceive them. They could not believe a *hiding* could be concealed where they stood. The Germans had the electrician give the password so that the *hiding* would open up to let him in. The electrician was shot together with those he had betrayed.

By April of 1943 the Germans realized how deeply dug in the remaining Jews of the Ghetto were. The daily raids got worse. The Germans were now using listening apparatus to detect us. We heard them screaming, 'Raus! Raus! Again we escaped detection. During the brief times that we were not in *hiding*, Max, Yakov Brezinski and Mr Greenberg worked hard to finish our new *hiding*. Finally the new *hiding* was completed and we moved in. Our new *hiding* was built into the remnants of an attic that was left under the roof of a small, deserted and ruined house at 60 Mila Street. The structure was nothing more than a shell; it only had walls and a few beams to support the roof which abutted the second- floor of the building we lived in at 58 Mila Street. No one could ever imagine finding a place to hide in it.

Max had built an undetectable entry to our new *hiding*. It was under a marble window sill of a second- floor apartment at 58 Mila Street that abutted the roof of 60 Mila Street. When anyone stepped into the room the only thing they saw was a table in front of the window. Scattered on the table were some cobbler's tools. It looked like someone had just rushed out. Max had constructed it so that to get into our *hiding* the heavy marble window sill had to be pulled back into the room. This exposed a narrow tunnel less than a meter high and about two meters long. It was just wide enough and high enough for a person to crouch through. The tunnel ran between the outer and inner walls of 58 Mila Street to the attic *hiding* under the roof of 60 Mila Street. The bricks between 58 and 60 Mila Street had been removed. To get into the tunnel we stepped off the table top. Once inside it we crawled the two meters into our attic *hiding*. Max had rigged a handle on the bottom inside of the marble sill so that it could be pulled back into place.

Our *hiding* had wooden benches running around the walls and was furnished with iron beds for the women and children. We had prepared a supply of coarse rye bread and sugar in case we would have to stay there for a very long time. No one would suspect that the attic of this ruined house hid thirty people who were praying for a miracle. We used to joke that with Passover approaching maybe God would perform another miracle and free us like he had the Jews from Egypt. Felunia and I stayed in the new *hiding* constantly. The only time we went out for some fresh air was immediately after each raid.

April 7, 1943, was Felunia's birthday. It was a beautiful, sunny day and when the raid had stopped we came out of our *hiding* to walk around the streets, checking to see who had survived. We stood in the street breathing in the fresh, spring air, to store it up, for who knew when, if ever, we would have a chance like this again. 'Felunia, what would you like me to give you for your birthday?' I asked her; she answered, 'A doll that I can play with while in hiding.' If she would have asked to go to school, what possible answer could I have given her? I said to Channa, 'It won't be hard to find a doll for her in all those empty buildings.' Channa was against my going, 'No. You will not go. There could be another raid at any time and you would be trapped somewhere and I wouldn't know where you were.'

Despite my sister's dire warnings not to go look for a doll, I set off. I went down to the lower numbers on Mila Street and hurriedly searched through the empty and deserted buildings, one after another. I ran from floor to floor without finding one doll. I thought to myself, 'Did these children go to Treblinka and take their dolls with them?'

I had been searching for a doll for over two hours when, just as my sister predicted, there was another raid. I did not know what to do. Suddenly I saw five Jewish men running straight towards me. They were running for their lives. It meant that the German SS were carrying out an action nearby. I had to run with them. We ran along the rooftops, jumping from roof to roof. The roofs varied in height from two to four stories. We were either jumping down or climbing up. At one point we had to jump from a higher building to a lower one and climb from the lower one back up onto a higher one. I could not keep up with them. They pulled me along. Without their help I would have been caught and shot. Somehow we managed to escape and hide. By five or six o'clock the raid died down and I ran home.

When I got back Channa screamed at me, 'I told you not to go! What does she need a doll for?' She was so angry with me for disobeying her, she almost struck me. I was now very upset that I had not found the doll I had promised Felunia. That night we heard that a number of German SS had been killed by Jewish fighters and the Germans were now bent on revenge and shooting everyone in sight. I wondered if the men with whom I had run were some of these Jewish fighters or if they were just fleeing from SS reprisal.[9]

On April 19, 1943, just before Passover, the Warsaw Ghetto Uprising[10] began. The almost weaponless Jewish Ghetto fighters engaged and beat back the mighty German Army, inflicting heavy casualties on them. I now found out that Max and some of the other men in our *hiding* had been buying ammunition and other supplies for the fighters, from the Poles. The Poles would bring us whatever we could pay for. And we paid exorbitant prices for everything.

As the Uprising raged, the young boys and men who were fighting came to our *hiding* to bid their relatives good-bye saying, 'We don't know if we will see tomorrow.' There was a lot of crying. When any of them survived the day's fighting and came back we were very happy to see them.

One fateful morning during the Uprising I watched a young boy, who had come to our *hiding*, say a final farewell to his aunt. He was laden with belts of grenades for the coming battle. At midday the men decided that a few women would go out and prepare some food while they stood guard. Channa was among the women who went out to cook. Just minutes after the women left, the men on watch saw a column of Germans and tanks advancing towards us. Max could not find Channa. He ran out to look for her, leaving me with Felunia in the attic *hiding*.

The German Army, having been humiliated by the almost weaponless Jewish Ghetto fighters, had now returned with their Panzer tanks, machineguns and fire bombs. The Germans no longer dared to enter the buildings. They fire bombed us instead. Their strategy was to burn down the buildings with us in them. 58 Mila Street was one of the many buildings set on fire that day.

From our *hiding*, where I huddled with Felunia, we could hear everything that was going on in the streets through the cracks in the walls. Above the roar of the spreading flames we could hear the Germans shooting and yelling orders. We could hear the screaming and yelling of people as they ran out of the blazing buildings into the street where they were shot or captured by the Germans. Others jumped from the windows of the upper stories to their deaths on the street below.

I did not know where my sister and Max had disappeared to. At one point I thought I could hear my sister's voice calling me to come down with the child. I became hysterical and cried to Mr Greenberg, who was in charge, 'Let me out! I hear my sister's voice in the street. She wants me to come down with the child!' He came over to me and said, 'Be quiet! If you will not be quiet I will strangle you to death. Not a word. Not a sound!' I sat there quietly.

At around five o'clock, as I was sitting and holding Felunia in my lap, I heard a faint voice above the sounds of the burning buildings, explosions and street battle calling, 'Fela! Fela! Fela!' This time I was sure that it was my name being called but I kept quiet for fear that Mr Greenberg would choke me to death. As I sat there weeping silently and wondering who was calling my name, there was an explosion just outside the *hiding*. Smoke began pouring into the *hiding* through its cracks and other openings. People grabbed pillows, blankets and whatever was at hand to plug the openings.

Finally the German SS troops withdrew. When it got dark and very quiet, Mr Greenberg went out to reconnoiter. After a few minutes he returned and went straight to Mrs Tola and started whispering to her. He knew that she was a good friend of ours. I saw her looking at me as he spoke. I wondered what was being said. Before she answered him, she looked at me again. I became suspicious but I did not know what was going on.

Mrs Tola was an elderly woman who had traveled the world and lived in America. She had come back to Poland to visit her family just as the war started. Because she was not a naturalized American, she could not return to the United States, and was trapped in Poland. Max always enjoyed her company and we all liked to listen to the stories of her travels.

Mr Greenberg waited a while before he went out again. A few minutes later he came back in. From his behavior towards me I was sure that Max and my sister had been taken and that now the child and I were alone.

58 Mila was on fire. We were all exhausted and sat in silence not knowing what was to come next. Suddenly, we heard someone walking on the roof. I thought, 'That's it, they've discovered us.' Through an opening we saw a

heavily booted foot come through the roof into the *hiding*. We were all dead silent as we heard a voice say, 'Don't be afraid! It's me, Wilczypol.'

Wilczypol was a very strong and brave nineteen-year old man who worked with Max. He was guileless and frank and had become very close to Max. When he came in he did not want to talk to anyone. He came straight over to me and silently asked, 'Who has left this *hiding*?' I whispered, 'Mr Greenberg.' He replied, 'I thought so.' He had two blankets with him and said, 'Don't be afraid, I'm taking you and the child to your sister. She is in the basement *hiding*. I will carry the child covered in a blanket because everything is burning and the walls are very hot. Cover yourself with this blanket and when you come out don't look into the room.' I asked myself, 'Why is he telling me not to look into the room?' In a harsh voice Wilczypol ordered Mr Greenberg to open the exit for us. Mr Greenberg obeyed and let us out. Wilczypol covered the child with a blanket and took her in his arms. With my curiosity aroused by Wilczypol's warning not to look, I looked into the room and saw a corpse burned like charcoal lying on the floor. The corpse had one boot missing from his left foot. I was not sure who it was because several of the men from the *hiding* were missing. Wilczypol took us down the rickety stairs through the burning building. We had to be careful not to touch or fall on the very hot, soot-covered walls. Wilczypol brought us through the burning rubble to the basement *hiding*.

The basement *hiding* was full of water which was running in from broken pipes. Everyone was covered in soot from the smoke of the raging fires. Channa's face was black with soot and she kept repeating, 'Max is dead. Max is dead.' I said, 'Stop talking like this. Who told you that Max is dead?' She said, 'My heart tells me that Max is dead. If he wasn't, he'd be here. He went to see where you and the child were. To see if you had been taken or if the *hiding* had been burned. I see how people are looking at me. He won't come back. Max is dead.' She started to cry and I tried to comfort her. She said, 'I want you to know that without Max we are nothing. We may as well give up and go with the rest of the people. Without Max we have nobody to protect us.' Yakov and Sala Brezinski comforted my sister and promised her that wherever they went, we would go. That we would always stay together.

I went over to Wilczypol and asked him, 'Can you tell me the truth? Was that Max? Is that why you didn't want me to look into the room?' 'Yes,' he said 'That was Max. He went out of the *hiding* to rescue you and his child from the fire. He called out your name three times. The Germans spotted him through the window as he was pulling the sill back. Before he could get it open the Germans killed him with a grenade.' Wilczypol then told me that when Mr Greenberg had gone out to reconnoiter he had seen Max dead. The reason Mr Greenberg had left the *hiding* a second time was to steal the money and jewels Max had hidden in his left boot. The incendiary grenade that had killed Max had also caused the fire whose smoke had entered the attic *hiding*. Now I knew what the whispered conversation Mr Greenberg had with Mrs Tola was about: he had asked her if she knew where Max had hidden his valuables. Somehow Mrs Tola knew.

As we waited in the basement *hiding* for the next German assault I asked Channa what had happened to her after she had gone out with the women to cook. Channa told me that when she saw the German tanks advancing she started running back towards the *hiding*. A young man, Yosele, was on guard. He saw Channa running and knew that she would not make it back to the *hiding* before the advancing German column arrived. He grabbed her and placed her into his own *hiding* and pushed a heavy wardrobe in front of her. Then he ran to find a cover for himself.

After the German attack was over Channa had managed to pull herself out from behind the heavy wardrobe and run down to the basement *hiding* where Max was. They were afraid to come up to our *hiding* for fear that the Germans would spot them and follow them. Max promised my sister that as soon it got dark he would go and see if Felunia and I were still alive. But Max could not wait, because the fire was spreading rapidly and he was afraid that the flames would soon reach our *hiding*.

Yosele was a smart young man whom Max had known before the war. Yosele's family had had a furniture factory and Max had done business with them. Yosele frequently came to our *hiding* to see me. Whenever he came around my sister would sing a Yiddish song about Yosele and Faigaleh. She wanted him to be my boyfriend. We never saw Yosele again.

The Germans came back the next day and gassed us. They carried sound detection apparatus to detect any noise coming from beneath the ruins, especially elderly people coughing. The water flooding the basement helped us to survive. Those suffocating from the gas could put their faces into the water. Once again we escaped undetected. We realized that it was only a matter of days before the Ghetto would be totally destroyed and all of us with it. With Max dead, Channa completely lost her will to live. No matter how I tried to persuade her to go on, if only for her child, she had only one reply, 'Without Max, we are nothing.'

That night Yakov said to us, 'I am afraid to remain in this place. Sala's friend Dora is in a good *hiding* on Ostrowska Street. They have asked us to join them. Let's all go there. You have to come with us. We won't go without you.' Channa said, 'They won't let us in with the child.' 'If they don't let us in with the child we won't go in either,' replied Yakov. Sala and Yakov tried to convince Channa to go with them. I, too, urged her, 'Let's go. Let's go. It's a good hiding place.' Finally she agreed. That night we helped each other crawl through the small debris-covered window that was the exit to the basement *hiding*.

Out in the streets the night was as bright as Christmas Day. Everything was on fire. All the houses. All the trees. Everything. Flames were roaring and leaping. I was afraid that the Germans would see us in the glare of the firelight. Ostrowska Street was just one block away. I held Felunia close to me, to protect her from the burning branches falling from the trees, as we hurried through the swirling cinders and over the hot street beneath our feet to Ostrowska.

The Brezinskis knew the exact address of the building their friend Dora's *hiding* was under, but when we got there the building had burned down. Yakov and Sala began searching for the entrance to the *hiding*. They walked around calling out Dora's name. Not another human sound was to be heard. Channa and I stood in the middle of the street to protect Felunia from the burning debris raining down on us. We waited silently in the light of the raging fires. In the flickering light of the flames, Yakov and Sala Brezinski disappeared from sight. It was as if the earth had opened up and swallowed them. We had lost them.

When we realized that we were alone, my sister, in her disillusionment and pain at being abandoned by our good friends, said, 'You see, without Max we are nothing. Nobody is here for us. It is better that they take us.' I argued, 'No. We have no choice but to go back to the basement *hiding* on Mila.' We returned to the basement *hiding* with Felunia fast asleep and re-entered it by the same window from which we had left.

We waited in the basement *hiding* until Felunia woke up. When she did she was hungry, but we had no food. I said to Channa, 'Let's go back up to our own *hiding* under the roof. There we have dried bread and sugar; we can give the child something to eat.' There was also a bed for the child that Max had prepared for her. We managed to crawl up to our attic *hiding* at 60 Mila. They had no choice but to let us back in.

Felunia was almost asleep again when we entered the *hiding*, but the bed prepared for her by Max was now occupied by Mrs Greenberg. I said to her, 'Mrs Greenberg, please let me put the child into the bed.' Mr Greenberg came over and said, 'Listen, I'm the boss here now. My wife is sleeping in the bed.' If I had had a knife at that moment I would have killed him with it. Killed him for his betrayal of Max's family and for stealing from Max's corpse. My sister, being a better person than I was, said, 'It's okay, Mrs Greenberg is a sick person, put the child down here.' We prepared some bread and sugar for the child. I had no choice but to be quiet.

Despite the fact that all of the surrounding buildings were ablaze, we survived many more raids in our *hiding* under the attic of 60 Mila Street. This was due to Max's clever planning. He had built the *hiding* into an already burnt-out shell of a building and there was almost nothing left that could catch fire. Through the cracks in the walls we could clearly hear every sound from the street below as the Germans assembled the people they had not killed outright and marched them away. Towards the end of the first week in May the German raids abated. The nights became quiet. We were unaware that the Germans were hiding and observing our every movement.

At the end of the first week in May a man who had lived with us at 58 Mila Street came to visit us in our *hiding*. Mr Greenberg opened the entrance and let him in. He sat with us and told us that his wife and child had been taken and that he was now by himself. However, he decided not to stay in our *hiding*. He did not like it. At nightfall he went back to his old *hiding*.

That very night, after our visitor had left, we heard the window sill entrance to our *hiding* being opened. Shots were fired and loud shouting ordered us out. '*Alle raus! Raus! Raus!*' The shock of being discovered and the fear of being killed was overwhelming; I began to menstruate. 'Everyone out! Hands up! Leave everything behind, money, jewelry! If we find anything on you, you will be shot!' Out! Out!'. My sister had a small cache of jewelry in a handkerchief. She threw it away. I protested, 'Why do you throw it away?' 'We don't need it anymore. Don't you see that tomorrow we will go out with the smoke in Treblinka.' We were all convinced that we had been betrayed to the Germans by our visitor.

With our hands above our heads we were marched at gunpoint into the street and herded to an assembly point. There we joined a group of other prisoners and all of us were marched off through the fire-lit streets together. Every building we passed was on fire. People were desperate to escape the flames. Those on the lower floors came running out to the street. Those trapped on the upper floors leapt from the windows to their death. We were marched to the *Befielshtelle*, the command center, on Zelazna and Novolipie Street.

At the *Befielshtelle*, the German SS handed us over to Ukrainian guards and then went back into the burning Ghetto to continue their murder and destruction. The Ukrainian guards surrounded us. Menacing us with their machine guns, they ordered us onto our knees. The cobblestones were cold and hard. Channa and I kept Felunia between us. I held my niece close to me; it looked like the Ukrainian guards were going to kill us. I thought, 'It will finally be over. We will all be killed together.' But we were not shot. Instead we were kept kneeling on the cold hard cobble stones for hours as more people were brought in by German SS units.

In the distance we could see the German SS throwing grenades into the ruins of a building. A short while later we watched a group of *Chassidim* appear out of the ruins, their hands in the air in surrender. The *Chassidim* were assembled and marched towards us. They were ordered to halt nearby. The Germans then started to beat the *Chassidic* men mercilessly. They used large scissors to cut off their side curls and beards. The Ukrainians joined in and cut off the *Chassidim's* beards with their bayonets. Blood ran from the *Chassidim's* faces as they called out their *Shma Israels*. It was a terrible sight to see. I hid Felunia's face, so that she could not witness such cruelty. I prayed that they would kill us right there, the three of us together, while we were holding onto each other.

We were kept kneeling on the cobblestones through the night, waiting for the German Commandant to wake up. When the half-asleep German Commandant finally came down from his quarters we were all ordered to stand up. The German Commandant's face, hideously pocked with livid red acne scars, contrasted with the crisp snow-white shirt he was wearing. He had one thumb hooked into the suspenders of his trousers, which were tucked into high black boots. He looked like an evil animal. Alongside him was a clerk with a sheaf of paper. The German Commandant gave the order to count us and to record how many of us there were. After we were counted and recorded we marched away from the burning Ghetto towards the

Umschlagplatz. As we marched I could see the Poles in windows watching us. Many of them were gleefully shouting to each other, 'Look at the Jews burn!' Others looked at us and ran their fingers across their throats. I turned away from them as we were marched on; their hatred was not a concern to me.

At the *Umschlagplatz* we were taken to a large building surrounded by an outer wall. As we marched through the gate in the wall and across a yard I saw an enormous jumble of confiscated packages and belongings piled against the wall. We were taken up to the third floor and into a large hallway where we sat on the floor, huddled together. We knew that we were going to be shipped to Treblinka to be gassed.

Felunia started to cry that she was hungry. This child never cried and never complained. I often wondered what a child like her was thinking. Did she see this life that she was born to endure as natural? I said to Channa, 'I'm going downstairs. I saw packages in the yard and I can find something for her there.' She replied, 'Don't go! Stay here! What's the use? So she's hungry. Tomorrow we'll be dead!' But I didn't listen to her and I ran down the stairs.

Without even looking around I quickly walked out into the yard towards a pile of packages against the outer wall. I bent down, picked up a knapsack and opened it to make sure there was food in it. A quick glance. A man's blue shirt. Dried bread and sugar. As I clutched the knapsack shut and raised my head I saw, a young man, a meter away from me, fall flat on his face, dead. I turned my head. Three meters behind me stood a young German in a black SS uniform looking at me as he fussed with the mechanism of his hand gun. I had not even heard the shot that had killed the young man. I realized, 'He just killed this boy and I'm going to be next. I'm not going to stay here until he kills me.' I gripped the knapsack and darted away. I ran past a huge dead woman lying in an immense pool of her own blood. There was so much blood; I could not believe how much blood had come out of this one person.

I ran across the yard and around the corner into the stairwell of the building. I stopped to look back around the stairwell wall to see what the SS man was doing. He had not moved; he was still trying to fix his gun. Some-thing else in the yard caught my eye. I recognized two sisters I knew from Mila Street. They had lived with two brothers who were both Jewish policemen. The sisters were dealing with a Ukrainian Guard near the outer wall. I saw them giving him money and jewelry and I thought, 'My God! They are going to buy their way out of here. Why did my sister throw away the jewelry? I could have made the same deal.' I watched as the Ukrainian Guard boosted the two girls over the wall. From the other side of the wall I heard two shots. In the next instant, the girls flew back over the wall, their limbs and heads limp. Their dead bodies thudded onto the ground of the yard. It was too much for me. I bolted back up the stairs. As I ran up the two flights of stairs, clutching the knapsack of food, I heard terrible cries and moans coming from rooms on each floor. I wondered what the noise was all about. I thought that there must be a lot of sick people in those rooms.

When Channa saw me she could not believe that I had come back alive and untouched. She said, 'I thought I would never see you again; I'm glad you weren't here. The Ukrainians came up here, picked out all the pretty young girls and took them downstairs. I was sure that they got you, too.' I gave Channa the knapsack with the dried bread and sugar. We took out the food and fed the child. As Felunia ate the bread and cubes of sugar I told Channa about the fate of the two sisters and how I did not hear the shot that killed the young man who fell near me. She told me that the SS man had used a silencer.

Some time later the girls who had been torn away from their relatives by the Ukrainians were brought back to us, their faces and bodies covered in blood. The moans and cries I had heard from the rooms below were made by these girls as they were being raped by the Ukrainians.

At four o'clock that afternoon the armed Ukrainians began striking and hitting everyone and screaming, 'Fast! Fast!' They drove us down the stairs and herded us like animals from the *Umschlagplatz* into the cattle cars. More Ukrainians stood guard on the cattle car roofs. We were packed into the cars standing up, like herring in a barrel, and the doors were slid shut. Bodies pressed against my back and sides. Channa and I pressed against each other face to face to make room between us for Felunia.

Despite the press of so many bodies I tried to keep us near the car door, close to the small, barred window. I had heard that some people had escaped through those windows. I looked at Felunia, an innocent child, and I thought, 'How can the world be so silent?' We were so helpless.

As the train rolled to our final destination, our attention focused on the small window in the cattle car. A man started to remove the iron bars, saying that he would jump and risk getting killed by a bullet rather than being taken alive to the gas ovens. I said to my sister, 'Listen, Channa, I have heard that people have saved themselves by squeezing through the window and jumping from the train. Now we have to try that. You will jump, then I will throw out Felunia, then I will jump.' She said, 'No, you jump first.' We argued. I knew that if I jumped first she would not throw me Felunia nor jump herself. We did not jump. Neither did any of the men. Nobody jumped.

The sound of the wheels rang in my ears. I looked out the window and saw the Polish people moving about freely, and thought, 'Why is this happening to us? Are we not human?' Suddenly Felunia started sliding to the floor. Channa said, 'Look, she's fainting, her lips are blue.' I panicked. Channa started to kiss Felunia, and gave her daughter her own saliva to revive her. It worked. Felunia became conscious again. I said to Channa, 'I'm going to push through the car and see if I can find some water.' But there was not a drop of water to be found.

Pushing through the hot, airless and crowded cattle car, I was stunned to see my cousin Rosa standing with her back against the wall, the arms of her fiancé protecting her from the crush. She was very pale. I was able to get to her and ask her about our Aunt Chaiah. Chaiah was Father's last surviving sister from Brandenburg, Germany. I knew that she and Rosa were always together. 'Rosa, where is Aunt Chaiah?' 'She is at the other end of the car. She is sick and lying on the floor.' I tried to get to her, but could not push through the crammed bodies. I could not understand how we could have been so close to each other, while being pushed into the same cattle car, and not have seen each other. I could not believe that we were in the same cattle car as my father's sister and the daughter of one of his brothers. I made my way back to Channa and told her whom I had just met. There was no water available in the cattle cars. Our thirst became so acute that our desire for water over-powered everything else, including the ever-increasing odors. We lost our ability to think clearly; we just stood there in a dehydrated stupor as the train labored on.

The train finally stopped. The doors were slid open and we were allowed to grope our way out of the fetid confines of the cattle cars, into the fresh air and sunshine. The grass was green and young on the ground. It was May 8, 1943, and a sign told us we were in Maydanek.[11] Treblinka had been too busy to take us in on this beautiful spring day. The children immediately started running and playing in the field besides the tracks. I was amazed at their resilience.

At last, pails of water were brought to us by a detail of camp prisoners. They put them down on the ground and were quickly marched away. The pails were mobbed. People were simply plunging their heads into the pails of water. I started to look for something in which I could fetch some water for Felunia. I searched the ground near the tracks and found an empty bottle. I broke the bottle with a stone. It broke at the neck, leaving a pointy and jagged edge. I scooped some water from a bucket with it and brought it to Felunia. As she drank from it, I held the sharp point with my hand so that it did not cut her lips. Felunia came back to life like a fish returned to water. She began to run around on the grass as if she were as free as a bird. My sister and I watched her run to three children her age that she knew from our apartment on Mila. In the distance we saw windowless barracks and some children playing outside them.

There was tremendous confusion and noise caused by the incessant orders and demands of the Germans. Within minutes, before we knew what had happened, the Germans had separated the men from us and marched them off. Immediately after that the young boys were separated and taken away. No one knew where they were going.

The Germans made it clear that they were taking only one thousand women to work. And they were taking volunteers now. Women were being formed into groups of one hundred and immediately marched off to work. The noise and panic went on. Channa and I stood and watched mothers pushing their daughters away, pushing them to enlist for work and kissing them goodbye. Young women and children were separated. We watched mothers abandon their children. They left infants lying on the grass. Young abandoned children huddled in groups, crying, 'Mama! Mama!'

The children Felunia had been playing with just a few moments ago were now crying. Those poor children had been abandoned. Their mother, and her younger sister, had enlisted for work. Felunia came close to my sister and asked, 'Mama, will you leave me like this too?' We hugged her to protect her and said, 'Never. Never. You'll stay right here with us."

As we stood there our Aunt Chaiah came looking for us. Her face was yellow, she was weak and tired-looking. She pulled me aside and said, 'Enlist for work. The Germans are assembling young people to work. Tell Channa to assemble with you.' I said, 'What about Felunia? We will not leave the child, like others do, we will not.' Aunt Chaiah then turned to my sister. She loved Channa dearly, and said, 'Enlist for work. You are young.' I did not hear Channa answer her. I do not know if Channa even listened to what she was saying. Rosa called her. Aunt Chaiah turned around and marched off with her niece to enlist for work.

The *kapo*, assembling the women, was a short, stocky Czechoslovakian man wearing a black beret on his bald head. He noticed my sister, came over to her and said in perfect German, 'You're young, you're beautiful. Enlist for work!' Holding Felunia close to her, she replied, 'Don't you see, I have a child. Take my sister.' To convince her, he said, 'Look over there in the field and you will see barracks for children. You will join your child later.' He knew better. We knew better. He just wanted to save my sister.

He turned away and started to assemble another group of one hundred women. After he had them marched off he came back to us again. Again he tried to convince Channa to enlist. He said, 'I must tell you, they are taking only 1,000 people from this transport for work. Your child will be in the children's barracks.'

Each time he sent away another hundred women he came back to my sister and tried to convince her to enlist. My sister said, 'Do me a favor, take my sister, she is young. I cannot go. I will go together with my child.' I said, 'What are you saying? I will not go! I will not leave you!' We began arguing. Channa was very mad. 'You will work. Take my shoes. They are better than yours. I want you to survive.' 'No!' I protested. 'Look, girls are leaving their mothers. They're saying goodbye. Maybe you'll meet someone if you survive. You'll tell them what happened to us.' She took off her shoes. Crying, I obeyed her. I took off my shoes and put on hers. She put on mine.

While we had been arguing, the *kapo* had sent off another one hundred; he came back to us yet again. Now he was in a rage. 'This is the last hundred. If you do not enlist now it will be too late. This is it.' The last hundred were almost formed up. Channa begged him, 'Take my sister! Enlist her!' I turned away from him; she pushed me towards him. He grabbed my arm and pulled me into the last row of five to complete the last group of one hundred women to be marched off. A woman grabbed my arm to hold me in place and we immediately started marching away. My sister ran towards me with a little piece of bread and sugar for me. We were both crying. I said, 'No, no, no! Keep it for Felunia!' Her last words to me were, 'Survive. Remember. Do everything you can to survive so you can tell what happened to us.'

Everything had happened so fast I did not have a chance to kiss Felunia goodbye.

BOOK FOUR

DEATH CAMPS

May 8, 1943 – January 18, 1945

Waves of overwhelming emotional agony and helplessness washed over me as we were marched away from the railroad tracks. Mrs Feldman, an elderly woman I knew from 58 Mila, took hold of my arm and asked, 'Do you mind if I hold onto you?' 'No, no, Mrs Feldman, hold on to me.' As we marched I could see children playing in front of a barrack surrounded by barbed wire and watchtowers. No matter in which direction I looked, high barbed wire fence and watchtowers, each manned by two guards, ran as far as I could see.

An SS man, holding a baton, waited for us in front of the building we were marched to. Each one of us had to step up to him for a visual inspection. Pointing with his baton he sorted us with orders: left or right, go into the building or stay outside. When it was our turn we stepped forward to be examined. He looked us over and said to Mrs Feldman, 'You stay here!' To me he said, 'You go in.' I was among the last to enter. Inside the building I found myself completely surrounded by strangers. Adding to my fear for my sister and Felunia, and what had become of them, was the realization that this was the first time in my life that I was entirely by myself.

Three SS men with sticks in hand stood waiting for us inside the building. As soon as they saw us they started screaming, 'Fast! Fast! Undress! Undress!' Once we were naked they called or just motioned us forward with their sticks. They turned us, like animals are turned, with taps and waves of their sticks as they inspected us one by one. I saw a pretty brunette, in her twenties, hanging back. She was afraid to step up when they ordered her forward. They screamed at her, 'Come! Come fast!' She went forward and held her clothes awkwardly in an attempt to hide something under her arm. They took away her clothes. I saw a terrible black and red tumor under her arm. The SS men immediately told her to get dressed and sent her back out of the building. I was terrified that the same would happen to me because I was still menstruating. I did not have anything with which to wipe off the blood that was flowing down over my lower body. They called me forward.

Prodding me with their wooden sticks they forced me to turn around. The three looked at me and asked how old I was. 'Nineteen,' I lied. I had just turned seventeen. I could see they did not believe me. They looked at each other to decide my fate. I heard one say to the other, 'This is her period.' And then to me, 'Get in fast! Wash up.' I quickly went into the shower area where the other women were. We all stood there in helpless silence and avoided each other's nakedness by looking up at the shower heads. We wondered what would come out of them: water or gas. We waited and waited. Those few minutes of waiting felt like endless hours.

Water. It was water. To the screams of, 'Fast! Fast!' we washed up. We were rushed out of the showers to where we had left our clothes, to find only our shoes. Our clothes had been taken away. Wearing only our shoes we were marched naked to another barrack where other prisoners stood at a table, handing us back our disinfected clothes. They gave us whatever clothes came to hand; big or small, it didn't matter. You took what you got. Supervising the table was the same Czech *kapo* who had torn me away from my sister and Felunia. I went over to him, hoping that he would remember me and perhaps tell me something about my sister and her child. I tried to catch his eye, to engage him, but there was no visible sign of recognition from him. I was afraid to ask him about my sister and Felunia. Instead I asked, 'Please, can you give me a comb?' He gave me a package of three combs and a bar of soap. This turned out to be a very valuable gift.

Again we were marched off, this time by SS women who yelled at us incessantly. 'You animals! You whores! Fast! Fast!' As we were marched towards another barrack we saw prisoners at hard labor, carrying large stones. I cried as I looked around with the hope that I could spot my sister and her child somewhere. I hoped that tomorrow I would be able to find out where the women and children's barracks were.

We arrived at a gate set in a barbed wire fence. Another group of German officers was waiting for us at the gate. Behind the gated barbed wire fence were more barracks. The German officers selected us again as we went through the gate. Again, many women were taken out. I passed through the gate. As we waited for the selection to finish I saw three girls I knew from 58 Mila. I positioned myself close to them as we were marched towards the barracks.

The four of us went into the same barrack. The interior of the barrack was windowless and filled with rows of wooden shelves, two tiers high. Each shelf was a *pritcha* and each *pritcha* had to sleep two people. I had no one to team up with. I stood there alone as the *pritcha*s filled up. Two of the three girls that I knew from 58 Mila Street were sisters, Rozia and Sala Birenbaum. Sala was a red-haired, freckled, twenty-year old with a fully developed voluptuous figure. Rozia was eighteen years old, a pretty, blue-eyed blonde, with very white teeth and a little turned-up nose. Their parents, whom I also knew, were very religious and modest people. The sisters climbed up into an upper *pritcha* and occupied one *pritcha*. I stood there looking at them, not knowing what to do. They pointed to the third girl from 58 Mila Street, Sala Beinstock, a small, skinny, bespectacled girl, and told me to team up with her. At least she was somebody I knew.

I did as the sisters suggested. Sala Beinstock and I shared a *pritcha*. She was twenty-two years old and very depressed. She had been separated from her two brothers, young men of eighteen and twenty, as they had come into the camp. Her parents were long gone. She did not stop crying and calling her brothers' names. At seventeen, I was the youngest of the four, and I, too, was crying. We both cried throughout the first night. It was much easier for the two sisters: they had each other. In my despair I resolved to find my sister and Felunia the first chance I had. Maybe what the Czech *kapo* had told Channa was true; maybe they would be in the women and children's barracks.

At first light there was an *appel*. This was an assembly for all prisoners, during which we had to line up to be counted, inspected, assigned work details, issued camp orders, to watch punishments and undergo selection. There were *appels* every morning and every evening. *Appels* could be called at any time of the day or night, any day of the week. Selections could be made at any of the *appels*, but those *appels* called at random were the most dangerous. They usually meant selections. The selection criteria were superficial. The Germans looked at our physical condition. If you were too skinny, too old, too weak, too sick or not fit to work, you were selected. Or they would just walk through selecting people at whim.

This first morning *appel* in Maydanek was a selection. Again the old and sick were sorted out and taken away. Among them was Mrs Greenberg. I almost did not recognize her. She was not an old woman but she had turned completely gray. I pitied her. I had known her so well. My sister had consoled her after she had lost her son. After she fell sick, Channa, whenever possible, would cook her something to eat. Despite her husband's behavior towards us I felt terrible as she was taken away. We were not formed into labor gangs during this *appel*. We were just left in the blocks.

I immediately went around asking where the women and children's barracks that I had seen yesterday were. I found out. When I got to the blocks in which the children had been, they were now occupied by adults. I was told that the children had been taken out during the night. Nobody knew where to. I had to accept that the women and children I had seen in those blocks yesterday had been put there by the Germans as decoys to prevent the men and women with children in the incoming transports from panicking.

With this delusion shattered, my despair deepened. I now needed to find my Aunt Chaiah and cousin Rosa. I needed to be with family. I wanted to join them. I knew that they had enlisted for work and were here somewhere. I started searching for them. I went to the first block and called out my aunt's family name, 'Chaiah Gothelf! Chaiah Gothelf!' There was no response. I went from block to block calling out her name. I searched all the blocks and nobody replied. I could not understand why I had not gotten an answer. 'Where is she?' I asked myself as I fought to control my panic. I forced myself to think logically and decided to start over again this time calling out her maiden name, 'Burman! Burman!' This was also my cousin Rosa's family name.

At the second block my cousin Rosa stood up and waved to me. She was surrounded by a group of friends. I went over and asked her where Aunt Chaiah was. Rosa told me that Aunt Chaiah had been taken away from her. I expected Rosa, who was a few years older than I, to ask me to stay with her, to be together with her. She did not. My hope of being with someone from my family was shattered. I did not know where to turn. I left her and walked back towards my block, broken-hearted.

When I returned to the girls I knew from 58 Mila Street and told them what had happened, they said, 'Let's all stick together.' This comforted me and I was grateful for their friendship. I gave them one of the three combs that the Czech *Kapo* had given me. With it they could remove the lice from their heads. Everyone in Maydanek was plagued by lice. I kept one comb for myself and lent the third to whoever needed it. I stayed close to the two sisters, Sala and Rozia. My bunk mate, Sala Beinstock, was not easy to be with. She never stopped crying. She seemed to be losing her mind. It took a few days before we were put to work. I used this time to walk around all the blocks searching for people I knew. I looked into everyone's eyes and everyone's eyes looked back into mine.

On one of those days I came back into the block around three or four in the afternoon and the two sisters were nowhere in sight. I went out to look for them. I spotted them behind the barracks. They were eating something. As soon as they saw me they wiped their mouths and hid what they were eating. This hurt me deeply. We were supposed to be friends and stick together. Now they had something to eat and would not share it with me. Why were they doing this? Why were they hiding from me? I could not understand it. I went over to them and said, 'You don't have to hide anything from me, nor give me anything. And I will not take anything away from you.' They felt guilty and offered me some white bread and a piece of salami. But I was so hurt I refused to take it. I said, 'Just tell me how you got it.' One of them had managed to hide a gold coin in her mouth which they had traded for the bread and salami.

My pain was so great I could no longer talk to them. I could no longer look them in the face. I turned and walked away from them without uttering another word. Once alone I had a good cry and realized that nobody could ever take the place of my sister, and that everyone in this place was on her own. I thought of taking away the comb I had given them, but I knew it was essential for them to have it. But I resolved that from now on I would not trust anyone.

When I woke up the next morning my shoes were gone. Stolen. I had been using them as a pillow. They had been stolen from under my head. I had not felt or heard a thing. These were the shoes that Channa had switched with me, as we were arguing, on our arrival in Maydanek. Now I realized that Channa had foreseen that she and her child were going to their deaths and that I needed better shoes because I was to go to work. I went into shock and started yelling, 'Somebody stole my sister's shoes!' Screaming and crying, 'My sister took the shoes off her feet and gave them to me!' I went through the entire block looking for my shoes. But nobody was wearing them. At that moment an *appel* was called. I had to stand barefoot in the cold May morning.

Even though I was not on speaking terms with them, Sala and Rozia took pity on me. They said that they knew how to sew and that they would make me a pair of shoes, *papuskas*. They were going to cut up a blanket and sew them for me. Cutting up a blanket in Maydanek was a criminal offence punishable by death. I said, 'No, you cannot do that! If they catch me wearing them they will make me tell where I got them and they'll hang us all.' I could see that they were willing to risk their lives for me and were truly sorry for not having shared their food with me. I forgave them. I now had to go out to all the *appels* barefoot. My feet went numb from the cold during the early morning *appels*.

A few days later the time to work arrived. Labor groups were called commandos. There were various kinds of commandos, each named for the type of work that was involved. One was either assigned to a commando during an *appel* or one could 'enlist' in one by lining up as it was being formed. Some commandos were less life-sapping than others. At first it was impossible to know which commandos to avoid and which to try to get into. In some commandos the work was very brutal, or the German guards and *kapos* were extremely sadistic, or there was a very poor chance of getting anything to eat. In the worst commandos it was all three problems at once. Once you knew which commandos to avoid it still took some luck to get into the less dangerous ones.

Our meals consisted of a daily ration of gray bread and a bowl of a watery green soup of indeterminable origin. Twice a week we were given a meager portion of salami. It was impossible to survive on these starvation rations while being forced to do hard labor and endure the constant beatings by the *kapos*. The deterioration of our bodies was rapid.

After a few days of hard labor on these starvation rations, time in Maydanek took on a new meaning.[1] It was time to eat, time to work, time for *appel*, time to die. It was either day or night, hot or cold, summer or winter. The calendar did not exist for us; hours were meaningless. We were always afraid, hungry, and tired. Our only concern was how to stay alive. To stay alive you had to *combineer*, to *organize*, to find a way to get some extra food for yourself so that you did not become emaciated and get selected for death during an *appel*.

I was still shoeless when I was put into a commando doing field work. A few days later, when I returned to the block after a day of field work Sala and Rozia presented me with a pair of *papuskas* they had sewn together using a piece of a blanket and lined with insoles of cardboard. They had made them despite my objections and had risked their lives for me. But by now the days of standing barefoot for the cold six a.m. *appels* and working outdoors shoeless had taken their toll. I became very ill. At the next morning's *appel* I was burning with fever. Sick as I was, I lined up for work. Not to 'enlist for work' and stay in the barracks, for whatever reason, was a death sentence. If you were found in the barracks you were taken away. By the time we marched off to work I was shaking with fever.

That day we were set to work weeding a field. I went out into the field but my fever was so high I could not do anything except crawl. I hid on the ground between the rows of plants hoping I would not be found by a German or a *kapo*. Whenever the girls had a chance they came by to see if I was still alive. The sun was very hot and the heat added to my fever. I became desperate for water. I could see a small building on the far side of the field. I thought to myself, 'I have nothing to lose. I'll work my way over there and ask for a little bit of water to put on my head and lips.' I forced myself to my feet and struggled to the door of the small building.

I slipped into the building unseen. The place was empty except for a large oven. An oven like the ones in Grodzisk to which we would bring our *chulent* for baking before the Sabbath. There was a wooden table near the window with shovels, long irons, and various instruments that I did not recognize. In my feverish state I did not realize what kind of oven it was nor what the tools were for, nor where I was. I just wanted water.

As I looked for water a short, stocky, bald Ukrainian with a round face walked in. He was startled to see me. He looked at me as if I had fallen out of the oven. He asked, "Where did you come from? What are you doing here?' He spoke in a mixture of German and Russian. I answered him, 'I work in the field out front and I'm sick. I need a drop of water. Please give me a drop of water.' He said, 'I have no water here. Just go out the way you came in. Go back to your commando and never tell anybody that you were here.'

I left the small building and went back into the field. Nobody had noticed me leaving and nobody noticed me coming back. With luck I managed to make it through the day undetected. Once back in the block I told the girls that I had been inside the small building looking for water. 'Oh my God!' they said, 'Why did you go there? It's the crematorium where they burn the bodies of the camp inmates who have died, or have been shot or hanged.'

My illness lasted several more days and then developed into dysentery. With every attack of dysentery, I ran, doubled over with painful cramps, to squat near the fence behind the barracks. It was too far to reach the latrines without fouling myself. I was not the only one running to squat near the fence.

With our behinds to the fence we were exposed to the guards up in their watchtowers. During one trip to the fence another dysentery-stricken girl squatting next to me suddenly sprawled dead in her own excrement. I had not heard the shot but knew immediately that she had been shot by a German guard in one of the watchtowers. The Germans shot us whenever it pleased them. I did not run away. I was too sick and miserable with my painful stomach cramps to stand up and run. At that moment I did not care if I was the next victim. If the guard shot me too, that would have been all right. But the German did not shoot. Doubled over, I crab-walked away holding my cramping stomach with both hands.

As I made my way back towards my block from the fence, I was stopped by the head *kapo*, an *Ofzayeren*, a powerful and feared camp figure. She was in charge of the daily *appels*. A Lithuanian named Janina, she was a very handsome woman with long blond hair and a large bust. She was always well dressed and always carried a leather riding crop. Whenever she accompanied the SS men on their duties they always walked beside her and flirted with her. She asked me, 'Why are you holding your stomach?' I was afraid to say anything, thinking that she would send me away for good. I thought of running away but the tone of her voice convinced me that she would not do me any harm. I said, 'I'm sick. I have to run to the bathroom all the time. She said, 'Stay right here. Wait for me, don't move, just stay here.' I did not know her reason for making me wait for her but I did. She came back with a handful of bread burnt like coal. She said, 'Eat this, it will help you. You will get well.' I ate most of it on the spot and returned to the block with a few pieces still in my hands. I didn't know what to think of this woman. I went to Sala and Rozia and told them about the girl who got shot right beside me and about my good fortune with the feared Lithuanian *Ofzayeren* Janina. They concluded that she must like me, since she helped me.

Three days later, my fever disappeared and the dysentery stopped. But now my shoes, the *papuskas*, were falling apart. We were afraid to make new ones because we had just witnessed the hanging of a girl who had tried to escape. One of the girls said, 'Nobody in this block is wearing your shoes. After our bread ration, when everyone is sitting on their beds, we will go block by block to look for your shoes.'

That evening Sala, Rozia and I walked around and looked at every woman's feet to see who was wearing my shoes. Sure enough, in one of the blocks I saw a tall, strong, blonde woman wearing my shoes. We followed her and saw her climb into an upper *pritcha*. We confronted her. I said, 'Those are my shoes!' The girls started to scream at her, 'You stole her shoes! Give her back her shoes! Those are her shoes!' She started kicking at us with her long legs from the upper *pritcha*. She came off the *pritcha* and fought the three of us.

She was older and taller than we were and she was stronger than the three of us combined. She was a giant compared to us and we could not do anything against her. She beat the three of us mercilessly, screaming that they were her shoes. No matter how I begged and cried she kept hitting us. We finally managed to get away from her.

When we returned to our block one of the girls said, 'Go to the Lithuanian *Ofzayeren* Janina and tell her that this woman stole your shoes.' I thought, 'My God, if I tell the *Ofzayeren* that this woman stole my shoes, who knows what she will do to her. I cannot do that.' But the girls insisted that I go over to the *Ofzayeren* to thank her for the burnt bread which had cured me and then tell her about the woman who had stolen my shoes. Finally the *papuskas* tore and I was barefoot again. The girls kept insisting that I ask the Lithuanian *Ofzayeren* Janina for help. Early on a beautiful Sunday morning I saw an opportunity to approach her. I went over to her, greeted her and thanked her for the burnt bread. As I hesitated to tell her about the woman who had stolen my shoes, because I still was not convinced that it was a good idea, a German SS man approached her. She turned to face him and he ordered her to call an immediate *appel*. His order caught her by surprise. She was totally unprepared to call an *appel*. She panicked and started lashing everyone in front of her with her riding crop, yelling, *'Einschtellen zu appel! Einschtellen! Einschtellen! Schnell! Schnell!'* 'Line up for ! Line up! Line up! Fast! Fast!' I too was caught by surprise and was too slow running away. As I turned to run, the end of her crop came over the top of my head on a back swing and caught me in the eye. My eye immediately swelled closed and turned black and blue.

Fortunately, there was not a selection during that *appel*. We were just counted and sent to our blocks. Back in the block nobody recognized me because now the whole side of my face was swollen black and blue. I said to the girls, 'God punished me for wanting to squeal about my shoes. Look at what happened to me because I listened to you.' I was sure that at the next selection I would be taken away. Surprisingly I went through several selections with my eye in this condition and I was not taken away to my death.

A few days later the Lithuanian *Ofzayeren* Janina saw me. Noticing my discolored eye, she called me over. 'Who did this to you?' she asked. She was sure that somebody had beaten me up. I said, 'You.' She was surprised, 'Me?' 'Yes, but you didn't know. It was on Sunday when I was talking to you and we had to rush for *appel*. Your crop caught me in the eye.' She said, 'I remember. Forgive me.'

By the following Sunday my eye had healed, but I was still barefoot and moving around was getting hard on my feet. We were not taken to work that day and I sat outside the blocks looking at the new faces walking by to see if I could recognize someone I knew. Transports bringing in the last survivors from the Warsaw Ghetto and other parts of Poland were arriving in Maydanek almost every day. New arrivals and camp inmates alike used every free moment to see who was still alive and to *combineer, organize* the necessities to stay alive.

Sitting there barefoot and scrutinizing every face that passed by, I saw Sala Brezinski and her friend Dora walking towards me. Both their faces were yellow. I did not stop them. I was still hurt that she had abandoned us on Ostrowska Street in the middle of the night in the burning Ghetto. I could not bring myself to go over to Sala Brezinski and look her in the eye. I looked away so they would not see me.

Unaware of my presence, Sala and Dora walked right by me. However, my curiosity overcame me. I wanted to hear her explain why she had abandoned us that night. I also wondered why their faces were so yellow. I was sure that with their faces like that, they were going to be taken away to their death in the next selection. I sat and waited for them to walk back. When they came my way I called out, 'Sala! Sala!' Sala ran over to me, happy to see me, and embraced me. Dora did not greet me. She just stood there, a very tall, yellow-faced woman.

I could see the guilt on Sala's face. I told her that I saw her pass by earlier but I had not gone over to her because I was so hurt. Sala immediately apologized and explained what had happened that night on Ostrowska Street. She said, 'We never saw the underground bunker open up. We were pulled into the *hiding* so fast that we did not have a chance to call out your names. We told them there was a woman outside with a seventeen-year old girl and a child. They told us, 'No children. If you want we can let you out.' Dora had witnessed this and confirmed her story.

I asked her, 'Why are your faces yellow? Are you both sick?' She explained that when the Germans discovered their underground bunker on Ostrowska Street they had refused to come out. The Germans gassed them, forcing them out. Swallowing the gas had caused them to vomit violently and turned their faces yellow. They were lucky to have survived. Their underground bunker was discovered before our attic *hiding* was. I told them about our fate and about my final parting with Channa and Felunia.

No shoes meant certain death and I was still barefoot. My sister's words rang in my ears, 'Do everything you can to survive, so you can tell what happened to us.' I needed shoes. Another *appel*. Another selection. Another disinfecting. After my group came out of the shower I took a pair of shoes from among the many pairs left outside by the group now in the showers. I did not know whose they were, nor did I want to. I now had shoes.

One day while I was working near the sauna I saw a small group of prisoners from a newly arrived transport being marched to the showers. Among them was Leon Kamerfux, a man from my hometown of Grodzisk. But it was impossible to speak to him. It was not until after I started working in the Gertnerie that I chanced to see him again. He was spading in a field. I told him, 'I saw you arrive here with about ten others.' He replied, 'We were the last few people taken out of the Warsaw Ghetto. There are no other Jews left there. If any were left there ... the Germans have gone in with bulldozers.'

Sala Brezinski and Dora worked in the Gertnerie commando. The Gertnerie was the camp vegetable farm. Sala advised me to find a way into it. 'After all, you work close to vegetables, so if you're smart you'll find a way to put something in your mouth, a piece of lettuce, a radish, anything. But you have to be very careful that Brigida, the SS woman[2], does not catch you.'

Brigida was a tall, slim, attractive brunette. She was a good-looking woman, and always rode her bicycle with her German Shepherd trotting alongside. What you could not see was the evil sadistic beast that resided within her human form. She beat and tortured women and men mercilessly at any offence. We had to be extremely careful around her because if she singled you out for punishment and did not kill you outright, there was not enough left of you to make it through the next selection.

Sometimes we were forced to watch the cruel punishments meted out by Brigida and the other SS as examples of what happened to anyone who committed any infraction of the camp's innumerable rules.

One day as Brigida was marching us out to work she saw two men carrying pails of water on yokes. She stopped us, got off her bike, and went over to them, saying, 'Put down the water.' While we watched she poured the pails of water over their heads. Then she started to kick them with her boots and beat them with her riding crop. She beat them mercilessly. Then she had them get more water and poured it over them again and repeated the kicking and beating. She did this at least ten times before she stopped and marched us off to work. The two men were barely conscious when we left. They were not likely to survive the next selection. We never knew what they had done to incite her.

On another day Brigida caught a woman eating a piece of lettuce. At the end of the day we were lined up to be marched back to the camp. We stood in front of the bushel baskets full of the mud-and sand-covered lettuce that we had picked that day. Brigida singled out the woman she had caught. In front of everybody Brigida shoved mud-and sand-covered lettuce into this woman's mouth until she choked to death. We had to watch. We were not allowed to turn our eyes away.

The Commandant of the Gertnerie wore a German uniform, but it was not an SS one. He was a very handsome, good-looking man, always riding about on a motorcycle. From the way he inspected the fields it was obvious that he was an agricultural specialist. He directed Brigida and the other *kapos* as to what had to be done. Whenever he saw Brigida beating someone, he would say something to her and she would stop immediately. I was never beaten by Brigida, but one day I had a terrible scare.

Brigida and the Commandant were sitting on an embankment having lunch, drinking milk and eating sandwiches. I was working nearby. The Commandant called me over and offered me the remains of his sandwich. Brigida knocked it out of his hand. I quickly turned my back so that she would not remember my face and recognize me, for fear that she would punish me later. I could hear them speaking loudly as I ran back to work, to get as far away from her as I could.

On another day the Commandant of the Gertnerie spotted me and said, 'You come here!' I obeyed. He picked up a switch cut from a tree branch. He gave it to me and said, 'Go run in that field and chase the birds away.' I was glad to get out to the far side of the field of sweet peas where nobody could see me. It was a blessing. I was away from Brigida and all the others and I could eat as many peas as I wanted to. I hid a few peas to bring back to the girls.

That evening I gave the two sisters, Rozia and Sala, and Sala 'the cry baby' Beinstock, as we now called her, the peas I had smuggled back for them. They were all working in other commandos and I said to them, 'No one will know that the Commandant assigned only me to the field. Come with me and we'll all chase the birds.' The next day the girls came to the Gertnerie with me. We all chased birds and ate sweet peas.

There was a fence at the far end of the sweet pea field. On the other side of the fence were some barracks around which we could see men walking and working. When Sala Brezinski heard this she re-enlisted for the Gertnerie commando. She begged me to help her to get close to the men. She insisted that we take a stretcher, put soil on it and carry it close to the men working there, to ask them if her husband, Yakov Brezinski, was in their barracks. I could not refuse her.

We filled a stretcher with soil and began carrying it towards a section of the fence where we saw some men working. Just as we got close to the men the Commandant roared up on his motorcycle and began yelling at us. 'You damn women! Where are you carrying that soil to? What are you doing here? That soil is supposed to stay on the other side!' We played dumb as if we had misunderstood. Our *kapo*, hearing the screams of the Commandant came running over and said, 'You will pay for this!' We were lucky that Brigida was not there at that moment. She would have had us eat that soil until we choked on it.

The *kapo* marked Sala and me down for punishment. Twenty-five lashes each. The whipping was to be administered upon our return to camp. A few other girls had also been marked down for lashes because they had been caught eating a piece of lettuce. As we were marched back to camp I was filled with fear. I knew that I could not survive twenty-five lashes. I saw what other girls had looked like after receiving twenty-five lashes. They could barely stand, let alone walk. They usually did not make it through the next selection. When we got to the gate leading into the blocks, the *kapo* pulled us out of the work group and stood us next to the gate to await our punishment. We watched the rest of the commando go through.

As we stood there, a small isolated group waiting for our punishment, I said to Sala, 'I won't survive these twenty-five lashes.' Sala told me that she was very sorry for having asked me to risk my life to help her find out about her husband. I was in such dread of the whipping I was about to receive that I did not see Janina, the Lithuanian *Ofzayeren*, who was always at the gate, but she saw me. She came over to me, took my arm and began to pull me through the gate. I instantly grabbed Sala Brezinski. Janina, the Lithuanian *Ofzayeren*, pulled us both into the camp and let us go without saying a word to us. We were both safe and out of danger. We could not believe our luck in escaping the twenty-five lashes. There was no going back to the Gertnerie commando now.

The two sisters and I enlisted in another commando that worked outside the camp, carrying bricks and wood for the construction of garden bungalows for the families of the SS. We had heard that some of the Polish girls who worked as nannies for these SS families brought out food, sandwiches and whatever they could, for the commando. Our constant hunger made this a very attractive idea.

We were marched out of the camp, burdened with loads of wood, to the construction site. We were disappointed to find the site deserted. There were no Polish girls there to give us some food. There was not even a drop of water to be had. Eventually we needed to toilet. Looking for a suitable place, we found a nearby fire pit and stepped into it. As we squatted among the ashes to do our business we noticed passports and bone fragments under our feet. We picked up some of the passports that were still intact. They had pictures and names in them. We began to read aloud the names of men and the cities they had come from. What we were witnessing dawned on us. 'Look at what we are doing. These men that were killed and burned here could have been our own brothers.' The three of us were sick with the horror that had occurred here. And yet the SS was building garden bungalows for their wives and children almost on top of the charred remains of their victims.

Sometime in July my cousin Rosa came looking for me. She said, 'I came to tell you that we are leaving here. We are going to a working camp.' I said, 'How do you know it's a working camp? Maybe it's a transport to Treblinka?' She replied, 'Well, I'm taking a chance and so are all the girls I'm with. I suggest that you also enlist.' My reply was, 'My friends and I are afraid. Maybe it's better to wait.' Had I gone with Rosa, I would have been far better off. They were sent to Skarzysko, near Chestochova, a working concentration camp where there were no crematoria.

A few days later there was a selection at morning *appel*. Those of us who survived the selection were marched straight into cattle cars. There were only a few hundred of us, so the cattle cars were not as packed as when we had arrived some ten weeks earlier from the *Umschlagplatz*. I had been in Maydanek from the beginning of May until late in July. This time we were certain that we were being transported to our deaths.

We read the station name as the cattle cars rattled into Birkenau's rail depot. Birkenau[3] was the largest part of the Auschwitz concentration camp complex. As soon as the cattle cars' doors opened we were immediately rushed out by the SS guards, who never stopped screaming and yelling. The sky was red and black with smoke billowing from the crematorium chimneys. The smell of burning corpses was in every breath we took. We were rushed through another selection. Once again, would we be sent to the left or to the right? To work or to die? Luckily all four of us were chosen to work. The unfortunate ones were marched off to the crematorium. The rest of us were marched into the camp.

Everywhere we looked we saw railway tracks, barbed wire, electrified fences and watchtowers. Deep ditches ran alongside the electric fences. Behind the electric fences ran rows of barracks in orderly blocks. Unlike Maydanek, these barracks had windows. We were marched past the ever-present gallows, always ready for those who tried to escape. Everything we saw was orderly. As we were marched through the gate into the camp we read the mocking inscription on the gate's overhead arch: 'Arbeit Macht Frei'.[4] Not one of us felt that we would get out of here alive.

We were marched to the disinfecting area. Our heads were shaved and our bodies were disinfected and showered. Still naked, we were ordered to sit on wooden benches and wait for our *pasiaks*, the striped, coarse-fibered dresses that were our concentration camp uniforms. With all our hair shaved off and our bodies now rail thin we looked like boys. I could not recognize anyone. I called out the girls' names. They did not answer me. It was not until we could get close enough to hear each others' voices that we could recognize each other. They had not answered my calls because they had not recognized me. The *pasiak*s were terrible itchy. It was torture to wear one. The girls said not to complain, it could be worse. It immediately was.

We were marched into a large hall. The Germans ordered us to line up in alphabetical order for tattooing. The four of us were lined up one behind the other; all of our family names started with the letter B: Sala 'the cry baby' Beinstock, the two Birenbaum sisters, and myself, Burman.

We were tattooed, one after the other. My number was 48378. The others were tattooed with 48379, 48380 and 48381. I cried when the needle stuck my arm. The girl tattooing me said, 'Don't cry. I will try to do it nicely.' I could not comprehend the meaning of what she said. I felt like an animal being marked for slaughter. I found myself wondering what was going to happen to us next. And then, in the next instant, I was thinking that it was not important. There was no need to worry because none of us was going to survive this place.

We were assigned to Block 15 in Camp A, Birkenau. The four of us got an upper *pritcha*. Our *blockeldeste* was Sara, a Slovakian Jewish woman, in her late forties. She was a short woman, with curly red hair and an ugly face splotched with freckles. We called her the Red Sara. She hated Polish-born women. She beat us mercilessly and called us 'Polish swine' and 'whores'. She was a beast. The only woman more brutal than her was Brigida the SS guard in Maydanek. Red Sara had an assistant, a *schtubeneldeste,* a brunette called Clara. Clara was a relative of Red Sara's; she was not as brutal, but she, too, beat us often.

One of the girls took offence when Red Sara called her a whore and called her a whore in return. Red Sara turned on her and beat this poor girl until she could no longer move. Then Red Sara turned on all of us. She beat some more girls and then said, 'If you Polish swine ever try to open your mouths I will show you what I can do!' Two women had to drag the girl who was beaten senseless back into the block. This was the fate of any Polish- Jewish girl who dared talk back to Red Sara or her assistant.

Our daily rations in Birkenau were identical to those at Maydanek. Again the daily gray bread and a watery green soup of indeterminable origin. Twice a week we were given a meager portion of salami or jam. Our hunger was constant. As our bodies wasted away from starvation and hard labor our thoughts were focused entirely on how to *organize* something to eat. Each of us knew that the quicker our bodies wasted away, the sooner we would fail to survive the almost daily selections.

Soon after we arrived in Birkenau I fell sick. My body and legs became covered with weeping sores and scabs. I had *organized* a pair of nylon stockings to protect my legs from dirt during the day. During the day the stockings covering my open weeping sores became encrusted with scabs. But at night I could not fall asleep unless I took them off. Pulling them off was terribly painful. As I slowly peeled the stockings off, the scabs ripped off the sores. Blood and pus ran down my legs. But at least they were now exposed to the air for healing and I could finally fall asleep. As I stood naked in front of the German doctors during the endless selections I could not understand why, with my legs covered with running sores and scabs, I was not selected for death.

We had to enlist for work every day. Every day the Germans came through the blocks to check whether anyone was too sick to go to work or had just stayed behind in camp. If someone was too sick to enlist for work they were taken out of the block and sent to the hospital. From there they were almost always sent to the crematoria. If anyone was caught not working for any other reason, their punishment was immediate death.

Whenever we went out to work the crematorium chimney was always spewing smoke, mostly black and red. Sometimes, however, the smoke was of various other colors. It always smelled of burning flesh. Some-times we were more aware of the sick smell than at other times. We had gotten used to it. I always thought to myself, 'One day I'm going to go out in that same smoke.'

The four of us enlisted in various commandos. I preferred outdoor work. We often worked in the 20th Auser commando, carrying stones from one place to another. The next day we carried the same stones back to where we had brought them from. Sometimes we were transported out of Auschwitz and taken to clear out swamps. Our work was to pull out all the weeds. I did not like this work. I was afraid of water, afraid that I might drown. Whenever possible I avoided these commandos. The most important factor about where one worked was the *kapos*. If the *kapos* were not brutal sadists, you could survive the brute work.

One day, overcome by hunger, Sala, Rozia and I did not enlist for work. We stayed behind in the blocks planning to get close to the kitchen, in the hope that someone working there would give us something to eat. When the SS man arrived looking for people who had not enlisted for work we barely managed to avoid him by running to hide in the latrines. From then on we went out to work every day, rain or shine.

Selections took place almost every day, usually right in front of the block during early morning *appel*. If we had to stand and wait for hours for the SS man to come to count us, we went into a state of panic. We knew that we were going to be selected right where we stood. If we were not formed into work commandos right after being counted we became panic-stricken, too, because we knew that we were going to be selected again. On these latter occasions we were taken to the saunas for a shower and were selected there.

During one of these selections, while we stood naked waiting for the water to run, I could not take my eyes off a striking young woman in her twenties standing near me. Cyla was a recent arrival and her figure was still full. She had slanted blue-green eyes and blonde hair, but I could not stop looking at her stomach. It was all wrinkled. I wondered why. I did not hesitate to ask her, 'Cyla, why is your stomach so wrinkled?' She told me, 'These are the marks left from the children I gave birth to.' I just prayed that they did not take her away because she had such heavy wrinkles.

One evening I heard someone cursing our lot from an upper *pritcha* across from ours. I said to the girls, 'Who could that possibly be? Aren't we cursed enough?' I looked towards the *pritcha*, and the women, from whom the cursing came. As I looked at them, I recognized them: they were two sisters from my hometown. Their name was Garber, and I had known their families. The younger sister was a year younger than I and we had gone to the same school. After a while I no longer saw the younger one; she had been taken away. I never spoke to the older one; she did not know me.

We heard that there was a commando run by an older German soldier who was rumoured to be a decent man. This commando consisted of about fifteen women. Our work was to push a wagon carrying a huge barrel of excrement from one of the latrines out to the fields, and then empty it there. A commando of men loaded the huge barrel of excrement onto the wagon for us. We were then surrounded by S.S. men and their German Shepherds as we started pushing.

The older German soldier was the commandant of this commando. He gave us rest stops and displayed a sense of fairness. When the noon soup arrived the German *kapos* would serve us the top watery part of the soup and keep the potatoes on the bottom for themselves. When the older German soldier saw this he yelled, 'Stop! Don't touch that soup! Wait for me!' He walked to a tree, broke off a branch, and trimmed off its bark with a knife from his knapsack. He used the clean stick to stir the soup so that whatever was in it was evenly distributed. 'Now give it out!' he ordered the German *kapos*. Thanks to him everyone got at least a piece of potato in their soup ration. The rumor was true; he was a decent man. I enlisted in his commando whenever I could.

One day as we were pushing the wagon loaded with its barrel of excrement, I looked up to see one of the young SS guards looking at me. I did not know why he was watching me. I could see him say something to his dog and then point at me. The dog immediately leapt into a run directly towards me. I started to scream. In a panic, I turned to run, but I fell. I picked myself up, stumbled and fell again. A piercing pain shot through me as I felt my left ankle break. The older German soldier, alerted by my screams, ordered the young SS guard to call off his dog. With one command the dog, who was almost upon me, stopped, turned and went running back to his master. I overheard the young SS guard say to the older German soldier, 'She wasn't pushing hard enough.' My ankle immediately swelled up. I was in excruciating pain. But I could not show that I was injured. My broken ankle was a death sentence if discovered. I had to work as if nothing bothered me. I continued holding onto the wagon.

From that day, my left ankle remained swollen. I did not dare return to this commando for fear that I might find only the younger German soldier and his dog there. I had already seen what these trained killing dogs could do. The German SS would sic their dogs on people merely for sport. It was horrifying to see a German Shepherd tearing chunks of flesh out of a person's groin and legs. You just prayed it did not happen to you. The day it did happen to me I was lucky that the older German soldier had been there to save me. I went back to the 20th Auser commando where we labored carrying rocks to and fro. I worked in other outdoor commandos as well.

Towards the end of the summer, the two sisters, Sala and Rozia, Sala 'the cry baby' and myself, were among a group transferred to block 26 in Camp B. Camp B was considered a work camp. Our new *blockeldeste* was Editka, a Jew from Slovakia. She was a cute brunette. Her *Einschrieberen,* the block clerk, Sara, was a tall, curly-haired girl. Sara had a kind and pious air about her. Editka's mother was an elderly woman who lit candles every Friday night in the *blockeldeste* quarters of the block. The Slovakian Jews were well educated and spoke perfect German.

Block 26 was right near the crematorium and we could see transports stopping in front of them. We were not allowed to be outside the block when the transports arrived. We were ordered inside so that we could not witness what was happening. But there were windows through which we could see the truckloads of people being taken to the crematorium. We did not want to look. We did not want to see it. We tried not to look. But some of us could not help ourselves. We looked. One day open trucks carrying little children arrived at the crematorium. The children had no idea where they were. The SS men shoved the children off the trucks to the *sondercommandos* waiting to put them in the gas chamber. Those children that were too slow were picked up and tossed off the trucks like sacks of potatoes.

On the other side of a fence next to Block 26 were the blocks where the Gypsies[5] were being held. They were in family groups. They had not been separated as we Jews had been. I rarely saw them outdoors. I never saw any of them being taken to work. The one or two people I saw walking outside their blocks were probably *blockeldestes*. Some nights we could hear them singing. They seemed oblivious to where they were. I do not know how long they had been there, but one morning their blocks were empty. All the Gypsies had been taken away to their death during the night.

The four of us continued to stick together and we worked together on Auser commandos whenever we could. Selections continued every day. Sala 'the cry baby' Beinstock had come into Maydanek short, skinny and wearing spectacles. Her glasses had been taken away from her and she had started to squint. In Birkenau the brutal labor and lack of food quickly wore her down. She became almost skeletal and was now always squinting. She was the first one of us to be selected. We were now three, the two sisters, Rozia and Sala and myself. We still had some shape to our figures.

One morning Rozia awoke with a high fever. She just could not get up and go to work. She decided to stay in the block. This was very dangerous; if she was found during the daily block inspections she would be taken away. When Sala and I came back to the block from work that day, Rozia was gone. She had been found in the block and taken away. We did not know where she had been taken.

We quickly learned that all the sick women were taken into quarantine in Camp A. We were in Camp B. Sala went out to learn exactly where in Camp A the quarantine was located. She came back and told me, 'I know exactly where Rozia is. She is in block eight. They keep all the sick in there because the hospital is overflowing. I would like to go and see her.' Camp rules forbid us to go between Camp A and Camp B. During the day the guards prevented it; at night there were no guards, but if you were caught the penalty was death. We were even forbidden to leave our blocks at night except to go to the latrines. I had pity on Sala and did not want her to go alone. I said, 'We'll go later on.'

When evening came we left the block and walked undetected to the gate. We saw that the gate separating the camps was unguarded. We walked through unseen and made our way to block eight. An overpowering stench came out of block eight. A sign outside the block read, 'Dysentery. Keep Out'. However, there was no one there to forbid us from entering.

We pushed opened the door and the revolting stench washed over us in full force. Sala walked into the dimly lit block and I forced myself to follow her. Every available spot on the three-tiered *pritchas* that filled the block was filled with sick women unable to move. They just lay there, prostrate. The excrement and vomit of those on the upper bunks ran down over the women on the tiers below them. More women lay on the bare floor in their own vomit and excrement. Not one of them, young or old, was able to move. Every one of them was burning with fever. All of them were crying and moaning, begging us to help them. I do not know how, but in the midst of this horror Sala found her sister, the beautiful, blonde-haired, blue-eyed Rozia, lying befouled and helpless among the other wretched women. Sala could not help her. There was nothing she could do. She just stood over Rozia and wept in despair. I could no longer bear the stench and the sight of what I was witnessing. I said, 'Sala, let's go. I can't take anymore. If we are caught here we won't be allowed out.' Sala kissed her sister a final goodbye and we left block eight. Miraculously we returned to our block in Camp B undetected.

Very soon after our visit all the women in block eight were taken to the crematorium. From that day on Sala was beside herself. She never recovered from the loss of her sister. Everyday she told me, 'I am not able to survive anymore. After what I have seen happen to my sister I do not want to live. I am sure it is the end of me, too.' I tried to encourage her to go on: 'Don't say that, maybe they took them somewhere, where they are being helped.' We both knew it was not true.

Another girl was assigned to fill Rozia's space in our bed. A very nice, polite girl named Sala Czarnalaska, who seldom spoke. I did not strike up a conversation with her either. One day Sala Brezinski came over to me and said, 'You have a very good girl bunking with you. I know her.' Because Sala Brezinski was our mutual friend, Sala Czarnalaska and I also became friends. She told me her history. She was from Warsaw. Her family had owned several men's clothing stores on Gesia Street. Her brothers had worked in the stores.

Sala Birenbaum and I continued to work with the 20th Auser commando carrying rocks back and forth. By now we were both very skinny. Even though I was seventeen and Sala Birenbaum was twenty, we looked like skinny fourteen-year olds. One day as we were carrying a stretcher heavily loaded with stones from one place to another, I noticed the behavior of the German soldier guarding us. He stood on top of a large pile of rocks, turning his head in all directions in evident disbelief at what he was seeing.

As we passed in front of him he came down from the pile of stones and said, 'Stop! Put down the stones!' We were frightened and did as he ordered. 'Why do you carry such big stones?' he asked. I answered, 'Because the *kapo* over there makes us do it.' He said, 'Unload these stones and when you go back for more don't take so many. Take just a small load.' We did as he ordered.

As we passed the Yugoslavian *kapo* carrying a small load of stones, she stopped us and started screaming. 'I've already warned you once to carry a big load of stones and you don't listen. If I see you without a big load again I will punish you!' We were afraid of her and did as she ordered. Carrying our stretcher heavily loaded with stones we again passed in front of the German soldier. Again he came down from the pile of stones he was standing on and asked, 'Did you not understand what I said?' We replied, 'Yes, we did, but that *kapo* ordered us to fill up our stretcher and has threatened to punish us.'

The German soldier walked over to the *kapo* and said to her, 'Why do you ask those girls to carry such big stones? Don't you see they are not capable of carrying such loads?' She started to protest that she had to, but her protests were cut short by a blow to the face that staggered her. She almost fell to the ground. I was not pleased with this. I said to Sala, 'This is not a good thing, because if we come back here tomorrow and he isn't here, we will be at her mercy.' We carried small loads the rest of the day but we never returned to the 20th Auser commando.

I dragged Sala to work every day. Left on the block, she would have faced the same fate as her sister Rozia. We went on. We went out to work. Sala and I had a red bowl that we shared. The bowl was a piece of property vital to our survival. If it was lost or stolen there was no way for us to get our soup ration at noon.

One autumn day as we were worked in an incessant downpour, wet, cold and miserable, I could think only of the soup we were going to get at noon and how it would warm me up, revitalize me. When we finally collected our soup Sala turned to me and said, 'Here Fela, eat my soup. I won't eat it today.' I was astonished, 'Why?' 'Don't you know? It is *Yom Kippur*.' 'How do you know it is *Yom Kippur* today?' I had no idea that it was *Yom Kippur*. I had never heard a soul in this place mention it. I do not know how she knew. She just replied, 'I know. No. I will not eat it.' Then I remembered her father, a red-bearded pious man. I said, 'If you will not eat and are fasting, I will fast with you.' We took our red bowl and I hid it behind some bushes so no one could steal it.

It rained all day. It was still raining when I retrieved the red bowl of soup after work. I hid it under the vest of my *pasiak* as we were being counted back into our block. The tall, curly-haired blond girl, Sara the *Einschrieberen*, kept track of the head count. As *blockeldeste* Editka counted me she stopped and asked, 'What are you hiding under your jacket?' 'It's our soup. We didn't eat it yet. I don't know if you know but today is *Yom Kippur*.' Editka answered, 'If I know that today is *Yom Kippur*? So you fasted?' She was so astonished to hear this that she called her mother out of the block to tell her. She then pointed to Sara the block clerk and said, 'Sara here is my first cousin. Her father was the rabbi of our city and you ask me if I know that today is *Yom Kippur*? It is so nice of you children to fast today.' Our fasting had really touched her. It meant something to her. She continued, 'You have the right to go to the stove and warm up your soup.' From then on Editka was friendly with me and always treated me nicely.

Sala Birenbaum's health deteriorated day after day. She had not been feeling well and had stopped eating. She now carried her uneaten bread ration in a small rag bag. She was becoming skeletal, a *musselman*. I considered her hoard a great wealth. She had so much bread. I was as hungry as a wolf, but I did not dare to ask her for any, believing that she would eat it when she felt better.

One night I dreamt that my father had come to my bedside and had brought me some cheesecake. He handed me the cheesecake and said, 'Eat this and don't be afraid.' I woke up abruptly, drenched in sweat. Sala Czarnalaska, wakened by my sudden movement, said, 'Fela, what is it? What is happening to you?' I told her about the dream and what my father had said to me. I then lay there wondering what the dream could possibly mean. My father and I both loved cheesecake.

The first thing we heard the next morning was that we were not going to work that day; we were going to be selected. As always, everyone panicked. I was able to remain calm. I focused on only one thought: if I am not selected today then I will be selected tomorrow. If only it could be over and done with.

It was raining as we were let out of the block for assembly. The selection would begin after our showers. While we stood in the rain waiting to be sent into the sauna for our showers, we asked each other, 'What do you think they will look for today, those who are too skinny or if the tongue is white?' People started to rub their tongues with garlic, passing the garlic bud from one to another. Sala was rubbing her tongue, but I refused the garlic when it was offered to me. I did not believe that rubbing my tongue with garlic would save me, nor would I, for the life of me, rub my tongue with the same garlic that everyone else had used. In my mind I could hear the words my father had spoken to me in my dream, '...don't be afraid.' So I was not.

There was only one German doctor. He checked our tongues. I could see the girl next to him write down the number of the person he was looking at whenever he blinked his eyes at her. Sala stood in front of me. I saw the doctor blinking to the girl to write down Sala's number, but I passed the inspection. In my heart I thanked my father for the courage he had given me. After the selection was over we were returned to our block. I pretended that I had not seen anything, but Sala calmly said to me, 'Now I am going to join Rozia.'

We were all kept in the block until they came to take away those whose numbers had been registered for death. We knew this would happen in a day or two at the most. Then the rest of us would be sent back to work. We all waited together.

It rained the day they came for Sala Birenbaum. It seemed like it was always raining on the days that they came to take people away. Her number was called out. Sala climbed off the *pritcha* and stood up straight. I got off the *pritcha* with her. She was carrying the rag bag filled with the bread that she had not eaten for days. I kissed her goodbye. She handed the bread to me and said, 'Here Fela, have the bread. You eat it. I don't need it anymore.' 'No, no, keep the bread, you'll get better.' I did not know what else to say. She walked out of the block. I waved to her. She waved back. She was taken away and I was left with the bread. Alone.

I sat on the planks of the *pritcha* and could not talk. Sala Czarnalaska tried to comfort me. Sala Brezinski came over to comfort me. She knew how much I had cared for the two Birenbaum sisters. She had also known them from 58 Mila Street. I missed Sala Birenbaum terribly. I had gotten so attached to her.

Again I was alone. The pain of once again losing someone close to me was so unbearable that I promised myself to never get attached to anyone else. I could no longer start conversations with anyone. If I was not spoken to, I did not speak. Sala Czarnalaska, my bunkmate, also rarely spoke.

Two new girls were assigned to our *pritcha* planks. Another day, another selection. The two new girls in our *pritcha* were taken out. Only Sala Czarnalaska and I were left. Sala Brezinski, who had also lost two of her bunk mates during that selection, came over and said to us, 'Instead of getting new girls in your *pritcha* why don't you two come and bunk together with Marisha and I?' Marisha was Sala Brezinski's friend from the Warsaw Ghetto. It seemed like a good idea. We did it.

Marisha was a big, rough girl who used to hawk cigarettes on Karmelicka Street, four for ten zloty, from a little tray hung around her neck. Marisha had a talent for always being able to *organize* something to eat. I could never figure out how she did it. Every time I went behind the block I would find Marisha and Sala Brezinski there, eating something. Whenever Sala Brezinski saw me she would give me something. Marisha would always say, 'Why do you give her anything?' She never wanted Sala Brezinski to give me anything. I hated her for that and to hurt her I'd start chanting, 'Four cigarettes for ten zloty! Four cigarettes for ten zloty!' She would become deeply embarrassed and always ask me, 'Did you see me on Karmelicka Street?' 'Of course!' I would reply; I did not want her to know that Sala Brezinski had actually told me so.

Sala Brezinski and Marisha could not withstand the hunger. They were always very secretive and very busy with their plans to *organize* something to eat. One way or another they were going to eat. Almost every night Sala Brezinski and Marisha disappeared from the block to *organize* something. I never heard them leaving or returning. It was forbidden to go out of the block at night. The penalty was death.

One night just after midnight my fingers caught in something sticky that was in my hair. I awoke in a panic and blurted out, 'What is this?' 'Jam.' Sala Brezinski answered. I was surprised, 'How come my hair is full of jam?' Sala Brezinski and Marisha quieted me down by telling me that my hair had accidentally dipped into a bowl of jam they had *organized*. I did not remember anyone having any jam when we had gone to sleep. We were rationed a spoon of jam with our bread twice a week. I hungrily asked them for a bit of jam.

Marisha said that she would only exchange it for bread. 'Where did it come from?' I insisted on knowing. Sala Brezinski hissed, 'Keep quiet! Keep quiet! I'll tell you later.' Sala Brezinski was afraid to tell me where the jam had come from in front of Marisha.

In the morning I climbed down from the *pritcha* and washed the jam from my hair with the coffee we were rationed. I never drank this coffee because I did not have any bread to eat with it. Whenever I got a ration of bread I immediately ate it all. I was too ravenous to save it for the coffee. Sala Brezinski then told me how they had gotten the jam. When she and Marisha went out at night they ran to the kitchen to find the empty jam barrels and then scraped them clean of any remaining jam.

Sala Czarnalaska and I decided to follow them the next night to see exactly how they went about getting the jam. We waited until they stole out of the block, then followed them. They walked towards the kitchen behind the barracks. Outside the kitchen were the big, empty containers of jam from which we were doled one spoonful of jam twice a week. Sala Brezinski and Marisha opened the containers, and using their hands they scraped whatever jam they could into their red bowl. Whenever someone came out of the kitchen they hid between the containers. We admired their daring. We did not have the nerve to do that. I said to Sala Czarnalaska, 'It's too risky for a little bit of jam. Let's go back.' We ran back to block 26 empty-handed.

A few days later I went behind the block looking for Sala Brezinski. I found her and Marisha eating from a full bowl of hot soup. Astonished I asked, 'Where did you get the soup? The soup has not yet arrived at the block and you already have a bowl of hot soup.' Sala said, 'Look at Marisha's hands.' I did: They were all red and scalded. Sala continued, 'When the two *Schtubeneldestes* carry the big kettle of boiling soup between them, she runs over to it, pulls off the lid and with her bare hands she dips her bowl into the soup and runs away.' The *Schtubeneldestes* could not put down the soup to chase her because then the entire soup would disappear. Sala said, 'What she can do no one else can do.' I agreed: The minimum penalty for this act would be a very severe beating. Again I realized that this was another act that Sala Czarnalaska and I could not copy.

The autumn of 1943 was very cold and there had been an early snow. The cold made me hungrier than ever. When I saw Sala Brezinski take a piece of bread out of her pocket and eat it, I wondered where she had gotten it from. How did she and Marisha always have pieces of bread in their pockets? I asked her, 'Where are you getting this bread? Are you stealing bread from others?' Sala Brezinski swore to me she had not stolen the bread from other people and added, 'Don't ask me how I got it; I won't tell you.' I was angry and turned away from her.

I discussed the mysterious source of this bread with Sala Czarnalaska. 'We already know where they get the jam, but where are they getting this bread? They must be stealing it from other people.' We decided that when they slipped out at night we would follow them again and see where they got the bread.

When they stole out of the block that night Sala Czarnalaska and I followed them. We had to stay well behind them because the snow cracked with every step we took and we did not want to give ourselves away. They went through the gate dividing camp B from camp A. We followed them to a ditch running next to the hospital block in camp A. Against a wall of the hospital block corpses were piled one on top of the other like firewood. Some of the corpses were still clothed. We watched in horror as Marisha and Sala Brezinski went through the pockets on the clothes of these corpses, looking for bread. We were sick to our stomachs. If we had not seen this with our own eyes we would have never believed it. I said to Sala Czarnalaska, 'It's a good thing that they never offered me a piece of bread. I would be sick knowing that it had come from a corpse. I would rather die than do that. Let's go back now.' As we stole back to block 26 I said to Sala Czarnalaska, 'My mother used to say that hunger can break iron and they have proven it.'

By November of 1943 transports from France, Belgium and Holland were arriving around the clock without let up to the ever-smoking crematoria. We could see them from our block only a short walk away. More and more selections took place as the blocks were emptied in preparation for the new arrivals. The women who had arrived in the transports from Italy and Greece were always among the first to be selected. They did not have a common language with which to communicate with the rest of us and learn survival skills. They did not last long. They became *musselmen* in no time.

Each day when we came back from work we heard that some of the lower numbered blocks had gone through another selection. The key question was, what percentage of the block had been taken out? If we heard twenty or thirty percent we had a chance of surviving a selection. If the percentage taken away was fifty, this was bad news. One day when we returned to our block from work we heard that the percentage that had been taken from the last blocks selected was higher than ever.

The day came for our block to be selected. To be selected to live or to die. We were marched to the sauna. Our clothes were taken away. We stood naked under the showerheads waiting for the water to run. We felt a drop and then it stopped. There was no water; there was no shower. Suddenly a rumor began to circulate. The Germans were not going to make any more selections. They were sick and tired of selecting; since we were the last block, we were not going to get showers, we were all going to be taken straight to the crematoriums. Trucks were already waiting for us outside. A terrible panic set in. People began running in all directions.

I saw Sala Brezinski running behind Marisha. I ran over to her and asked, 'Sala, where are you running to?' She angrily barked at me, 'I can't tell you!' I stood there unable to move, transfixed by the pain of her rejection. Sala had never spoken to me like that before. I thought, 'My God, one moment she is like my sister and in the next she doesn't want to tell me where she is running to, or want me to follow her.'

I saw our *blockeldeste* Editka, wringing her hands as she ran by me, saying, 'Oh my God! Oh my God!' There was nothing for me to do but to resign myself to my fate. What will happen will happen. I waited.

In the commotion I heard that *blockeldeste* Editka had run over to Hoessler[6] and Mengele[7] and begged them, 'Please make a selection, select my block. Even if you leave me twenty per cent I will be happy.' Editka had her mother, cousins and other relatives in this block: with a selection she might be able to protect most of them. After a short wait we heard that the Germans had agreed to her request. They were going to select us. Mengele, Tauber[8] and the other SS men gave orders that we be given a shower and assembled for selection.

The showers were running. '*Schnell! Schnell!* Fast! Fast!' Naked, we were assembled in front of Mengele, Tauber and several other German officers. Kathy, the Czechoslovakian clerk, sat at a nice wooden table writing down the numbers of those selected for death. We passed in front of Mengele, Tauber and the other Germans. Left, right, left, right, healthy, not healthy, it made no difference. They were not even looking at us. I saw Sala Czarnalaska, selected for death. I saw her walk over and give her number to Kathy. I stepped in front of Mengele and Tauber. They did not even look at me. They selected me for death.

This was the day for me to die. I was to go to my death. I thought of the many times when the commandos I was in had marched past the crematorium and the girls had said, 'See, that is the door you go into when you go to the crematorium.' I used to answer, 'I wish it were already a few minutes after that and the end of me.' I had always prepared for this moment, but now that it had come, I was not ready. Now that I was going to be taken to the crematorium I could hear my sister's plea as we were parted in Maydanek, 'Do whatever you can to survive so you can tell.' I thought, 'Now I will be unable to fulfill her wish. What can I do? How can I survive now? How will I tell?'

One by one the girls selected for death were walking up to Kathy and showing her the numbers on their arms. I hung behind desperately looking for a way, a chance, to save myself. Once my number was registered it would be over for me.

I looked at the *schtubeneldestes* and other Slovakian girls whose linked hands formed a human fence that prevented anyone selected from fleeing registration. It was only these girls who separated those condemned to death from those allowed to live until the next selection. I had nothing to lose. I ran at them and tried to break through the human fence. I could not. They pushed me back yelling, 'Go back! Go back! Give your number! Go back!' My time was quickly running out. Almost everybody selected had given Kathy their number. I still hung back, looking for another chance.

Just then Editka ran by me again. She was wringing her hands and crying, 'My God! My God!' I pushed my way close to her and said, 'Editka! Tell them to let me through!' '*Puskai!*' She ordered the girls. One word. It meant 'let go!' With that one word I was able to push through the human fence and was instantly on the other side. I could not believe my luck. I started to cry. I covered my eyes with my hands and cried hysterically.

I felt a touch on my shoulder. I did not know who it was but I recognized the soft voice of Sala Czarnalaska saying, 'Fela, why do you cry? You saved yourself. You are okay. Stop crying. You are okay. I will go to my death. I gave my number, but you didn't.' I did not know what to say to her. I could not face her knowing that tomorrow they would come and call out her number and that she would be taken to her death.

At that very moment we heard the Germans start to laugh uproariously. Sala Czarnalaska said, 'Look there, Fela! Look what's going on?' I saw two girls, their naked bodies completely blackened. I could not figure out how they had gotten so black, nor could I recognize who they were. Mengele, Tauber and the other Germans could not stop laughing. They could not control themselves. They were laughing so hard that they were bending over, clutching their stomachs. Their laughter went on and on.

The Germans had found the two girls hiding in the chimney and both of them were covered in soot from head to foot. Looking at the two girls I said to Sala Czarnalaska, 'You know who that is? It's Sala Brezinski and Marisha.' And it was them.

When the Germans finally stopped laughing at the sight of these two helpless creatures, they decided to spare their lives for their courage and because they had been so amused by them. They had the showers opened so that Sala Brezinski and Marisha could wash the soot off. The secret Sala Brezinski had not wanted to share with me before the selection was that she was going to hide in the chimney with Marisha. I was happy that she and Marisha had found a way to save themselves, but I was very sad about losing Sala Czarnalaska. The selection was over and we were sent back to the block to wait. We were to wait with those selected until they were taken away.

In the block there was only silence and tears. Daughters were being taken from mothers, mothers from daughters and sisters from sisters. Sala Czarnalaska did not speak at all. I did not know what to say to her. We both knew that at some time during the next day the Germans were going to come and take her to her death. They were going to gas her to death and burn her dead body. Finally she said to me, 'Fela, tomorrow I will be taken away. With luck you will survive the war. If you do, I want you to promise me one thing.' I thought to myself, 'Who is going to survive this war?' But I asked her what I could do. 'If ever you meet someone after the war with the name Czarnalaska they will be my family. They will have known I had brothers, that we lived in Warsaw on Gesia Street and that we had stores of men's clothing. Tell them how I died.' She then took out a piece of Pulsa, a very popular Polish scented soap she had been given by a friend who worked in the *Canada commando*, and said, 'Take this soap and go into the Polish women's blocks and trade it for a piece of cake. Before I go to my death I want to taste a piece of cake again.'

Non-Jewish prisoners were allowed to receive packages from home.[9] They had all kinds of goods to barter. I went into one of the Polish women's blocks and said to the women there, 'I have Pulsa soap. Who has a piece of cake for it?' A woman traded me a nice piece of hard, dried-out cake for the soap. I returned to the block very happy to have found some cake and gave it to Sala Czarnalaska. She took a little piece of it, put it in her mouth and gave me the rest. 'I don't need it. I just wanted to taste it. You eat it.' I ate it.

The next day they came. The four of us were sitting together on the *pritcha* when they called her number. She stood up and kissed Sala Brezinski and Marisha goodbye. She then turned to me and took off the beautiful, hand-knitted gray and burgundy blazer sweater that she had been given by a friend of hers in the *Canada commando*, and said, 'Here Fela, I want you to have my sweater. It will be useful to you. It is cold now and I want you to have this sweater to keep you warm.' We kissed goodbye and she climbed off the *pritcha* and went out as if she was going to a party. I started to cry. The other girls said to me, 'Why do you cry, who knows, maybe we will go tomorrow?' Once again it was the end of someone I had gotten close to and loved. Sala Czarnalaska was such a sweet, intelligent and quiet person.

The next day I went back to work in the 20th commando carrying stones from one place to another. I continued sleeping on the same *pritcha* with Sala Brezinski and Marisha. Other girls were assigned to our *pritcha*, but I was not interested in making friends with any of them. Every time I got close to anyone they were taken away. Sala 'the cry baby' Beinstock, Sala and Rozia Birenbaum, Sala Czarnalaska, all of them had become very dear to me and then been taken away. Their loss was more pain than I could bear. The only person I had left was Sala Brezinski and now I was closer to her than ever. I began a period where I did not know if I would be better off if I also went to my death. I was losing my will to live. Many times I thought of ending my life on the electric barbed wire fence, but I could always hear my sister's voice in my head telling me, 'Live so that you can tell.' Every morning I went to work and every evening I came back to the block, but I just wanted to be on my own.

Sleeping in the *pritcha* across from ours were two sisters from the Polish city of Pultusk. They both worked in the *Klaidenskammer*, sorting out all the clothing confiscated from the transports. This was a highly desired job because one could always find something to trade for food. One day they called me over, 'Come, we want to talk to you.' I went over. They said, 'You are so different from all the other girls. You never fight, you always address older people formally, you're such a nice girl.' They gave me some bread and added, 'We work in the *Klaidenskammer* and we like you a lot, so come and see us often. We will always have some food for you.' These two sisters were very good to me.

During the early part of 1944 I walked back into the block from work to find

Editka the *blockeldeste* waiting for me. She called me over and said, 'While you were at work, the Camp Commandant Franz Hoessler came here and asked if I had young girls with delicate fingers in my block. He needs them for a special job in the Union munitions factory.[10] I would advise you to enlist. You will be transferred to the Union workers block.'

I remembered Hoessler from an earlier incident. One day while standing near the gate waiting to go out to work, I had seen two women I recognized approach him. They fell to the ground before his feet and began crying as they kissed his boots. He ordered them back onto their feet, spoke to them, and they left. They were two sisters who had come to my block where their younger sister, a young, pretty girl, was a *schtubeneldeste*. The younger sister had been chosen to serve as a prostitute for the German Armies. However, orders from the Third Reich forbid the use of Jewish girls as military prostitutes because it was *rassenshande*, race disgrace. The army could take Ukrainians, Poles or girls from any other nation, but not Jewish girls. Somehow there had been an oversight and this young and pretty Jewish girl had been included among those chosen as prostitutes. Hoessler had told the two older sisters not to worry; she would not be sent away. And she was not.

I took Editka's advice. The Union blocks were never selected. Editka handed me a document and I went over to the munitions block to enlist. I gave the document to the *blockeldeste* there and became a worker for the Union munitions factory. I was transferred to a different barracks, a low- numbered block. They did not have any more room in the upper *pritchas*, so I was told to bunk on the cement floor. I wasn't alone in the *pritcha* on the floor: there were already two girls there.

One of the girls was from Litva. She had such a deep *Litvack* accent I had difficulty understanding her. There was also a Hungarian girl who cried relentlessly. My first night in this bottom *pritcha* was a difficult one. Not only did the dirt from the upper *pritcha* fall on my face as I tried to sleep, but the incessant crying of the Hungarian girl kept me awake. During the night I finally told her, 'Stop crying! Let me sleep!' She replied in German, 'I don't know why I'm here. I'm not Jewish. Why am I here?' I was surprised. 'You're not Jewish? Then who are you? And where are you from?' 'I'm from Hungary.' 'And you are not Jewish? Your parents are not Jews? What did your parents do?' 'They had a farm with pigs on it.' I realized that this girl came from a very assimilated family.[11] She did not even know that she was Jewish.

In the morning I went to the *schtubeneldeste* and complained, 'Please, you have to assign me another *pritcha,* I cannot sleep there with the dirt falling on my face.' She said, 'As soon as I have another place, I will.' By the next night I was exhausted. Despite the dirt falling on my face and the non-stop crying of the Hungarian girl, who claimed she was not a Jew, I slept. I woke up to find that the beautiful sweater Sala Czarnalaska had given me before she had been taken to her death had been stolen from under my head. I went berserk, screaming and crying. To calm me down the *schtubeneldeste* said, 'I found you a good upper *pritcha*. There are two girls in it; you are going to be the third.

I soon joined the two girls Tola and Esterka, in their upper *pritcha*. The *pritchas* were grouped together three across and we were in the middle one. The third *pritcha* was occupied by a thin-faced, red-haired, freckled woman and her sister-in-law. Her name was Dora Klein; she was a doctor and ran the clinic in the munitions factory. The first *pritcha* was occupied by a Mrs Goldberg and two incredibly beautiful young girls. One was her raven- haired, black-eyed twelve-year-old daughter, Sara, and the other was Wanda, a fourteen-year old blond, blue-eyed, Nordic-featured girl.

Mrs Goldberg was from Belgium. She told me that when camp Commandant Hoessler caught sight of her black-haired, black-eyed, twelve- year old daughter Sara, coming off the transport from Belgium, he grabbed Sara and herself by their arms and took them out of the selection. Wanda and her aunt were in the same transport. Hoessler saw Wanda, took hold of her and brought her over to Mrs Goldberg, saying, 'I want you to be a mother to this little girl as you are to your own daughter. Take care of her.' Wanda's aunt was then sent to her death.

Masha was yet another tall, fourteen-year-old girl taken out of a transport by Hoessler. She came from Czeladz in Poland. She was assigned to our bed. We were now four girls in one *pritcha*.

A few days later Sala Brezinski came to see me with good news. She had managed to get into the *Canada commando*. The *Canada commando* was the best possible work one could have. It not only increased your chances of survival but you could prosper as well. The work in the *Canada commando* was sorting out all the belongings taken away from the victims, as they were unloaded from the incoming transports. Every item of baggage and clothing had to be checked for hidden diamonds, gold, jewelry and money. Food was also separated. If you had courage you could always manage to eat something you found or bring back an item that could be bartered. Sala Brezinski assured me that from now on I would not be hungry. She had even managed to bring me a good pair of shoes.

Every night that Sala Brezinski came from the Canada block to the Union block to see me, she brought me something. It was always something that I could trade for more bread. She would say, 'Trade it or sell it for anything you can eat, bread, a piece of salami. Eat! Eat! Eat!' From the way she looked after me everyone assumed that she was my sister. Sala Brezinski risked her life to provide me with things she smuggled out of the *Canada commando*. She brought me enough that I was able to exchange some of them for cigarettes.

Cigarettes were valuable currency and I stored them against the day Sala Brezinski might no longer be working in the *Canada commando*. I made a little cache for the cigarettes between the planks above my bed. I always waited until the girls were out of the block and carefully looked around to ensure that nobody was watching before I stored any cigarettes in my cache.

At first I had Esterka trade for me, but soon Masha told me that Esterka was cheating me and that she could do far better. It turned out to be true. And Masha did bring me more for each item she traded for me. I shared my good fortune with her and also helped the others. Masha was only fourteen years old and wild with hunger. She would risk anything for a piece of bread.

I had told Sala Brezinski that I was trading the extra things she brought me for cigarettes. She asked, 'Why are you buying cigarettes?' 'In the event you get kicked out of the *Canada commando* we will be able to buy your way back in.' She said, 'Don't think about that! Just buy yourself enough bread and a piece of salami!' I always told her how many cigarettes we had saved ... thirty cigarettes, forty cigarettes. She said, 'Do what you want.'

One day Tola's sister, Regina, was assigned to our barrack. They were from Bedzyne, Poland. Regina wanted her sister to be with her and insisted that we let her sleep in our bunk. We were already four in the bunk and the other girls refused, saying that we would be too crowded. I convinced the others: 'They are sisters, let them be together.' The other girls agreed with me because I had been helping them out with the goods I was receiving from Sala Brezinski. Consequently, we were five girls tightly crammed together on one *pritcha*. At night when someone wanted to turn everyone had to wake up and we all had to turn in unison. I was always blamed for the over-crowding.

By the summer of 1944 the Hungarian transports were arriving daily. The railroad tracks ran to within a short distance of the crematoria. When the crematoria were too busy, the transports had to wait their turn. I knew first hand how much they were suffering from their lack of water. How delirious they were. When the *blockeldeste* would come calling for volunteers to bring pails of water to the people in the cattle cars, I always volunteered, even when I knew that the Germans allowed them only enough water so that they could revive enough to walk into the gas chambers on their own. The Germans did not allow us to get too close to the cattle cars, but we could hear the noises coming from them. The hardest to bear was the sound of children crying. The sky was constantly red from the flames and the billowing black smoke produced by the burning of thousands of humans every day. The odor of their burnt flesh pervaded the air. I thought, 'This is how I am going to die.'

Every morning we were marched the three kilometers from the camp to the munitions factory, which was situated, between Birkenau and Auschwitz. After work we were marched back. We were 1,000 women working the day shift and another 1,000 women working the night shift. We were glad to walk from the camp to the munitions factory, because it meant that we did not have to endure the constantly smoking crematorium chimneys, nor think that one day we, too, were destined to go out with the smoke like all those before us.

Working in the Union munitions factory improved our chances of surviving the war. We were no longer highly disposable slave laborers but useful cogs in the German war machine. The Union blocks were free from selections; we had access to showers and we could receive medical attention.

The soup at Auschwitz for the Union workers was not much better than what we had as slave laborers in Birkenau. It was made from whatever the Germans confiscated from the daily transports. At lunchtime we would go outside to get our soup. I always shared my red bowl of soup with Masha. One day as we were standing in line for our soup the *kapos* distributing it began laughing. One of them removed a sanitary napkin from the soup and showed it to us. I said to Masha, 'I won't eat today. You can have my soup.' There were pieces of meat and potatoes in the soup that day and even though I was as ravenous as a wolf I could not touch it. The sanitary napkin floated in front of my eyes. Masha ate undisturbed. She felt sorry for me and said, 'Eat just the potatoes or some pieces of meat! What is it to you?' I just could not.

Nor were the *kapos* in the Union as brutal. Maria was the head *kapo* at the Union munitions factory. She was a German and wore the red triangle of a political prisoner. She liked me. When we filed out for our soup we had to go through the entire factory. A short cut through the factory led through the cloakroom where we hung our jackets. The cloakroom was also where Maria and her German boyfriend trysted. One day a few girls decided to take this shortcut and I followed them. We walked in on Maria and her lover. Maria did not take kindly to this sudden intrusion on their privacy. She started beating the girls remorselessly. I was afraid that she would start beating me next. But when she got to me she just yelled, '*Raus*! Out!'

The huge hall I worked in was called the montage. In it were two assembly lines and a steel wire cage. The first assembly line was stationary and the second one was conveyorized. There was a small table inside the steel wire cage. Each assembly line had a German civilian as foreman. The foreman of the first assembly line was Maister Paul Vonendem. He was a German civil engineer, a very decent and nice man. I worked for him and was assigned to the table inside the steel wire cage. I worked there with Chanka Libman, a girl from Warsaw.

Supervising the conveyorized assembly line was Maister Krigsmann, a short man with mysterious eyes. Whenever he passed me, he smiled at me. I did not know why he was so friendly with me. Maister Krigsmann's supervisor was a German Army officer, who was always in uniform, and who was very friendly with all the women. Erna Laufer, a Jewish prisoner, was also our supervisor.

Next to my workstation was the powder room. Estusia Wajcblum and Regina Safirsztajn were in charge of the powder room inventory. The powder came from the pulver room. It went to the stationary assembly line where four girls, Dorka Koplowicz, Hilda Friedman, Lonia Kazimierska, and Sheva, received the oval-shaped *schlageboltzen,* firing pins. Their job was to load and close them. Then they put the firing pins on carton trays, laid out like eggs, and passed them on to Chanka and me. I counted how many of them were brought into our cage and noted the number on a sheet of paper. I then counted and noted how many we sent out of our cage through its window. They were usually taken out to another part of the assembly line by our foreman, Maister Paul Vonendem. He always cautioned me, 'Count and carefully mark how many you received and how many you send out.' He knew that I would be held responsible for any errors. He collected the tally sheets from me when my day's work was finished. He was happy with my work and I was happy to be working there.

Workers in the Union blocks were privileged with access to showers. From the shower area in Birkenau we could see the transports arriving at the crematorium. One hot summer day as I was showering I heard the orchestra[12] start playing. This meant that a transport was due at any minute. By the time I got out of the shower the transport had arrived. I was listening to the orchestra as I left the shower and began walking back to my block. I could see the Germans, Alsatian dogs at their sides, formed up alongside the sealed cattle cars. Then the cattle car doors clattered opened.

The camp orchestra's violins were playing beautifully as an entire wedding party tumbled out of the cattle cars: the bride in her white wedding gown, the groom with his long side locks dressed in his finest Chassidic attire, the rabbi wearing his fur *striemel* and white stockings, and all their guests dressed in their best. All their eyes were wide and searching. The smoke pouring out of the chimneys, the stench in the air, told these people where they were. And why. The orchestra's beautiful music had not lulled them as it had so many countless others. Panic set in. They stretched their arms to the heavens and screamed, 'God! *Shma Israel*! Hear O' Israel!' A few ran towards the electric fences and into the ditches only to be dragged out by the dogs that were set upon them. They were brutally beaten into the crematorium. Horrified I ran back to the block and told the girls what I had witnessed.

On another occasion I was among some two dozen other women who volunteered to carry pails of water to an incoming transport. We were marched outside the camp toward the woods. The German guards and the German *kapos* ordered us to leave the pails in a field. We heard terrible shrieks, hysterical crying and indescribably terrifying noises coming from the nearby woods. The Germans began screaming at us to start singing. The German *kapos* started singing and ordered us to sing along with them in German. They yelled at us to sing louder and louder in order to drown out the horrific screams of the people who we now realized were being burned alive in the woods. After this atrocity, I stopped volunteering.

The day came when Sala was kicked out of the *Canada commando*. She came running to me saying, 'Fela, you were so smart to save those cigarettes. Now I can buy my way back into the *Canada commando*.' By now I had fifty cigarettes in my cache, a life-saving sum. I went up to my cache to get my cigarettes. My fingers pried into the cache to retrieve them. I could not find a thing. My heart plunged; my stomach sickened. The cache was empty. There was not a single cigarette in it. My hand desperately fingered through my cache again. Everything was gone. I told Sala. She said, 'I thought I could depend on you. I was counting on you.' I replied, 'Sala, it's all gone, stolen. Don't you believe me?' She left. I was very hurt by her remarks.

When I went around asking who had stolen my cigarettes I could see by her reaction that Regina had been the thief. I recalled that she had once busied herself with her shoes and other minute details until I had finally gone out first. I accused her, 'Regina, you stole my cigarettes.' She would neither answer me nor look at me. When Sala Brezinski returned to see me I did not want to talk to her. After some time, I regretted my reaction.

One day as were marching back to camp from work at the Union, the sirens started wailing. We were halted at the entrance to the camp and saw all the women lined up for an *appel*. We wondered what all the commotion was about. We were counted through the gate and marched towards our block. As we were marching we saw a woman, with her hands behind her back, between two SS men walking away from the *appel* towards us. She passed directly in front of us and we saw her face. We all recognized the good-looking brunette, as she looked straight ahead. It was Mala, a prisoner from Antwerpen, Belgium. Everyone knew who she was because her job was to help organize *appels* and keep track of the prisoners. She was flanked by Mengele on one side and another German officer on her other side.

We had not known that she and her Polish lover, wearing German uniforms, had escaped from the camp a few days earlier. The wailing sirens now told us she had been recaptured and had been brought back into the camp and was going to be punished. The Germans had been preparing to hang her as an example to the rest of us. Somehow, Mala managed to cut her own veins denying the Germans the opportunity of making her death an example for the rest of us.

One day early in the autumn of 1944 all the women who worked in the Union munitions factory were transferred from our blocks in Birkenau to blocks in Auschwitz. Being in Auschwitz meant we no longer had to look at the crematorium that was constantly in front of our eyes in Birkenau. A rumor quickly spread that we would be under the power of Brigida, the SS woman. This was a terrifying prospect. Fortunately the rumor proved false. I never did see Brigida in Auschwitz. My only anguish at being transferred from Birkenau was that I would never see Sala Brezinski again. She had remained in Birkenau. I now felt very guilty for being mad at her for not believing that the cigarettes had been stolen. She had been very good to me.

Compared to the wooden barrack blocks in Birkenau, the three-storey- high brick barracks and the clean *pritchas* in Auschwitz were a real improvement. The *pritchas* were set up four across and we were only two women in a *pritcha*. We were really astonished to see our bedding. We could not believe the Germans were supplying us with clean, warm blankets until we picked them up and read the names and addresses of their previous owners sewn into them. They had belonged to the Jewish victims who had brought them here on the transports. I had a blanket that had belonged to a Jewish family from Paris. Masha and I were assigned to a *pritcha*. She was working for Maister Krigsmann. In a *pritcha* next to us was Cyla and another woman called Cypka. Our beds had to be made each morning before we were marched to work in the Union factory.

One morning as we were rushing to straighten out our beds to be on time for *appel* and work, Cypka started screaming and cursing, 'Someone stole my bread!' She then started accusing Masha. I did not believe it because I was always with Masha. I got mad and responded by yelling at her not to accuse someone without proof. Cypka told me, 'I'm not accusing you so don't mix in!' I told her she was crazy. In an insane rage she pointed her finger at me and said, 'One day I will show you who is crazy! I have a child hidden with a Polish family; I promised them that when I return home I will give them all of my possessions for saving my child.' Everyone who heard her was now convinced that she was indeed mad. I wondered how Cyla, who was so soft-spoken and gentle, the complete opposite of Cypka, could put up with her. I later asked Cyla and in her shy way she said, 'I need her; she is my pillar of strength.'

Sometime during the autumn of 1944 we heard that the crematorium had been blown up.[13] I had no idea who had been involved. But all the girls who worked with the powder were suspect. Among them were Hilda, Lonia, Dorka, Sheva, Chanka and myself. We were the team on the day shift and all the powder that left the powder room went through our hands. We did not know that the Gestapo was going to investigate.

Foreman Maister Krigsmann was constantly walking by me. His mysterious eyes always watched me work. Whenever I looked at him he would smile gently. When I saw him talking to my foreman, Maister Paul Vonendem, as they both watched me, I became very anxious and uncomfortable. I did not know what was going on or what to expect. A few days later they both approached me and my foreman said, 'Maister Krigsmann wants you at his assembly line.' I started to cry. I did not want to go. I pleaded with him, 'Are you not happy with my work? You always say I work well. Why are you letting someone take me away from this job?' He replied, 'There is nothing I can do.'

Maister Krigsmann took me by the arm and as he led me away he patted my shoulder. I asked, 'What do you need me for, Maister Krigsmann?' He replied, 'It will be better for you. Believe me.' I wondered what he was doing that would be to my benefit. He took me to his assembly line, assigned me a spot and showed me what to do, how to do it, how to be careful and how not to make a mistake. He said, 'Remember this is very responsible work.' I was given a little apparatus with needles poking out. I had to poke those needles in and give the device to the girl next to me.

She was a very sensual and refined girl in her twenties, named Henia Jakubowicz. Henia's dark black hair framed smoldering black eyes. She had a mouthful of beautiful white teeth. When she smiled at you the warmth of her eyes and the flash of her teeth hypnotized you. For two days she ignored me and did not talk to me. She spoke only to Maister Krigsmann in fluent German. It made me feel badly because all around us the other girls were talking to each other. But I said to myself, 'The hell with her, she can keep to herself. I won't talk to her either.'

On the third day of working together she spoke to me in German and said, 'Forgive me for not having spoken to you. I must tell you that I hate the Polish girls. I hate it when they talk in Polish. They are so loud. But I see that you are different; you are a nice girl.' I did not reply. She added, 'You will be surprised to know that my father was from Poland?' Now I asked her, 'So why do you hate the Polish girls?' She replied, 'I hated my father, too.' I was amazed. 'You hated your father? Why? What city was he from?'

Henia's father had been a Jew from Wloclawek. Her mother had been a German Christian. After Henia's parents married they lived in Leipzig where her father had been a prosperous furrier. They had two children, Henia and her brother. Every year her father would take Henia to Wloclawek to visit his mother. I asked Henia, 'Did you hate your grandmother, too?' 'Oh no! She treated me so nicely. What I remember most about my grandmother was the *challa* spread with goose *schmaltz* and slices of goose meat on top of it. Was it ever good! I would like to live through the war and once more in my life eat *challa* spread with goose *schmaltz* and slices of goose meat on top of it.'

When Hitler had come to power, Henia's German uncles joined the Nazi party. Her father had to step off the sidewalk whenever his brothers-in-law walked by. In 1936 as the situation continued to deteriorate for Jews, her father took his family and fled to Belgium. They did not run far enough. In 1943 they were arrested by the Germans and deported from Belgium to Birkenau. When the Jews were rounded up in Belgium her mother could have saved herself. But she refused to abandon her family, saying, 'If I cannot have my husband and my children, I don't want to live.' Henia had arrived in Auschwitz on a transport from Belgium. The days flew by as I listened to her endless stories. Henia and I became best friends and she appointed herself as my guardian.

Maister Krigsmann was satisfied with my work. He rewarded me with coupons that I could use to buy things, like mustard, mussels and red cabbage, in the canteen. I always kept some mustard in a red cup. Whenever I was hungry I ate some mustard. One day I ate too much mustard and broke into a cold sweat. My head started spinning. I could not work. Henia told Maister Krigsmann what had happened to me. He cautioned me, 'You have to be careful not to make any mistakes. This work is serious. Any mistake can lead to an accident that can be considered sabotage.' From then on he gave me permission to go to the bathroom and freshen up whenever I wanted to. One day while in the bathroom a woman approached me and asked me if I worked near the pulver room. I said, 'I used to, but now I work at another table.' She said nothing more to me and walked away.

On another occasion as I was returning to my workstation from the bathroom, I saw Camp Commandant Franz Hoessler standing in the corridor. He was looking at everyone and everything around him. He called me over to him. He was a man in his fifties and looked like a father figure. He also called a few other women over and asked us, 'How is the work here?' We all answered, 'Good.' 'Now,' he said, 'repeat after me. Herr Hoessler is your father and the Union is your God.' We repeated it as he asked and then he said, 'Now go back to work.'

As I was walking back to my table I saw Mamuska coming towards me, wringing her hands. I stopped her to find out what was wrong. She told me that her daughter Feluska was sick with malaria and had been sent back to the blocks. Mamuska and fourteen-year-old Feluska were yet another beautiful mother and daughter that Hoessler had taken out of an arriving transport. Mamuska had been to the clinic and the doctor had told her that she had the medicine to cure malaria but she needed permission from a German official before she could give it to her. I insisted that Mamuska go over to Hoessler right away and ask him for help. She was afraid to do it. I grabbed her by the arm and said, 'You speak German well and I'm coming with you.' Holding onto her I steered her towards Hoessler. We stepped in front of him. Mamuska asked him to forgive her for being so forward and asked him to help her. He gave her permission for the medicine and Feluska was cured.

A couple of months after being moved into Auschwitz from Birkenau, I heard that many people from block 26 had been sent to other camps in Germany. I wondered what had happened to Sala Brezinski and Marisha. I told Henia about Sala Brezinski and how Sala had shared everything with me but now I did not even know if she was still alive.

Our daily bread ration was brought to the Union by a German prisoner. Somehow he met Henia and immediately fell under her spell. The next day he brought her a buttered ham sandwich. She brought the sandwich to me and gave me half. She shared whatever food she *organized* with me.

One day while Henia and I were working, an SS woman approached our assembly line to speak to Maister Krigsmann, who was busy nearby. While she waited to catch Maister Krigsmann's attention, Henia started to speak to her in fluent German. The SS woman, taken with Henia's charm, asked, 'You speak such good German; where are you from?' Henia replied, 'From Leipzig.' 'If you are German, how come you are here?' 'I'm here because my father married a German woman. I'm half Jewish. That is why I am here.' The SS woman was shocked and hurried away. Even though I already knew Henia's story, I, too, was shocked. One had to have guts to address an SS woman in that way. From then on, whenever that SS woman passed us, she always greeted Henia with a gentle, '*Guten tag*. Good day.' There was never a dull moment working with Henia.

Until Officer Apple, a young German Wermacht soldier, came to work as an engineer at the Union factory, we did not know how the war was progressing. Officer Apple had come to inspect some machinery for Maister Krigsmann.

He was a man in his late twenties, sandy-haired, and of average height and appearance. Once he saw Henia, he could not take his eyes off her. Henia said to me, 'Watch me.' She started to talk to him. He did not stop asking her questions. She told him the story of her life. When he left she told me, 'Fela, this man is already in love with me. I can see it in the way a man looks at me.' I thought she was having delusions, that she was dreaming, not being realistic: a German falling in love with her! The next day the young German officer returned to talk with Henia again. He said that he had just returned from the Russian front and had been assigned to work here at the Union. When I heard him say, 'The war is almost over... ' I could not believe my ears.

Officer Apple was so infatuated with Henia that he could not work. Day after day he stood at our assembly line watching her and talking to her as he furtively looked around to see if he was being observed. Maister Krigsmann could see that Officer Apple was madly in love with Henia, but he never said a word. He was a mere civilian and Apple was a Wermacht officer. To Henia, Officer Apple's infatuation was amusing. To me, the way he spoke to her, how serious he was about her, was frightening. Here in Auschwitz, a German in love with a Jewess was madness.

One day Officer Apple told Henia that he had received a letter from his mother saying that the situation in Germany was very bad. They were now spending most of their time in bunkers to save themselves from the Allied bombardments. She had written that the Americans were dropping napalm bombs. This was the sweetest music our ears could hear. But we doubted that we would live to see the fall of Germany and the end of Hitler. It was impossible to imagine that the Germans would let us survive.

Officer Apple and Henia started to exchange notes. Then he started to invite Henia into his office for a drink and she would go. She was fearless. I told her to do neither, that it was too dangerous. Then he confessed to her that he was helplessly in love with her and that he was writing his fiancée in Germany to break their engagement. At this point Henia and I both agreed that Officer Apple was insane. Henia said to me, 'You see, this is what I can do. I can drive a man crazy.'

On another day Officer Apple came to our table and carefully looked around before he spoke, 'I can tell you girls that the war is almost over. The Russian front has collapsed. Believe me, the war will soon be over. You must be strong.' This boosted my morale immeasurably.

A short time later he came over to Henia and threw a ring down on the table in front of her. It was the ring his fiancée had sent back to him after receiving his letter.

The last time we saw him he had tears in his eyes. He said to Henia, 'Tomorrow I am leaving and I won't to be able to see you again. Remember my name is Apple. Will you promise me that you will look for me when the war is over?' She promised that she would. But to her it was all a joke.

With winter upon us we were lined up and issued winter coats from the *Klaidenskammer*. The coat one got was at the whim of the *Kapo* handing them out. You could end up with a thin cloth rag or something that would keep you warm. The *Kapo* I stepped up to picked out a heavy woolen coat for me. She handed it to me saying, 'Here, this will keep you warm.' I took it and moved on. When I tried the coat on I found the wool to be intolerably itchy. After a few days I traded it for a coat of a less abrasive material; it was also a lot less warm.

Masha fell ill with tonsillitis. Being a skilled Union worker, she was given medical care. The clinic doctors removed her tonsils and she was allowed to stay in the block to recover. When I returned from work Masha said to me, 'Go to the bed and see what's in it.' I saw bulges under the blanket and wondered what it could be? Was it a dead person? I pulled the covers off and saw six loaves of bread. I couldn't believe my eyes, six loaves of bread. I quickly covered them up and asked her, 'Where did they come from?' I thought she had stolen them. She said, ' I went down when the man passed by with the bread and he said, 'Put out your two hands.' When I did, he put three loaves in them and said, 'Come back. I ran up here, put them down and went back. He gave me three more loaves.' We were suddenly the richest people. We ate and we were happy. The six loaves lasted us quite a while.

I developed a toothache. It throbbed with every step I took as we marched to work through another cold and rainy morning. I was in misery. As we marched past the front of a block I saw a woman looking out of a window. She stretched her arms out in a way that reminded me of a Greek goddess. She looked so serene, so healthy. I said to the woman next to me how I wished I could be in that block. The woman I had spoken to was much older than I and she snapped back, 'Bite your tongue, you don't know what you are talking about.' Henia than explained to me that that was the block in which experiments were done on women.

The next morning I went to the clinic and the doctor pulled out two of my teeth without any anaesthetic. I decided to stay in the block because of the pain. While I was there the young man from Lodz who was delivering bread passed by. I went down to see if I would have the same luck that Masha had. The young man said, ‘Here!’ and gave me two loaves of bread. I came back and he gave me two more loaves. That was the day the Gestapo came to the Union.

The Gestapo arrested Estusia Wajcblum, Regina Safirsztajn, Rosa Robota and Ala Gertner, four Union girls who worked in the powder room. They were suspected of stealing the gunpowder that had been used by the *sondercommando* to blow up and destroy the crematoria.

Estusia Wajcblum and Regina Safirsztajn worked with Hilda, Lonia, Dorka and Sheva, during the day shift. The Gestapo entered the Union and were in the process of arresting all of them when a uniformed German foreman intervened saying, ‘You will not take these four young girls. They are innocent. I guarantee that they had nothing to do with this incident and I will not allow you to take them away.’ Hilda, Lonia, Dorka and Sheva were not taken away. They had not even been aware that they had been also under surveillance. The four Union girls arrested were all tortured.

The German investigation had concluded that the powder used to blow up the crematorium had come from the night shift of our section. Maister Krigsmann had done me a favor by taking me away from my previous work. Being transferred to Maister Krigsmann’s assembly line had removed me from suspicion and from the surveillance that the other girls had been under.

January 5, 1945, was another rainy day. That morning, before going to work, we were forced to stand and look straight at the gallows to watch the execution of Estusia Wajcblum and Regina Safirsztajn. They slowly strangled to death dangling at the end of a rope. Chanka, Estusia Wajcblum’s younger sister, was kept in the block by their friends so she would not witness this terrible scene. The other two girls, Rosa Robota and Ala Gertner, were hung in front of the night shift.

In the days following the murder of Estusia Wajcblum, Regina Safirsztajn, Rosa Robota and Ala Gertner, air raid warnings became more frequent. Henia and I had heard from Officer Apple that Allied planes were bombing Germany and now we knew they were flying somewhere overhead. We wondered if the camp would be bombed. Was this how we were finally going to die, together with the Germans?

Before long hardly a day went by when we were not kept waiting in the montage until another air raid warning was over. Sometimes we waited for hours. During one of these waits the Germans, to relieve their boredom, decided we should entertain them. They told us that we were to stage a talent show for them and asked for volunteers to perform. The performances took place as we waited for the raiding airplanes to fly by. Some of the girls were singers and some were dancers, but no one impressed them more than Kiki, the belly dancer. Kiki was a Moroccan Jewess who had been working the Paris cabarets when she had been taken by the Germans. The Germans had us stage talent shows for them more than once. It kept all our minds off the bombs.

One morning I had a scare when Henia did not appear for work. I was relieved to learn that she had been sent to the hospital because of an appendicitis attack.

At approximately three p.m. on January 18, 1945, we were told to stop work and assemble. We wondered what was going on. Once assembled we were marched back to the blocks. We found the camp and the blocks empty. We waited for our bread rations but instead we got orders to come down and assemble again. There was chaos all around us. Germans were running around everywhere. We did not know what was happening. Rumors started circulating. We heard that we were being evacuated from the camp. The night shift had already been taken out. Daylight was fading quickly and in the gathering night I could see the Germans panicking to rush us out. I knew that we would soon be liberated. I begged Masha to hide under the *pritchas* with me. She began crying, 'No Fela, let's go with the others. What if they come to check? They will find us and shoot us.' I listened to her and came to regret it.

BOOK FIVE

DEATH MARCH

January 18, 1945 – May 3, 1945

Tired and hungry, Masha and I went down to the assembly. We saw that some women had brought their blankets down with them. It was too late for us to go back and get ours. We were already under the rifles of the SS men who had their dogs at their heels. We were immediately formed up and marched out into the cold dark night. All the SS men wore knapsacks on their backs and all the SS women were on bicycles to which they had strapped their knapsacks. We were ordered to march. *Schnell!* Fast! Shots were being fired continuously. Fast! The road was covered with dead bodies, their red blood contrasting darkly with the white snow. Those who could not keep up with the pace demanded by the Germans were being shot on the spot.

Gusting winds blew the snow from the empty fields on both sides of us as we marched. The swirling snow both blinded us and made us barely visible. The women in front of me were vague hunched-over forms disappearing and re-appearing in the whirling snow. In no time my shoes were wet and started to come apart. My main concern was that I would soon be marching barefoot.

Masha could not withstand her hunger. It overpowered all her fears. Without a word to me she disappeared into the blowing snow. I do not know how she found me again but in a short while she reappeared by my side whispering, 'Here Fela, take this.' She handed me a knapsack. 'Where did you get it?' 'I stole it from a SS woman's bicycle. Open it, see what's in it.' 'Now they will catch us and shoot us.' I said. She kept watch for any SS that might happen upon us as I quickly went through the knapsack. What a fortune! I took out a few sandwiches, bread, butter, ham and a few pairs of silk stockings. As soon as I had emptied it, Masha got rid of the knapsack. We ate the sandwiches as we marched and for those few brief moments of chewing and swallowing food, we forgot where we were. As we marched on I managed to pull the silk stockings over my torn shoes, one pair on top of the other. How I wished I hadn't traded away that woolen coat the *Kapo* had given me.

Masha and I spoke to each other continuously as we marched. Suddenly I heard my name being called out. I looked around and saw that the voice was coming from under a blanket that was covering the heads of two marching women. I went closer and looked under the blanket. It was Dorka Koplowicz, with whom I had worked in the Union, and her sister Haddasa. Dorka had recognized my voice as Masha and I were speaking. She and Haddasa took Masha and me under their blanket with them. It sheltered us from the snow blowing in our faces and gave us some warmth.

We marched throughout the cold night. We stopped only when the SS men were tired. We marched through the next day and into the next night. We received no food. The only thing we had to eat was snow. I was fortunate that I had my red enamel cup with me, since it was always tied to my waist. I melted snow in it. I shared my cup with many people but I never let it get out of my hands.

As we marched on we overtook a bent, hobbling woman. As we passed I looked at her to see who it was. It was Henia Jakubowicz! She was holding both her hands across her abdomen. A few days earlier she had been hospitalized for an appendectomy. She told me that all the patients had been ordered to march out as they were. She was now hobbling along holding her incision together. I soon lost her amid the shuffling mass. She could not keep up.

I lost track of how many continuous days and nights we were marched through the cold and snow. At some point we were divided into groups and sent off in different directions.[1] When the SS needed to sleep, we slept. We slept wherever we were stopped. Sometimes we slept in barns. To keep us from being seen by the civilian population the SS always marched us on side roads and we were taken through villages only at night. Whenever civilians did see us in daylight, they quickly turned away. As we were marched through villages and past farms we could see the lights in their windows and the smoke coming out of their chimneys. We could not help but think of those people in their homes, sleeping in their warm beds and waking up to a hot meal with their families and children, while we were outside their doors being marched to death in the heart of winter.

One night we were stopped and herded into a school. The floor was spotlessly clean, the place was heated and it was cozy and warm. When I lay down I prayed that I would never wake up. I was physically and morally finished. But as day broke we were already marching. March or get shot. Schnell! Fast! As we were marching the SS guards suddenly jumped into the roadside ditches, ordering us to do the same. Obeying, we jumped into the ditches. We did not know why we had been ordered to do so until a few moments later when Allied war planes came roaring by low overhead. The thought of escaping ran through our minds at the sight of the planes, but we feared falling into the hands of other Germans or hostile Poles. We did not know which would be worse.

By now my shoes were almost gone. My feet were frozen and I was very weak. Masha spotted a woman carrying a pair of extra shoes. She went over to her and asked her to give me the shoes. The woman, a Hungarian, refused. Masha, tall and still strong, grabbed the shoes and tried to take them away from her. As they were fighting, an SS guard intervened. He was an older Hungarian[2] serving with the Germans. He ordered the woman to give me the shoes. She had no choice. I now had shoes again. We marched on. March or be shot.

I do not know how long we marched for or where we were when we were finally ordered onto a train. It was a regular passenger train. It had seats. Real seats. Passenger seats. Exhausted, we sat on these seats and almost felt like human beings again, even as we rolled on towards our deaths in some unknown destination. We traveled for the better part of the day before the train stopped. We were ordered out of the rail cars. The rail signs told us that we were in Germany.

We were immediately formed up and marched off again. Blocks, barracks and the chimney of crematoria came into view. We marched past a sign that read Ravensbruck.[3] We had been marched to yet another concentration camp. Another concentration camp with crematoriums. We said to one another, 'This is our final destination. They did not have time to finish us off in Auschwitz so now they will spread our ashes here on German soil.'

The blocks in Ravensbruck were overflowing with Poles, Ukrainians, Yugoslavs, Czechs, Dutch, Russians, Slovaks and Gypsies. There was not any space for us, the new arrivals. Here we learned that it was February. We had been marched non-stop for more than two weeks. I spoke to several Polish women, asking them why they were prisoners. They told me about the November 1944 Polish Revolt in Warsaw.[4] In reprisal, the Germans had arrested these women at random and deported them to various camps.

Since there was no place for us in Ravensbruck, we were formed up and marched out again after a few days. We did not know where we were being marched to this time. But now I could no longer keep up. I had had enough. I could not go on. I told Masha, 'Leave me. Go on. You're still strong.' She argued with me, urging me not to give up. I pushed her away from me. I fell back. As I walked I thought of my dear sister and asked, 'Forgive me. I have tried everything; I even rescued myself from Mengele's death sentence, but I cannot go on. I cannot fulfill my promise to you, to survive ... so I can tell.'

It was February, the month both my parents had died, and now, three years later, it was my turn to die. I had a simple plan. A simple plan to end my life. I would walk up to a German guard and tell him that I could not continue. He would not have any choice but to kill me on the spot. I could see my body sprawled dead in the snow. The snow splattered red with my own blood. I would be buried in an unmarked grave like countless others before me.

I singled out a German guard, walked up to him, and said, 'I can't go on.' He unslung his rifle from his shoulder and pushed me away with the butt yelling, 'Weiter machen! Go on! Weiter machen!' I did not move. I stood in front of him not moving. The German guard was hesitating, but I knew he would have to shoot me. As I stood there no longer thinking, frozen and waiting for the bullet, two hands grabbed my arm and pulled me. My feet were uprooted from the spot as a voice wrenched into my consciousness saying 'Hold on to me! Don't be a fool! Don't you see the rail cars waiting for us?' I looked at the Older Woman who had grabbed my arm as she had walked by and I said, 'And where will they take us? To another concentration camp with crematoriums?' 'No, no! The war is almost over.' She pulled me along as she told me her story.

She had been deported from Brussels, Belgium, to Birkenau. I told her that I used to write letters to my maternal aunt who lived in Brussels, on 28 Nancy Street. The Older Woman helped me climb onto the roofless rail car and she disappeared. I never saw her again.

The German guard who had refused to kill me was in the same roofless rail car as I. I watched him set up a steel drum and prepare a fire in it. I positioned myself nearby hoping to get some warmth from his fire. He took out a sandwich and began to eat it. It was torture to watch him eat while we were starving to death. Another train with roofless rail cars rolled slowly past us on another track. A skeletal man was standing up in one of them. We asked him if he was alone in the rail car. He replied, 'Yes. I alone am alive.'

After a few hours of travel the train stopped in the middle of nowhere. We were disembarked from the train and marched toward a nearby wood. We were sure that we were going to be shot there where nobody could see us. We marched through the woods until we came to a small camp containing a few barracks filled with Ukrainian women. It was almost nightfall and we were put into a large shed for the night.

Everyone picked a spot on the floor. I recognized two sisters, Dora and Adela Bauxenboim, whom I knew from block 26 and the munitions factory in Auschwitz. Ever since I had urged Masha ahead after we had left Ravensbruck, I had been by myself. Now I wanted to be with them. They were nice girls, devoted sisters. They could be relied upon. My instinct told me that the best place to spend the night would be near the German *kapos*, but the sisters thought differently. I tried to convince them to position themselves closer to the German *kapos* along with me, but they refused.

These German *kapos* wore the green triangle indicating that they were criminals, thieves or prostitutes. In the middle of the night the German *kapos* urinated into the red soup bowls from which they ate and flung the urine over the sleeping mass of women. When the women realized that they had been befouled with urine, they began to scream in indignation. Their voices were shrill in the dark of night. Because I had chosen a spot close to the *kapos* I was not fouled by their urine.

In the morning Dora and Adela come over to me and said, 'We should have listened to you.' From then on we became a trio and did everything together. When a truck came into the camp bringing a few potatoes there was a frenzied scramble to get some. The three of us shared whatever we were able to grab. Later on some trucks arrived bringing us a meager portion of watery soup. We reasoned that since they were feeding us maybe they would not kill us.

Every morning we broke off the icicles that hung from the roof eaves and washed our bodies with ice and snow. We sheltered each other as we took turns taking off our clothes and rubbing our bodies. Our bodies warmed up and we felt better. Others followed our example and did the same. Towards the end of February we were taken out of this camp and again transported in roofless rail cars, this time to Malchow.[5]

Malchow was a small concentration camp with a hospital, a kitchen and barracks. It did not have a crematorium. We were put into one of its small barracks, and we slept on thin mattresses on the floor. Dora, Adela and I stayed together. Sleeping nearby was Mamuska and her daughter Feluska. In the morning we were given coffee. At noon we got soup. The soup was made of white beets. It was impossible to eat it; just the smell of it could kill you. We were not put to work and at night we were given a bread ration.

Whenever I got my bread ration I ate it immediately. I was too hungry to keep a piece to savor with the next morning's coffee. I was always afraid that it might be stolen as I slept. Dora and Adela ate only one of their two bread rations at night. They kept the other ration for their coffee the next morning. But Adela, the younger sister, could not swallow her bread knowing that I did not have any. She would always sneak me a piece of her bread when her sister was not watching. Out of fairness I would refuse her offer but she would insist, pleading on her life that I take it until I was overpowered by my hunger and could no longer refuse her.

Sala Brezinski had never left my mind. Even in the worst of times I thought about her. She was my last living link to the family I had lost, my sister Channa, my brother-in-law Max and our precious Felunia. In the never- ending quest to find a loved one still alive a few girls who had been in Birkenau and were now working in Malchow's munitions factory came to visit us, the new arrivals. We were sitting on the thin mattress when one girl recognized me and screamed, 'Oh my God, you are here! I have to run and tell Sala that you are alive.' I asked her, 'Which Sala?' She answered, 'Sala Brezinski. She does not stop talking about you, wondering if you are still alive.' I could not believe my luck when Sala Brezinski came running into my arms. We cried as we embraced like sisters. We were together again. My desire to live was reborn. My desire to struggle to survive ... to keep my promise was rekindled.

Sala Brezinski worked in the munitions factory and was assigned to a different block than me. But every night she came to visit me and always brought me something to eat. She shared the margarine and the piece of salami, which her work entitled her to, with me. She spent Sundays with me. She always managed to find a potato or a carrot that we cut into small pieces and then added some potato peels. We would make a fire between two bricks and start cooking. The thin soup we made this way was delicious.

We were kept in the blocks. There were not any *appels* or any work commandos. We were left alone. We watched the handsome camp Commandant openly flirt with the camp Doctor, a very beautiful Jewish inmate. What was he doing? This was unthinkable. Punishable by death.

Our block was separated from the kitchen by a narrow alley. From the window of our block we could see down through the barred window of the kitchen cellar. It was a deep cellar in which food was stored. This food was not for us; if we were caught trying to get at it we would be put to death. One day I sat looking out the block window and noticed that one of the bins in the cellar was brimming with potatoes. The kitchen had just been resupplied and those potatoes were piled high and near the window. As I looked at those forbidden potatoes an image from my childhood came to mind, that of a long stick with a nail on it being lowered through a kitchen window, hooking a schnitzel and pulling it out.

I called the girls together and told them my plan. We scrambled to scavenge the materials we needed. In no time we had a nail, some sticks and lashings. We assembled our stick and nail and went out into the alley. While someone stood guard we lowered our pole and nail through the barred cellar window. It was too short. We quickly rushed back into the block and lashed another stick to our pole to lengthen it. We went back into the alley and again lowered the pole down through the cellar window. This time it was long enough. After a few tries we nailed a potato. We fished out a few potatoes and ran back into our block. Our pole was disassembled and the parts hidden. Flammables were quickly gathered, a fire built and a potato soup was cooked. After several more potato fishing expeditions, we could no longer reach the rapidly dwindling pile of potatoes.

April arrived and with it the fresh air of spring. Being out in the open strengthened my desire to live, but every day we were given less and less food. Some days we received nothing at all. I started feeling extremely weak. I was constantly fantasizing about the food my mother used to make for me. I was so faint from the constant hunger that I saw stars in front of my eyes. In my starved state of mind I reasoned that if cows could survive by eating grass, so could I. I started to eat grass. I picked the tender spring grass, chewed it, swallowed the juice and then spit out the pulp. My frail body broke out into a sweat from this.

One day they asked for volunteers to clean the blocks where the Germans lived. I volunteered, hoping to find something to eat there. We found the German living quarters empty. They were deserted. It gave us hope that the war would soon end. I looked through their garbage for something to eat, but there was nothing.

At the end of April the Swedish Red Cross[6] arrived in Malchow. The girls from the munitions factory were assembled. Five-kilogram parcels were distributed to some of the barracks but none reached us. Sala Brezinski came running to bid me goodbye. She was being taken out of the camp by the

Swedish Red Cross. She said, 'Soon they will come and take you too.' Once again we were separated. We never saw each other again. The Red Cross never came back for us.

On the first of May, 1945, we were assembled and marched out through the gates of Malchow in columns of five abreast. Dora, Adela and I marched out together. As we left Malchow we received a five-kilogram parcel that the Red Cross had left behind. We had to divide it among the five of us.

Once again we were on a forced march. This time most of the guards were Hungarians. On the second day out of Malchow we noticed fewer and fewer guards walking beside us. Whenever any guards passed us they, too, were dragging their feet, but they would always order us to march on. We decided to rest and sat down on the edge of a roadside ditch. Two other girls, Hilda and Lonia, who had worked with me in the munitions factory under Maister Paul Vonendem, joined us.

A young man walked out to the road near us and addressed us in Polish. He said that he had heard us speaking Polish and that he and some other Poles, who had been brought to Germany as forced labor, lived in the house nearby. He was very friendly. We asked him to bring us something to eat. He replied that they did not receive enough food themselves. He then pointed to a small house just off the road and said, 'The Germans have left in a hurry. If you are not afraid to go in, maybe you can find something to eat.' Afraid that the Germans might see him speaking to us and accuse him of aiding and abetting prisoners to escape, he soon went back to his house.

Adela and I went into the small house that the Germans had hurriedly left. On the table was a large bowl of hard boiled eggs. We took them back to the girls and five of us began to eat them. As we ate the camp Commandant, dressed in civilian clothes rode by on a bicycle. He saw us sitting there and said, 'Girls, keep going. Go to the Americans because the Russians are not far behind.'[7]

The young Pole came back out again and said, 'Girls, don't go any further. We may be liberated tomorrow. Wait here till nightfall, and then go into the next house. It's empty. Hide there.' We decided to follow the young Pole's advice. We went into the empty house and went up to the attic to hide, in case the Germans came back during the night. We found three other women already hiding in the attic. Among them was Bella, a girl I knew from Birkenau.

During the night I began to have severe pains in my stomach, chest and back. I could not breathe. I was sure that I was going to die. I went to where the Poles lived, hoping they could help me. I told them that I had eaten hard boiled eggs and felt like I was dying. They were sympathetic but were afraid to let me into their house because of the striped jacket I was wearing. They could be accused of hiding prisoners if any Germans showed up. They suggested that I put my fingers down my throat and bring it all up. I tried but it did not work. I had never vomited in my entire life.

I went back to the house we were hiding in and staggered around yelling, 'I am dying! I am dying!' Adela came down from the attic to look after me. I was standing with my back to a warm stove. Adela began to rub my back and chest. After a while I started to feel better. Thanks to Adela I made it through the night.

The next day, May 3, I visited the house where the Poles lived. We were all looking out the window for the Russians. We watched a few very young German soldiers appear and take up positions among some trees and bushes in a field across the road. They were merely teenagers, probably Hitler Youth[7]. The Poles cursed them vehemently.

Around 3 o'clock that afternoon the young Pole came running into the house screaming, 'We are liberated! The Russians are here in our yard!' I ran out and saw two Russian soldiers dismount from their horses. One immediately ran to help a third soldier who was wounded. One soldier came near me, looked at my striped clothes and said in Russian, '*Plochoy zyzna w Germany?* Life in Germany was hard?' I answered, '*Da, da.* Yes. Yes.' I understood the Russian language because my parents spoke Russian when they did not want the children to understand. I ran up to the attic and told the girls to come out: We were liberated.

More Russian soldiers arrived. One was hit by rifle fire from the field across the road where the young German soldiers had taken up positions that morning. They did not stop shooting. More Russian soldiers arrived and we watched them attack and silence the Germans. We could not believe that we were finally free.

BOOK SIX

FROM THE ASHES

May 3, 1945 – March 20, 1951

We were liberated! We were no longer prisoners with death sentences. No longer slaves of the Germans. We were liberated from the SS and their guns, whips and dogs. Liberated from forced labor. Liberated from *appels*, selections and the smoking crematoria. But we were not free of the knowledge that our families, those we had loved and those who had loved us, had been murdered, reduced to ashes around us. We had survived, but we were not free of the crushing weight that we were only a pitiful remnant of our people. We were incapable of rejoicing in our deliverance, for each one of us was still captive to one unvoiced fear: that we would not find any other members of our families alive.

Caught up in the sudden mania of liberation, the young Pole and his fellow workers hurried off to the now-abandoned local German headquarters. The girls and I followed them. We arrived at a large building surrounded by a farm. The place was swarming with high-ranking Soviet Army officials and Russian soldiers. Everyone was busy helping themselves to the vast quantities of flower, sugar, rice and the innumerable variety of goods that the Germans had stored there. We could not believe the vast array of wealth our eyes beheld. Our minds were overwhelmed with the realization that now we, too, could have anything that we wanted.

We ran through the building in a feverish frenzy, grabbing everything in sight. Each new thing we saw was better than the last. We quickly filled our arms until we could not hold anymore. We started to drop some items to pick up new ones. We saw people rushing up to the attic. We wanted to follow them up the stairs, but we did not have the strength to carry everything we now held in our arms. We dropped everything and joined the run up into the attic. The attic was crammed full of wooden crates brimming with the most beautiful furs. We went through the crates until our frenzy finally exhausted us. Our exhaustion brought us back to our senses. We left the attic empty-handed. We went back down to the farmyard and found it full of Russian soldiers pulling down the Nazi's black swastika flag and replacing it with the red Soviet Hammer and Sickle.

We decided that the best thing to do would be to catch one of the chickens scratching in the farmyard and make chicken soup. Most of us had never chased a chicken before and now we did not have the energy to do so. As we floundered after the chickens in the farmyard the Russian soldiers watched us and roared with laughter. We finally caught one. Now we had to kill it. We began arguing about who would do it. None of us had the heart to kill the chicken. Finally Lonia, who was holding the chicken, let it go. The Russian soldiers watched us in disbelief. One high-ranking soldier, his chest covered with medals, called me over and said in Russian, 'It is hard for us to believe that you girls, who survived such slaughter and endured so many sadistic tortures, are incapable of killing a chicken!' We all knew enough Russian to understand every word he said. We were deeply embarrassed.

Some of the Soviet soldiers then came over to us and invited us to a victory celebration that night. We decided that the former German headquarters building would be the safest place for us to stay. We went back inside and chose a room large enough for all of us to sleep in. Before long there was a knock at the door. A handsome Russian lieutenant was standing in the doorway. He pointed at Lonia and motioned for her to come out. Lonia was the most mature looking one of us; she was the least emaciated. She went out to see what he wanted. Within a minute she came back, red-faced, and told us that the Lieutenant had propositioned her to spend the night with him. We immediately left the German headquarters and went back to the house in which the Poles were living. We spent the night there in safety.

The next day we searched for a safe place to live. Bella, whom I had found hiding in the attic, joined us. We were now six girls. We found an abandoned house and moved in. We all slept in one room, hoping for safety in numbers. The Russians had set up a command post in the tiny village and Military Police patrolled to keep order. The Commandant ordered the MPs to check on us every two hours, but it was not often enough. Russian soldiers came to our house every night. They were often drunk, but would leave when asked to or when we told them that the MPs were about to come by.

During the day Russian soldiers, high-ranking officials and their wives came to visit us. There were many Jewish men and women among them serving as doctors in the Soviet Army. They were all very polite and asked us many questions. We told them about the problems we were having at night with soldiers coming to our door, and that we were more afraid now than when we were in the concentration camps. We added that the MPs checking on us every two hours was not enough. After that the MPs were sent by more often. However, one night Mongolian troops came to our house and we fled in terror. We ran to the Commandant's headquarters to escape being raped. From then on a Soviet Army Major was in charge of our security. We saw him regularly and he had endless questions about our experiences in the death camps.

Following our liberation, the local German population disappeared from sight. It was now their turn to go into hiding. They feared the Russians and they feared us, the concentration camp survivors. They feared we would revenge ourselves on them. But the Germans had to eat and after a few days, they slowly began to come out of their hiding places for a short while during daylight. By night they were all in hiding again. It reminded me of how we had come out of our *hiding*s in the Warsaw Ghetto when it was quiet and we thought it was safe to prepare something to eat.

One day the Soviet Army Major and I were discussing revenge. He said to me, 'You see that German woman and her child over there? Go do whatever you want to them. Take the child. Throw it out of the carriage. Smash it to the ground. Nothing will happen to you. Go ahead.' I started to cry. 'You see,' he said, 'you cannot do it. You are not like them.'

The German family whose house we were living in finally emerged from hiding. They were furtive and afraid of us. They knew we could treat them as we pleased. We decided to be on good terms with them and not deny them their home. They came in during the day to prepare something to eat, and after they ate they would disappear until the next day. Sometimes I had the urge to ask them how it felt to be afraid and to be hiding for their lives.' But I did not have the heart. I knew how it felt.

During one of the German family's furtive visits we asked them if they had any extra food to share with us. They began crying and told us that they hardly had any food at all. After they left we searched the house to find their food cache. We discovered the entrance to their cellar. It was packed with huge jars of meat conserved in lard, all kinds of pickled vegetables, especially asparagus, and all kinds of confitures. There was enough food hidden here to last for years. It was essential in the recovery of our health.

For the first time in years we were free of hunger. Free of fear. Free of fatigue. Our freedom seemed like a dream, and we were afraid that we might wake up at any minute and find ourselves back in the death camps. We reunited with our friends who had also survived the death march. Together we enjoyed the good food that had been hoarded in the cellar. We could now do as we pleased, come and go as we pleased. We could eat and sleep. We could heal. Heal until we had enough physical and emotional strength to confront our final fear: had anyone else in our families survived this Holocaust?

One day as I was on my way to visit Marysia, a friend who lived nearby, I realized that I was being followed. I turned to see a Russian officer behind me. The intensity of his stare terrified me. I ran to Marysia's house. She and her mother lived in an upstairs flat. The Russian Officer followed me. I ran up the stairs believing that I was now safe and that he would just go away. Two hours later he was still standing outside looking up at the windows. Marysia offered to walk me home thinking that this would finally discourage him, but he was not deterred and followed us back to where I lived. The Russian Officer went to the German woman who owned the house and told her that he wanted to occupy the room next to ours. He ordered her to bring him a lot of pillows. She had no choice but to oblige.

We could hear him through the walls, bouncing up and down on the bed and telling the German woman it would do for tonight. This frightened us even more. Hilda and I slipped out of the house and ran to where the high-ranking Soviet officials lived. We told them about the Russian Officer and how we felt threatened by him. We asked them to help us. They began to laugh. They found our situation funny. I said, 'I will not leave this place if you will not come and convince this soldier to leave us alone.'

Two Soviet Military Police escorted us back to the house and confronted the Russian Officer. He said that he was on leave and showed them his papers. They examined his documents, saluted him and walked away. They told us that they had no authority to forbid him from staying there while he was on leave. But they offered to guard us for the night. We accepted and invited Marysia to join us. The five of us had an all-night party with the two Soviet MPs, who were perfect gentlemen. The Russian Officer left early the next morning.

On May 8, 1945, the war was officially declared over. We had learned that we were some one hundred kilometers north of Berlin. By now we had regained enough physical strength to face the unanswered question that hung over us. We could not leave Germany quickly enough and begged the Russian

Command to have us taken back to Poland. They proposed a travel plan to us and asked us if we would agree to it.

Germany's dairy herds were being confiscated for shipment to Russia. The Russians asked us to walk the cows to the rail head in Brandenburg. Once in Brandenburg, Soviet soldiers would escort us into Poland. We were to be taken to a farm where they were assembling the cattle and then trained to milk the cows. Dora and Adela, who came from a farm, were capable of milking cows. The rest of us could not. Two older women also joined us. We had to promise that if we could not find German women along the way to milk the cows, we and the soldiers would milk them. We all agreed and fllled out the necessary forms with our names, our parents' names and the dates and places of our birth. Sixteen soldiers were assigned to guard us. The soldiers swore to protect us and to be loyal and correct to us in every way.

We began our journey back to Poland to find the answers to our final fear. We walked all day and stopped wherever we found good pasture. The local German women gladly agreed to do the milking for us once they heard that they could keep the milk. They even cooked our meals. At night they would prepare nice clean beds for us in their homes, after which they would disappear into their hiding places. They did not trust the Russians even though we assured them that no harm would come from our soldiers.

On days when we could not find local women to milk the cows, we and the soldiers did it ourselves. I was the only one who could not milk a cow. One day the soldiers called me over and assigned me a cow to milk. As I hesitantly approached the animal, puzzling over where her teats were located, the soldiers started convulsing with laughter. The other girls, attracted by the commotion, came over to see what was going on. They quickly pointed out that the cow the soldiers had assigned me to was a steer. I went beet red with embarrassment.

After almost two weeks of cow herding we arrived in a field on the outskirts of a city where a sign identified the Brandenburg railroad station. Memories of my Aunt Chaiah, who had lived in Brandenburg, flooded me. Finally we were near Berlin and not very far from Poland.

Other groups of women herding cattle arrived in Brandenburg as well. They were Russian and Ukrainian girls who had worked in Germany. When it was time to milk the cows these girls began to taunt us, 'Jewish girls cannot milk cows.' They also began flirting with our soldiers. We decided that we had better leave before hostilities broke out. Bella and the two older women left immediately. The rest of us, knowing that our soldiers would be held accountable for us, did not want to jeopardize them by leaving. They had sworn to bring us to Poland and to set us free. We went to the soldier in command and asked his permission to leave. He asked us to sign forms that attested that we had been well treated and that we had left of our own free will. We left our soldiers and walked towards Brandenburg. I never did learn how to milk a cow. I was too afraid to go near one.

It was almost dark when the five of us reached the railroad station in Brandenburg. We walked into the rail yard to find somewhere to sleep. We saw many box cars loaded with sacks of grain. We climbed into one, picked a corner where nobody was likely to spot us, and settled in for the night. We were in a deep sleep when a whistle blasted and the train started moving. By the time we were all awake the train was moving too fast for us to risk jumping off in the dark. We had no idea where we were heading, but with all the wheat on it we knew it was headed out of Germany. We went back to sleep.

Again we were awakened. This time it was by two Russian soldiers patroling the train to prevent the wheat from being stolen. Their faces were all smiles as one said to the other, 'Nice young girls.' Their intentions were obvious as they advanced towards us. We warned them that we had survived the camps and that they should leave us alone. Suddenly the rail car started rattling heavily. We looked out of the car and saw that we were on a bridge crossing over a river. We knew that no one would hear our screams for help above the racket the train was making on the bridge. Our only route of escape was to jump off the train into the river. Just then the train whistle blew. The two Russian soldiers stopped advancing towards us, turned around and ran to another box car, never to return. Luck was with us again. We knew that the river below us had been the Odra that runs between Germany and Poland. The train stopped just before dawn. Half asleep, I saw a sign announcing the city of Torun.

We jumped off the box car happy to be safe and back in Poland. Torun was a big city and it was still asleep as we walked in through the dawn. We walked out of our past into a world where we did not know what to expect. In the growing daylight we saw people rushing to work. Life was normal for them. They did not acknowledge us and did not appear to see us. It was as if we were invisible. For a moment I wondered if I was really alive.

We stopped the first person that came close enough for us to talk to. We asked where the city hall and the police station were. We followed directions to the police station. Being concentration camp survivors, the police gave us Polish identity documents bearing our names, place of birth and where we had lived. We received food coupons and rail passes that allowed us to travel anywhere in Poland for the next six months. A Polish policeman then escorted us to a hostel.

The hostel was clean and we were its only guests. Shortly after we arrived a young Polish man with a knapsack on his back and guitar slung around his neck appeared at the hostel. He came over to us and introduced himself. He had been one of the many Poles forced to work in Germany. He began playing his guitar for us.

An hour later the policeman who had brought us there came back to check on us. Seeing this young man near us he ordered him to sit on the other side of the room. The young man, angered by the policeman's authoritarianism, called him a German collaborator. They started fighting. The policeman subdued the young man and took him off to jail. A little later the policeman came back and ordered me to collect the young man's guitar and belongings and to bring them to the jail. The young man had requested this so that he could bid me goodbye.

We decided to leave Torun that same day. But first I went into a store on Torun's main street and asked the woman working there if she had lived in Torun before the war. Had she known the Leon Szyldszrajber family? Leon Szyldszrajber was the brother of my brother-in-law Max. Leon had been a prosperous man in Torun before the war and I wanted to know if anybody in Torun even remembered him. 'Yes,' she replied, 'I remember him and his family. I know where his business was and his villa is not far from here.' I left the store with my heart breaking. Leon, his wife Sara, their daughter and their good-looking, blue-eyed young son had been among the first taken to Treblinka when the deportations started in the Warsaw Ghetto. I recalled how Franka Michalska, Leon's sister, had cried hysterically when she told me about it.

We walked back to the train station. Our intent was to travel to Warsaw to find other Jewish survivors. But when we asked the local Poles where we could find other Jews, they told us that most of the surviving Jews were now in Lodz. Lodz was the city where my oldest brother Chaim had married and lived. He had fled the city when the Germans planned to close its ghetto.

We arrived in Lodz in the late afternoon of a very warm July day. We walked straight to the Jewish Committee on 32 Srodmiejska Street. We met many other Jews there. Some were concentration camp survivors like us, others had been partisans in the woods, and yet others had been lucky enough to have been hidden by good Polish people. Everyone was constantly searching each other's eyes in the hope of recognizing someone who had managed to survive the last six years. We did not find anybody we knew.

When we finally tired we asked where we could spend the night. We were sent to an address on Kilinskego Street. We found the building deserted. It had no doors or windows. There was garbage and litter everywhere. We decided to return to the Jewish Committee and look for someone who would take us in for the night before it got dark. Next to the deserted building was a small overgrown plot of land. It appeared to be an abandoned cemetery. A few broken monuments rose above the bushes and tall grass. We hid the few belongings we had in the overgrowth.

Our hope was that since Dora and Adela were from a farm not far from Lodz they might have a chance to find one of their brothers. We pledged that if any one of us found a relative, she would not abandon the rest of us. As we were walking down Kilinskego Street, I spotted my cousin Rosa, whom I had last seen in Maydanek. I could not believe my luck. I ran towards her. We embraced. I called the girls over to meet her.

Rosa had come to me in Maydanek to tell me to enlist for a work transport that was sent to Skarzysko near Chestochova. I did not listen to her advice and was later sent to Birkenau. She now told me that she was on her way to see Basha, one of our cousins, whom I had taken smuggling with me during the time we were in the Warsaw Ghetto. Basha had also survived in Skarzysko. Rosa's sister Lena had survived the war by assuming a Polish alias and working as a maid for a Polish family. Baruch, one of her brothers, had also survived by using a Polish alias. He had been a forced laborer in Germany. What a stroke of luck: out of my Uncle David's ten children, three had survived. It raised my hope that perhaps someone else in my family had also survived.

Having found a few relatives, I considered myself to be very fortunate. We went to see Basha. We began walking to 16 Swietgo Jakuba Street, where Basha was sharing an apartment with her friend, Tema, and an old friend of my father's, Mr Aron Lichtenstajyn. Mr Lichtenstajyn was an elderly man and somehow he had survived the war. As we approached our destination I said to Rosa, 'Let me go on ahead; I want to see if Basha recognizes me.' Both

Basha and Mr Lichtenstajyn were standing in the courtyard with some others. As soon as she saw me she recognized me. She was overjoyed to see me. She introduced me to Mr Lichtenstajyn. 'This is Motta's daughter.' He looked at me and said, it cannot be. I remember the youngest one was a little boy, Moishele. He was then about three or four years old. That was in about twenty-three, twenty-four.' I said, 'You didn't think another child was born after him?' His face broke into a welcoming smile. Now he, too, was happy to see me. Basha said, 'You will stay here with us.' This was wonderful music to my ears but I said, 'Thank you, but not unless my girls can stay with me.' Basha welcomed all of us saying, 'There Is a big couch you can all sleep on.' We were very happy.

The first thing the next day we set out to find work. Only Dora found work as a maid. Now she was able to support herself and her sister Adela. The rest of us could not find any work. After a few more fruitless days, Hilda, Lonia and I decided it was time to go back to our home towns, the cities from where we had come.

It was time for me to confront the gnawing terror that had been growing in me since our liberation. Had anyone else in my family survived the horrors that I had witnessed? Did my brother Tusha survive by some miracle? Had Chaim? Was Schloime going to come home from Russia? The first stop was my city, Grodzisk Maz. I prayed for a miracle. I hoped I would find someone waiting for me there. Someone who would take me in their arms, someone to whom I could tell what had happened to our sister, someone with whom I could mourn.

A few hours on the train brought us into Grodzisk Maz. The station master from before the war was still there. Seeing him triggered an avalanche of memories. How often had I walked through these station gates with my parents on our way to Warsaw? My heart sank. I almost fainted. As Lonia and Hilda walked with me into the streets of Grodzisk I began pointing out houses and describing the people who had lived there. I became hysterical with the anguish caused by the torrent of memories that the sights and smells of Grodzisk released in me. The girls had to hold me up until I could control myself again. We walked on and approached another house. Again I began telling the girls about the family who had lived there and about their son, Luzer Schulman, with whom I had spent all my school years. As I uttered his name, Luzer stepped out of the house. I could not believe it. I screamed, 'You survived!

You survived! Who else?' He told me that his father had survived by making boots for the Germans. His younger sister, Zelda, had also survived. 'Now, calm yourself.' He then named a few other people who had survived and had returned to live in Grodzisk Maz. He asked me if I remembered the Wajcer twins, brothers. I said, 'They are my second cousins.' 'Well, they have survived and have taken back their property. Almost all the surviving Jews who have returned to Grodzisk, around fifteen people, live there.' I asked, 'My brother Schloime, who was in Russia, is he here among them?' 'No.'

We walked over to the Wajcers' house. The twin brothers were happy to see me, a relative who had survived. I was happy to see them. They were now twenty years old, grown men. They were identical twins, impossible to tell apart. Both were quick-witted, blond-haired, green-eyed, handsome, athletic men. My father's cousins Leya and Moshe Schgimek were also there. Their beautiful, curly blond-haired little girl had been torn out of Leya's arms by the Germans and was never seen again. I was told that Moishe Apfal, one of my brother Schloime's best friends, was also here. I knew that Moishe Apfal had been in Russia with my brother. I had to see him immediately. When he heard I was back in Grodzisk he came to see me. He told me not to worry; my brother would soon come back from Russia. I felt that he was lying to me.

Later in the day, I decided to go and see the Fuchses on Koronkowa Street. I knew that if someone in my family would show up, they would go to the Fusches. I did not know what had happened to the Fuchses. Were they alive? Had they been thrown out of Poland as collaborators or worse? The Wajcer twins tried to discourage me from going to see the Fuchses. Besides, '... the countryside was dangerous for a woman ...', since anti-Semitism was always a danger. But I needed to see the Fuchses.

Hilda and Lonia, unwilling to let me go alone, reluctantly walked the two kilometers with me to the Fuchses' home. I had told the girls about how good-hearted the Fuchse family was. I had told them how I had spent my summer vacations in the beautiful villa, about the gazebo in the garden where I used to write compositions that were always displayed on the classroom wall, and about the Polish woman whom I had saved from the poison. As we walked I showed them the field where my younger brother Tusha had played football instead of going to Chaidar and how his new shoes had been stolen by the Polish boys and he had to come home barefoot.

When we arrived in front of the Fuchses place I stopped and stood there speechless, my insides churning. Nothing had changed. The multi-color pansies were where they had always been planted. Everything was exactly the same as it had been the last time I was there during the summer of 1939. I asked my friends to wait for me. I walked around to the kitchen and opened the door. Basha Fuchse, the youngest daughter, was at the table washing vegetables. She was not surprised to see me. When I closed the door, she asked, 'Where is your mother?' It was normal for her to always see me with my mother. I turned away from her and started to sob convulsively. She put her arms around me. She asked me if I had come alone. I replied that two friends had accompanied me. I asked her if anyone from my family had shown up here. She replied that no one else had.

I wanted to ask about her family but knowing that her brother Vladek had been forced to serve the Nazis, I feared what I might learn. Awkwardly I asked her if Vladek was still alive. She said, 'Yes, he is alive and well. He lives with his family in Ursus near Warsaw.' She added, 'I want you to know that we are Poles in bone and blood and that my brother Vladek worked for the underground, not for the Nazis.' That lifted a heavy burden from my chest. I remembered what mother had said to father, 'Even though he drives a Volkswagen with a swastika on it, Vladek can do no harm to anyone.' I left Basha Fuchse my address in Lodz so that she could tell anyone who might return to Grodzisk where I was. The girls and I returned safely to the Wajcer home.

The next morning I showed Lonia and Hilda around my city. As we walked through the market place we overheard people talking behind our backs, 'How come the Germans left so many of them? Why are they still roaming the streets here?' We ignored them. Then another Polish woman said, 'They are like worms, they crawl out from under the earth.' I could not take it anymore.[1] I went into the shop of a Polish woman from whom I used to buy supplies and began crying. She said, 'Don't take it so hard. These are people who have lost their homes and have come here and moved into the Jewish homes. Now they are afraid the Jews will come back and throw them out. They are not good people.' We returned to the Wajcers' house.

There I asked the other Jews, 'How can you stay here; this city is full of anti-Semites?' They replied, 'Everywhere you go, you will encounter anti-Semites. The Poles are afraid that the Jews will come home and take back their houses and possessions.'

That afternoon the girls and I left for Warsaw, Lonia's hometown. We were going to look for the place where she had lived on Pava Street. But when we got to Warsaw there were no streets to be found. Warsaw was in ruins. The entire city had been reduced to rubble. We learned that all survivors registered with the Jewish Relief Committee on Targowa Street in Praga, a suburb of Warsaw, on the other side of the Vistula River. We went there.

As I went up the stairs of the building housing the Jewish Relief Committee a man noticed the number tattooed on my arm. He asked me where I had worked in Auschwitz. When I told him, 'In the Union munitions factory,' he grabbed me and kissed me, saying, 'I am alive because you girls helped us to destroy the crematoria with the gun powder you smuggled out.'

We received some money, coupons for soup and a shelter to sleep in. The shelter was a building with bare rooms and a clean floor to sleep on. But the place was over-crowded and the noise was unbearable. We could not fall asleep. We decided to travel to Otwock, Hilda's hometown, in the morning.

It was cold and raining the next day as we walked to the train station for the trip to Otwock. The train was not going to arrive for quite some time so Lonia and I decided to leave the train station to buy some bread. When we returned with the bread, Hilda was gone. We could not figure out what had happened to her. We were sure she had not left for Otwock without us. We considered going there to look for her but we had never been there and did not know anyone there. We waited hours for her to show up. When she did not reappear we lost hope. How could she have just vanished? Had someone kidnapped her? Had she been the victim of anti-Semitism after all that she had been through? We were dismayed; our hearts were broken. We decided to return to Lodz.

Of the 3,500,000 Jews in Poland before the war, just a handful of us had survived. With our wounds still raw, it was shattering to be afflicted by anti-Semitism everywhere we went. The hopes I had dared to entertain of finding other members of my family alive turned out to be fantasies. After several weeks back in Poland they were shattered forever. My final unvoiced fear proved to be the grim reality.

It was summer and I was nineteen years old. It was now several months after liberation and I still looked like a fifteen-year old. After everything I had been through I felt like I was fifty years old. The only feelings I had were of loneliness, emptiness and bitterness. I wondered how a person could endure all this and still continue to live.

We took the late afternoon train back to Lodz. It was a six hour trip from

Warsaw and the train was packed. A gentleman made room for me to sit down next to him. When I fell asleep my head rolled onto his shoulder. I heard a whisper in my ear, 'Amchu.' The word woke me up. It was a code word used by Jews during the war to identify each other; it meant 'one of us'. I opened my eyes and looked at the elderly gentleman. He introduced himself and gave me his business card. He was a lawyer and told me that if I had any property to claim in Poland, he could arrange everything for me. He said that I should call his office in the event that I ever needed anything. The war was over but in Poland we still had to identify each other furtively. I returned to my cousin Basha's home.

For six years I had been denied and deprived of my freedom, the most valuable and essential requirement of the human spirit. For six years I had been on a perpetual sentence of death. At fourteen years old I had endured the daily stress and fear of being a smuggler in order to keep my immediate family alive. At seventeen I had been condemned to die by terror, starvation and exhaustion as a slave laborer. Again I went looking for work. Work in order to support myself. The only thing I found were endless marriage proposals. But marriage was far from my mind. I was not ready mentally or physically. Now I just wanted to be free.

Walking down Lodz's Kilinskego Street I saw a young woman slowly making her way down the street, her body hugging the walls of the buildings. I could see that she was lost and forlorn. As I got closer to her I recognized her. She and her identical twin sister had worked at the same table as me in the Union munitions factory. Their names were Bella and Regina. I could never distinguish one from the other and even now I did not know which one I was speaking to. I asked her, 'Where is your sister?' 'Dead,' she replied. 'She was shot. Killed along with seven other girls just after being liberated by the Russians. We were afraid of being raped by Russian soldiers so nine of us banded together to live in one room in a German village. One night several drunken Mongolian soldiers came into our quarters intending to rape us, but we started to scream and they left. A short while later one of them came back and started shooting us. I was hit and crawled under a bed and pretended to be dead. He killed all the others.' After hearing her story I understood her state of mind. I never saw her again.

One day that summer I met two girls I knew from Birkenau. They spoke a heavily accented *Litvack* peculiar to Vilnius. This was where Cyla and Cypka, two of my former *pritcha* mates, were from. I asked these two girls if by any chance they knew my friends. To my surprise they not only knew them but also told me that they were right here in Lodz, and I was given their address. I went to see them. I arrived at the address and started up a narrow staircase. I had climbed no more than a few steps when I heard people talking behind me. I looked back and saw a Polish Army officer accompanied by a beautiful woman dressed in an elegant gray tailored suit topped by a wide brimmed hat. She looked like a Hollywood movie actress. I stepped aside to let them pass. As she passed our eyes met. We screamed, 'Cyla!' 'Fela!' We hugged and kissed and before she could say anything I asked her, 'Tell me, does Cypka have her little girl?' 'Yes. Come up and see.' Cypka opened the door to let us in. She was happy to see me. She asked us to talk quietly while her little girl was napping. I waited until the child awoke and said to Cypka, 'You were right. You were not crazy. You were smart to save your child.' I considered her smart and lucky, and I considered the saving of the child a miracle.

Our cousin Baruch Burman often came to Basha's to visit us. On one occasion he gave me some money and said, 'Go out and buy yourself a good pair of shoes.' His presence always cheered me up. I saw a lot of my father in him: the similarities of voice, his good nature and the family resemblance. He was now the only Burman male left alive to carry on our family name.

I walked to the marketplace to shop for a pair of shoes with the money I had received from Baruch. Among the crowd I recognized David, a man I knew from the Warsaw Ghetto. He had been one of my neighbors at 63 Mila Street. He was with a friend whom he introduced as Benek from Otwock. When I heard he was from Otwock I asked him if he knew Hilda Fridman. 'Of course,' he replied, 'she is in Otwock right now.' I was overjoyed to learn that she was alive, but I was also very angry with her for the misery she had caused us by her disappearance at the train station. Now I swore that I would never speak to her again because she had not even bothered to inform us of her whereabouts.

As I continued through the market I was overjoyed to meet Dorka Koplowicz. She and her sister Haddasa had taken Masha and me under their blanket on the horrific Death March that had started on January 18, 1945. It was a joy for us to see each other alive. I told her that I had not found any other members of my family alive and that I could not find any work. She informed me that a religious *kibbutz*, Adath Israel, was being organized under the supervision of her sister, Haddasa. It was to be located on 33 Piotrkowska Street and on 66 Zachodnia Street.

As soon as the *kibbutz* was established Lonia and I joined. Dora and Adela were not willing to join the *kibbutz*. *Kibbutz* Adath Israel was under strict religious supervision. I was not religious, but thanks to my mother's insistence, I had attended *Beis Yakov* as a child and was sufficiently knowledgeable to fit in. Lonia and I were satisfied to be living and working on the *kibbutz*.

We worked in the *kibbutz* factory cleaning and restoring religious objects which had been taken back from the Nazis. We also cleaned and sorted captured Nazi photos to be sent to Israel. The *kibbutz* took in the Jewish children that had been hidden among the Polish population. The Jewish Agency worked hard and efficiently to unearth these children. At the *kibbutz* we began their Jewish education before they were sent to Israel. As *kibbutz* members we knew that sooner or later we would all be going to Israel.

One day as I was walking down Kilinskego Street to visit my cousin Basha, I met Hilda coming my way. She was coming from Basha's, *kibbutz* address in hand, to find Lonia and me. Hilda was unruffled. It had never occurred to her that she had wronged us by abandoning us at the station in Warsaw. After all we had been through together, I could not help but forgive her. She, too, joined the *kibbutz*.

By autumn of 1945, groups were leaving the *kibbutz* for Israel every few weeks. Hilda and I were losing our patience. Why were we not being sent to Israel? I went to Haddasa with my question. Her reply was that this was not her department and that I should talk to Malka and Fajga. Hilda and I confronted them and demanded that we be sent to Israel on the next transport. Fajga replied with anger, 'You have to work more for the *kibbutz* and wait for your turn.' By this time we had been hired out by the *kibbutz* to work in a knitting factory. The man for whom we worked was very pleased with us and always told us, 'I am paying good money for your work!' We realized that this was the reason we were being kept behind in Poland. After six years of having my life and freedom determined by others I could not accept this reasoning. I made a pledge that I would leave Poland at the first opportunity.

Bella, who had herded cows with us to Brandenburg, Germany, was also in Lodz. She was about to get married to Leon, a young man who had fought in the Russian army. One day Bella told me that she felt closest to me and needed my support. She asked me to promise her that I would be there with her on her wedding day. I promised.

Moishe, the elder of the Wajcer twins, came to Lodz from time to time to visit me. He had survived the war under the alias of Stashek. He was still using this alias to deal with the Poles. Whenever a survivor came back to Grodzisk from Russia, or from wherever they had managed to survive, he told me about them and reported whatever news they had brought. I was always glad to learn of them. Unfortunately, the reports were few and none of them were of my family. During one visit, Moishe told me that his twin brother, Berel, and the few survivors who had returned to Grodzisk after the war had all left for West Germany. They had all gone to a displaced persons (DP) camp in Zelsheim near Frankfurt Am. He had stayed behind in order to find a responsible person to take care of their family property that was now occupied by eleven Polish tenants. He said that as soon as his brother Berel returned from West Germany they would both leave Poland. He asked me if I would go with them. I agreed.

During Moishe's visit I was busy preparing for Bella's wedding. I invited him to come to the wedding with me. I introduced Moishe to Bella. Bella took my hand; she was cold and trembling; she said to Moishe, 'Fela is my sister.' Moishe replied, 'How many sisters does she have?' Bella did not let go of my hand until she went under the *chuppah* for the wedding ceremony. Moishe had to fend for himself among the guests. When Bella finally let go of me I went to look for Moishe. I spotted him sitting next to the groom. I was embarrassed and thought to myself, 'What a *chutzpah* he has; he doesn't even know the groom and he has seated himself next to him at the head table.' Suddenly a commotion erupted. Leon had taken a good look at Moishe and jumped up when he recognized him. The groom introduced Moishe to his guests as one his of comrade-in-arms during the fighting in the Polish Revolt in Warsaw.

In December of 1945, Moishe and his twin Berel came to Lodz to prepare me for our departure. When Hilda learned that I was leaving her behind she was devastated. She began to cry hysterically. At my suggestion Moishe agreed to take her along as well. We left the *kibbutz* in secrecy. The only person we said goodbye to was Haddasa.

The journey was short but not easy. We had to cross from Communist territory into West Berlin, which was under Allied control. By now we had learned that anything could happen under the communists and we had no faith in them. We took a train to the Polish city of Szczecin close to the German border. In Szczecin we and a few dozen others paid a man with a truck to drive us into East Berlin. Once in East Berlin we went to the large Rykier Strasse synagogue which served as both an assembly and transit point from which survivors who had left Poland could find transport to get past the communist police into West Berlin. From there our destination point, Zelsheim, would be easy to get to, but first we had to get into West Berlin.

After a number of days in East Berlin we boarded a train going to West Berlin and freedom. Before the train rolled into West Berlin it came to a stop. We could see both Russian and East German police boarding the train. They made their way through the rail car, questioning and searching everyone. Berel, who had survived with the partisans in the woods during the war, had a gun concealed in his bag. The East German policemen demanded to search Berel's bag. Berel quick-wittedly asked the Russian police why these Nazis thugs were not in prison camps. The East German policemen, incensed by the insult, started beating him. In the midst of the mêlée the train whistle blew and it started to roll forward. The East German police had to stop beating Berel to jump off the train. Berel was left covered in blood but he had succeeded in distracting the East German police from carrying out their search. This search would have led to him, and possibly all of us, being arrested. Luck had been with us and we rolled into West Berlin and freedom.

We arrived in Zelzheim, Frankfurt Am on January 1, 1945. The displaced persons' reception center was overflowing. However, anyone who already had a relative there could be registered and stay in one of the DP camps. I wanted to stay in the same facility that my cousins, who had arrived before me, were in. My cousins supplied me with the registration of a woman, an Anna Gruber, who had already left the facility for Israel.

Moishe proposed to me and we were married in Frankfurt Am in a synagogue, under a canopy, in the traditional Jewish manner. All of my surviving cousins were present as was Heniek, Moishe's only surviving first cousin. As a married couple, we received a one room apartment on 31 Paffenviesse Strasse from the Jewish Joint Distribution. As a married woman I tried my hand at match-making and matched Hilda to Heniek, with great success.

My cousin Baruch came to visit us. He asked me if I had tried to locate my Aunt Schifra who had been living in Belgium before the war. I told him that I had remembered her address by heart and had sent her a letter from Poland, but I had never received a reply. He urged me to write again and this time to send it through the agency of the United Nations. I did. In my letter to her I stated that I was the youngest child of her sister, Chavcha, and the only survivor of my family. I also told her that I remembered her visit to Poland in 1933.

Several months later a tall man in an American Army uniform appeared at our apartment. He had a letter and picture of my Aunt Schifra for me. He had been sent by her to bring me to Belgium. Not knowing whether my first letter had ever reached my aunt, I had not written her that I had married. I now wavered about leaving for Belgium. I did not know if my aunt could deal with taking in two people instead of one. My cousin Baruch insisted we not miss this chance.

The tall man who was to take us to Belgium was a young Pole serving with the US Army. He supplied us with American uniforms and documents. We boarded a train with instructions to let him do all the necessary talking. In June of 1946 we arrived in Belgium without incident. My fears were baseless; my aunt received us warmly. She had aged a great deal in the twelve years since we had seen each other. She was a childless woman and we now became her cherished possessions. She also had some priceless gifts for me; some photos of my parents, my sister Channa and my brother Schloime.

Life in Belgium was not easy but the fact that there was not any blatant anti-Semitism of the sort that we had endured in Poland made it a good country to be in. We were classified as temporary residents. We were not to be granted permanent status. Our papers indicated that we would have to leave, emigrate. We had no idea where we would go, but until that moment arrived we had our lives to live. Moishe, ever resourceful, always found work and we found a flat and began to a live a normal, peaceful life.

On October 7, 1946, I gave birth to my first-born son, Israel Mordechai, named in memory of both his grandfathers. During this time Belgium did not permit the registration of non-Christian names on birth certificates. Consequently our son was also given the names Simon Mathieu. For the first time since my liberation I felt true happiness. I felt a sense of belonging, of having someone to hold on to and to care for. My mother always said, 'Material things have no value.' I now understood what she meant. All that mattered to me was my son. My Aunt Schifra also adored my son.

In 1946 Brussels was a temporary home to many Jewish refugees. We met the Goldfarbs, a family we had known in Grodzisk. They had been among those smart enough to flee to Russia at the very beginning of the war. Despite the hardships they had to endure there, all of them had survived the war.

Shopping in a department store one day I saw a familiar face focused on the lipsticks at the cosmetics counter. It was Henia, whom I had last seen hobbling along, bent over double holding on to her incised abdomen on the death march. She looked terrific, beautiful and well dressed. She had not seen me. I stood beside her but she paid no attention to me as she inspected a lipstick she was holding. I snatched the lipstick out of her hand. Startled, she looked up. She started screaming when she saw me. We fell into each other's arms, kissing and crying. People around us were wondering what all the commotion was about. Henia, in her fluent French, explained the encounter. I invited her to my house to meet my husband and to have some *challa* spread with goose *schmaltz*, topped with slices of goose meat. Henia could not believe that I had remembered her wish to eat the food that her grandmother used to prepare for her. This time it was my Aunt Schifra who prepared it. Henia was still single but there was no shortage of suitors. And her stories were as exciting as ever.

Henia told me that Masha, with whom I had been on the death march, was also in Brussels. Fate had been kind to Masha: all her siblings had survived, three brothers and a sister. One day while walking my son in his pram, I bumped into Dorka Koplowicz; she and her sister Hadassa had sheltered Masha and me under their blanket from the driving snow on the first night of the death march. She, too, was now married. It was a joyful reunion. All the girls helped me celebrate my son's first birthday.

Life soon took us all in different directions, often so quickly that we could not even notify each other. My Aunt Schifra's husband learned that his children, who had been hidden in an orphanage in Belgium, had been found and evacuated to Israel. He and my Aunt Schifra left for Israel to join them. Henia left for Australia.

On May 21, 1950, I gave birth to my daughter Chavcha. She was named in memory of my mother. The name entered on her Belgium birth certificate was Evelyn. A little girl was a dream fulfilled, a replacement for my beloved Felunia whom I had loved so much.

When the Korean War broke out, those fearing a major war with the communists panicked and started to leave Europe. The most desired destinations were Australia, Canada and the United States of America. We applied to emigrate to all of them and let fate choose. Moishe had a cousin in Montreal and that facilitated our acceptance by Canada. We knew nothing about Canada except that it was a new country that offered us a new life, a new beginning.

Lodz, end of summer, 1945. Three months after my liberation.

The *Kibbutz* in Lodz. I am in the top row second from the right. Hilda is to my right.

Moishe and I at our wedding January 1946 in Zelzheim, Frankfurt Am.

Wuppertal, Germany, June 1946. Moishe and the tall Polish American soldier who guided us to Belgium.

My first born, Simon at two months. December 1946.

My Aunt Schifra, six month old Simon and I.

My husband and I with ten month old Simon.

1947. Masha and I stroll on a Brussels boulevard with my husband and son.
Just two years before, in 1945, we were struggling for our lives
on a Death March in the midst of winter.

BOOK SEVEN

SO YOU CAN TELL

April 1, 1951 – January 7, 2001

With two small children, very few possessions and little money, we boarded a former troop transport ship, the United States Naval Ship 'General Harry Taylor' on her last mission, transporting immigrants to Canada. Moishe volunteered to work as a ship hand during the trip. We crossed the heaving Atlantic at the end of March, in bad weather. When we docked Moishe received a letter of thanks and recommendation from the ship's IRO Escort Officer, William Hunt, for his service. We arrived in Montreal on April 1, 1951. We were taken in by my husband's cousin Ella Waitzer and his wife, Fania. Their son, Jack, and Simon became close friends. We spent a year with them in their spotless apartment on Esplanade Avenue. We had a wonderful time together. Moishe immediately began working for the Jewish Joint Distribution Committee and I was a housewife. To learn English, I subscribed to several English magazines. We managed nicely with what my husband provided for us. A year later we settled into a flat on St Urbain Street.

Many of our neighbors and friends in Montreal were also survivors and immigrants; we formed a large community and we kept to ourselves. No one who had not lived through our horrors and loss could begin to understand what had happened to us. On the weekends, when the weather was good, everyone would dress their children and themselves in their best clothes and promenade with them along Park Avenue looking for familiar faces. During the summer we would picnic on the lower slopes of Mount Royal meeting each other and exchanging our stories of survival while our children romped and played. Slowly, painstakingly and over a period of many years, I, like all other survivors, linked the remaining fragments of our families together. Those few who had survived the Holocaust and others who had left Poland before the war were scattered across the globe.

During our first few years in Montreal we were able to re-establish a number of contacts. Moishe ran into Mala Schweitzer, a girl who had also worked in the assembly line at the montage in the Union munitions factory. She was in Montreal with her husband and their two young children. I was re-united with

Masha, with whom I had shared a *pritcha* in Auschwitz and started off on the Death March. She landed in Montreal with her new husband, Jacob, and their infant son. The Beckers from my hometown of Grodzisk, who had been among those who had fled to Russia, were also here. Dora, with whom I had joined up prior to arriving at Malchow concentration camp, now lived in nearby Toronto; her sister, Adela, had gone to France. The Goldfarbs had also left Belgium and were now in Toronto. Chaiah Korcarz and her family were in New York City, as was my cousin Baruch Berman.

My cousins Lena, Rosa, Marga and Shlamit were all in Israel. Hilda and Heniek, and Moishe's twin brother, Beryl, had also immigrated to Israel. I found out that Schmulek Slak had settled in Venezuela and had a family there. I was able to establish contact with them. No matter how faint the chance, I always clung to the hope that my brother Schloime was still alive.

That hope was finally dashed when on a visit to Israel, Moishe Apfal, who had been in Russia with Schloime, finally told me the truth. A truth he had wanted to protect me from when we met in Grodzisk immediately after the war: Schloime had died of typhus fever. When his best friend Beryl Goldfarb was hospitalized with typhus, Schloime brought him food every day. He too fell ill. They both died.

Not all survivors were keen to be found or be recognized. On one occasion as I was on my way to the market with my two children, pushing a stroller down St Lawrence Blvd, I came face to face with the *Kapo* that had given me that itchy woolen coat. We recognized each other immediately. She turned away from me and walked on.

That summer as Masha and I were walking our children on the grassy slopes of Mount Royal, Masha stopped abruptly and hysterically screamed, 'Fela, look who is here!' She ran up to a woman sitting on a park bench next to a stroller, grabbed her by the hair and started to rain blows on her. I immediately recognized her as the *Kapo* that I had recently seen on St Lawrence Blvd. I stopped Masha from assaulting her and led her away. Masha was beside herself, 'Why did you stop me? Do you know how hard she beat me in Auschwitz? She beat me on the head so hard that it took me weeks to recover my senses.'

Many years later on a trip to Miami Moishe and I stayed at a hotel which many survivors patronized. As we were re-entering the hotel lobby we saw this same woman, blood streaming down her face, run past us, fleeing a mob of people. Another Auschwitz survivor had recognized her as a *Kapo* and cried out. Life for this woman was always plagued by the fear of a survivor recognizing her and exacting retribution.

On June 29, 1954, we were blessed with another daughter. I named her Channa Schifra in memory of my sister Channa and my Aunt Schifra who had since passed away in Israel. Her Canadian name is Anne Shirley. On June 14, 1956, I bore another son, Chiel. His name in English is Holden. He was named in memory of his paternal great grandfather. Our youngest daughter, Devorah, was born on September 6, 1958. She was named in memory of my aunt and is known as Debbie.

Shortly after bringing Debbie home I was rushed back to the hospital with a rapidly advancing blood clot in my left leg. It was caused by my permanently swollen left ankle, the one that I had broken trying to run from the German Shepherd set upon me by the SS guard in Birkenau. To have gone to the camp hospital for my broken ankle would have been a self-imposed death sentence. I had continued walking and working on the broken ankle and let it mend as best as it possibly could under those circumstances. It had remained swollen since that day and now I was paying the price.

Five doctors agreed: they had to amputate my leg. I was only thirty-two years old and after everything I had gone through I did not want to be an amputee. A Yugoslavian doctor supported my decision not to amputate and took responsibility for my treatment. When he saw that I was going to recover the use of my leg, tears streamed down his face. Only then did he tell me how close my leg had been to being gangrenous, which I had not known. I had often wondered if there was any compassion left in this world. I am forever grateful to this wonderful human being.

As my children grew older I was confronted with questions like, 'Mother, what is that number on your arm? Where are my grandparents?' The questions were simple but the answers were difficult. How could I begin to explain to my young children the murder of their families when I myself could not come to terms with it? How was I to explain to them that all their missing relatives were among the 6,000,000 Jews that had been murdered for only one reason, because they were Jews? How could I explain to them why I had survived when I had no rational explanation for it? How was I to explain to my children about Germans, Nazism, and anti-Semitism? With each passing day they asked more and more questions. When we moved to a neighborhood where they played with children who had entire families, their questions became even more probing. I knew that I had to be strong to deal with these issues and to explain them carefully so that I would not instill any hatred towards others in my children.

Slowly I made my children familiar with the names of our deceased family, our parents, brothers, sisters, uncles, aunts and cousins ... and the horrible things that were done to them during the Holocaust. I also promised them that one day, if circumstances ever permitted, I would take them to Poland to visit Grodzisk.

Before I realized it, I was being asked the same questions by my grandchildren. I now wondered who was going to tell the next generation, my great grandchildren, about what had happened to their ancestors during the Holocaust? My adult children could not.

When my children grew up I realized that they could barely remember the names of their parents' families and the events that I had recounted to them many times. My son Simon told me that no matter how many times he had memorized my tattooed prisoner number he could not remember it. My adult children and I attended a Children of Survivors seminar.[1] There we learned that their inability to recall the history of their family's Holocaust experiences was a phenomenon common among children of survivors. A psychological study showed that it was a reflex of self-preservation. Their consciousness could not retain the details of their deceased family members and the horrible things that happened to them and still be able to function normally. I realized that I needed to record my witness to the Holocaust for my descendants.

In March of 1989, I was contacted by Rena Seligman from the Holocaust Center in Miami Beach, Florida. They were videotaping survivors' testimonies and had been given my name. Would I agree to be interviewed? I gladly agreed. Despite the conscientious efforts of those involved in interviewing and taping me, I was not happy with the results. And it was my fault. My nervousness in front of a camera inhibited me from describing my Holocaust experiences in the depth and detail that I had intended. I realized that the videotaped testimony I gave had not fulfilled my promise to my sister. I now knew that I had to write it down, but I had a formidable obstacle to overcome. I was not a writer. I could not type or use a word processor. The task was daunting. I kept postponing the writing of my witness.

During December of 1992 I was rushed to the hospital and underwent open-heart surgery. With my life hanging by a thread I had only one thing on my mind: that I had not properly recorded my witness of the Holocaust for posterity. If I died, I would not have fulfilled my promise to my sister: to live so that I could tell my children and grandchildren what had happened to their relatives during the Holocaust. I realized that I could no longer postpone writing about what had happened to my family and myself during the Holocaust.

In April of 1993, four months after undergoing open-heart surgery, I left for Poland, with my husband and our son, Holden, to participate in the Commemoration of the Jewish Ghetto Uprising in Warsaw. We were going to stay with a cousin of ours, Bolek Rojzman, who lived in a Warsaw suburb.

Bolek Rojzman had never left Poland. He had survived Treblinka, where he had lost his entire family and his only child, a three-year-old son. He himself had walked naked towards the gas chambers down the infamous passage called *Himmel Strasse*[2]. While Bolek was walking down *Himmel Strasse* to his death, a pharmacist from Grodzisk by the name of Elfrand, who was working in Treblinka sorting out the victims' clothing, spotted him among the new arrivals. Elfrand pointed him out to SS Commandant Miller as a young, strong man who could be of use in helping with their growing load of work and asked to have him assigned to his work group. SS Commandant Miller agreed.

As Bolek Rojzman was sorting clothes he picked up his own son's little coat. He held it for a moment in anguish. While he was lost in pain he was being observed by the brutal SS Franz Kurt.[3] Treblinka inmates called SS Franz Kurt, 'Lalka', the doll, because he was so handsome and extremely meticulous about his appearance. SS Franz Kurt set his attack dog on Bolek. His dog was trained to attack a man's crotch and tear out his organs. The victim was then finished off by a bullet from SS Franz Kurt. The dog leapt towards Bolek. Bolek saw it rushing towards him and turned to face it. Bolek had an uncanny ability to communicate with dogs. As the dog approached him Bolek started to play with it, using his elbow, as if it were a puppy. SS Franz Kurt looked on in sheer amazement as his trained killer dog began licking Bolek's hands and face. Bolek Rojzman's life was spared again.

Bolek Rojzman was one of the organizers of the revolt in Treblinka. Out of the approximately 200 men who participated in the revolt, only twenty-six survived. After the war, Bolek Rojzman was called as a witness to testify against Franz Kurt, who was sentenced to 15 years in prison in Treblinka where 900,000

Jews perished. Treblinka was commanded by a small number of German SS and operated by Ukrainian SS volunteers.

On the day we arrived in Poland our son, Holden, insisted that we immediately go to our home town of Grodzisk. Bolek and his stepson, Zbyszek, drove us there. As we entered Grodzisk I felt my heart jumping out of me. Every street, every house evoked overpowering, vivid memories. Standing on the street not far from where I had lived, Holden was overcome with emotion. He said, 'I always dreamed of coming here. My roots are here. It means so much to me. Now I can see everything you told us about this city with my own eyes.'

The house where I had lived on 15 Pilsudsklega Street had not changed at all. It still had the same iron gate. Standing in the yard I pointed to the four windows on the second floor where my sister Channa had been married and where my father had worked side by side with his sons. This was where we had celebrated the holidays, where we had had our family gatherings and where we had sung our songs and laughed with joy. We were also standing right on the spot where Helena Skoblewski, the Polish girl, had refused to play with me and had spit in my face as she called me 'Jew'.

As I stood in deep reminiscence an old woman wrapped in a wool shawl asked us what we were doing there. I asked her if she remembered the Burman family who once lived there. She shrugged her shoulders indicating that she did not. But when I asked her about the Skoblewski family and about Mr Skoblewski I could see that she knew whom I was talking about. I looked deeply into her eyes and asked her, 'Are you Helena, the Skoblewski girl?' She admitted that she was. She was my age, sixty-six years old, but she looked eighty years old. She felt very uncomfortable and shuffled off. Our son could hardly believe that it was her.

We walked towards 11 Listopada Street and the large wooden dwelling where I was born. The house was now gone. It had been replaced by a huge cement building. I called out the names of all the families who had once lived there. From there we went to 15 Boleslawa Limanowskiego to visit the three-storey brick building which had been built by my husband's father in 1925. It had been occupied by my husband's parents, their seven sons and eleven tenants. After fifty-four years of communist neglect the building was now in extreme disrepair and dilapidated to the point of ruin. Incredibly, six families still resided in it, some without running water or electricity. Holden touched the oak rails to feel where his grandparents' hands had once been. Where a *mezuzah* had once graced the door to the family apartment, only a faint spot was now visible. Holden did not want to leave Grodzisk. We had to promise him that we would come back soon. That property still belongs to my husband. We left for Warsaw where my husband had a mission of his own to carry out.

After my husband Moishe's family had been captured in a Nazi action in the Warsaw Ghetto and taken to their death in Treblinka, he escaped the Ghetto into Aryan Warsaw. There he lived by his wits, posing as a gentile under the Polish alias of Stashek. During this time he met Jerzy Muszynski and they became close friends.

Jerzy Muszynski was an only child who lived with his widowed mother. His father had been killed fighting the Germans. When Jerzy and his mother found out that Stashek was Jewish, they sheltered him despite the risk to themselves.[4] Jerzy and Moishe, always under the alias of Stashek, fought together in the Polish Revolt in Warsaw. In the last days of the uprising Jerzy and Moishe's battle group were backed up against the Vistula River by the German Army. They could either swim across the ice- cold river to where the Red Army was or surrender to the Germans. Jerzy could not swim and surrender meant certain death for Moishe.

Moishe tied himself to a large piece of cork that he found in the debris of a factory they were fighting from and swam the Vistula under fire. He was wounded twice. When he got to the opposite shore he was disarmed and taken prisoner by the Communists. The Communists interrogated him. Realizing that he was not a threat to their plans for Poland they released him. Jerzy was taken prisoner by the Germans and was released at the war's end. Moishe and Jerzy met again briefly after the war but when the Communists took power they lost contact with each other. Now that Poland was free again and we were here, Moishe was determined to find his lost war brother, Jerzy Muszynski. His first step was to start calling all the Muszynskis in the Warsaw telephone book. Within several calls Moishe located him. After 50 years, they had a very emotional reunion.

April 18, 1993, was a very overcast, wet and bone-chilling day. Bolek Rojzman and his family drove us to Treblinka. Today, Treblinka is only a two-hour drive from Warsaw. In Treblinka we joined the Canadian delegation and the many other national delegations in a torch-lit memorial service. After the speeches, cantors sang. Their beautiful voices, the flickering flames and the dismal weather evoked in each of us the pain and suffering that our people have endured for two millennia. Chilling winds and rain whipped at us as we concluded the service, walking among the stones engraved with the names of all the cities Treblinka's victims had come from. We called out the names of our loved ones who had been among the 900,000 men, women and children who had perished in Treblinka.

After the emotional day we had just gone through, I was eager to attend the evening program to be held at the Congress Hall of the Palace of Culture as part of the *Yom Hashoah* and Warsaw Ghetto Uprising memorial events. Returning to Bolek's home from Treblinka, we received a telephone call from Dieter Birkenmeir. Dieter is a German diplomat with the European Union. Our daughter Evelyn had met him and his Polish wife, Yolanda, while vacationing in Italy. Dieter had arranged for us to attend the evening program. He and Yolanda escorted us to the event. The three thousand people in attendance listened to the moving testimonies of survivors of the Jewish Warsaw Ghetto Uprising. This was followed by a play directed by Szymon Szurmiey featuring his wife, famous Yiddish actress and singer, Golda Tenzer. It was an evocative and memorable evening.

The next morning we went to the Gesia cemetery where my parents were buried in mass graves. I had often taken a route through this cemetery when I had smuggled food. I showed Holden where I used to hide when the German patrols appeared. Now that I was back in the Gesia cemetery, in a free Poland, I did something I had promised myself to do for many years; I arranged to have a plaque installed in memory of my parents. Later that afternoon we assembled at the Rappaport Monument, [5] a very evocative sculpture dedicated to the Warsaw Ghetto, where a plaque was unveiled in memory of Szmul Zygelblom. [6]

That evening, surrounded by heavy government security, we stood in a chilling rain holding candles at the Ghetto Heroes Monument. Wreaths were laid and speeches made by Lech Walesa, the President of Poland; Yitzhak Rabin, the Prime Minister of Israel; Al Gore, Vice President of the USA; and Edgar Bronfman, President of the World Jewish Congress. A message from Pope Jean Paul II was read. Jewish music was played and cantors sang. As I stood there with my husband, Holden and friends who had joined us on the *March of the Living*,[7] I relived all the suffering Channa, Max, Felunia and I had endured. I could see and hear the cracking and roaring of the burning trees, the black smoke billowing out of the houses, the terrified screams of our people and the SS yelling, *'Hende hoch! Hende hoch!* Hands high!'

The next day we joined the *March of the Living* to Auschwitz and Birkenau. While sitting on the bus to Auschwitz I was asked if I would talk about what had occurred in this dreadful place. I refused. I was too over-whelmed by emotion, too afraid that I would break down and cry. Our guide, Nathan Leipciker from Toronto, spoke about his experiences in the camps over the bus microphone. In the middle of his testimony he broke down and cried. Later he told me that each time he speaks about it, he breaks down and cries. I had thought this only happened to me. It was reassuring that others had the same reaction. It gave me the confidence to speak uninhibitedly to strangers about my experiences.

In Auschwitz I went directly to the block I had slept in. My family and friends gathered around me as I recounted what had happened there. Other people nearby overheard and gathered to listen. I told them how we had been forced to watch the hanging of Estusia and Regina for their part in smuggling gun powder, used to blow up the crematorium, to the camp's resistance movement.

From Auschwitz we had the option of walking or taking a bus to Birkenau. But the vividness of the memories and the emotions evoked by Auschwitz again left me feeling weak and tired; I took the bus. As we drove past the former Union munitions factory where I had worked, the rush of memories simply overwhelmed me. I wept.

In Birkenau we assembled around the ruins of the crematoria. The Star of David, the flag of Israel, flew in the air as the names of martyrs were called out over loudspeakers. The ground that I was standing on once again reminded me of all whom I had walked here with and who were no more: the two sisters from 58 Mila Street, Sala and Rozia Birenbaum, and Sala Beinstock. All of us had been tattooed one after the other. Prayers and speeches by delegates from many countries followed. Young students carrying Star of David flags offered the hope that what had happened here would never happen again.

I returned once again to Block 26. But this time I was a free woman, the mother of five children and the grandmother of six more. I went directly to the wooden *pritcha* I had slept on and pointed it out to my husband and son. I recalled the names of the girls who had been there with me. I told them the story of how I was helped by the *blockeldeste* Editka when I was selected for death one day in November of 1943. One of the men standing nearby, listening to me, asked me to talk facing his camera crew. They were filming a documentary. Afterwards he introduced himself as Professor Irving Abella,

President of the Jewish Congress of Canada. As I walked out of the block, his wife, Rosella Abella, and another woman stopped me. They wanted to know how I had survived this place under such conditions. I replied that I did not know. It was a combination of luck, faith, and most of all my desire to fulfill my promise to my sister to do everything I could to survive, so that I could tell what had happened to us.

There was still one death camp for me to confront. Maydanek. The night before we left for Maydanek, I could not fall asleep. Maydanek was the worst place to return to. To me it represented the cruelest suffering a human being is capable of enduring. Maydanek was where I was painfully separated from my sister and her child, knowing that we would never see each other again.

As my family and I walked the grounds of Maydanek I pointed out various parts of the camp I had been in and recounted the experiences I had lived through there. My testimony was familiar to my family, but being in the very places where these events had actually happened had a powerful impact on them. My son stood by my side in the sauna where I had been sent to take a shower after the SS men had decided that the blood flowing down my legs was only a 'perioda' and selected me to work. We stood in the exact spot where I had stood, waiting and wondering if gas or water was going to come out of the shower heads, unaware that right next to me were the ovens where my sister, her child, my Auntie Chaiah and hundreds of others were to be burned that very same day.

I walked to the dome memorial under which the ashes and slivers of bones, the only remains of those cremated, are protected. The pieces of glass among these human remains reminded me of the bottle which I had broken off at the neck to fetch some water for Felunia. I retold how I had held the jagged glass edge with my hands so that Felunia would not cut her lips as she drank. I could not control myself anymore. I broke down. My sobbing frightened the other visitors. My son and Jerzy had to explain my strong reaction to them. No one but survivors themselves can comprehend the emotional impact caused by being in a place like Maydanek.

After we returned to Warsaw from Maydanek, Holden insisted that we go back to Grodzisk. He was determined to find its Jewish cemetery, if there was still one left. What remained of the cemetery was surrounded by a gated iron fence. The gate had a heavy iron padlock on it and a large sign giving the restoration date and where one could ask for further information. Holden climbed over the fence to inspect the head stones. A few were still intact. He wiped them off and read us the inscriptions.

Before leaving Poland for home, we took Jerzy Muszynski to *Yad Vashem* in Warsaw and filled out the forms so that he could be honored among the *Righteous Gentiles.*[8] That summer Jerzy Muszynski, his wife Christina, and our cousin, Bolek Rojzman, spent their summer vacation with us in Canada.

I still had some unfinished business in Poland. The rest of my children also wanted to visit Grodzisk. We decided to join the next *March of the Living.* On April 2nd, 1994, my husband and I, accompanied by our oldest son, Simon, our daughters Evelyn and Anne and our niece, Sarah, daughter of my husband's late twin brother, landed in Warsaw. We were greeted with flowers by our cousin, Bolek Rojzman, Jerzy Muszynski, both their families, and Dieter Birkenmeir. Like Holden, our children insisted on immediately going to our home town of Grodzisk. The day had finally come for them to visit the place that they had heard so much about, a place they had always longed to see, and a place where they could feel the centuries-long presence of their ancestors. They did not want to wait any longer.

As my family once again walked through the streets of Grodzisk, the grim reality sunk in. They were among the very few descendants of an entire vibrant Jewish population that had lived here for generations. They felt the absence of the Jews who had been forced to leave behind their property, possessions and livelihood and been herded into the Warsaw Ghetto with only what they could carry. There, without money and a place to live, they had died of hunger in the streets.

When we arrived at the building that my husband's father had built in Grodzisk, some of the Polish families living in it learned who we were. They kindly invited us to come into their homes so that my children could get a better look at the rooms in which their paternal grandparents had lived.

We returned to Grodzisk's Jewish cemetery. This time the gate was open. The heavy metal padlock was now missing. We discovered a few headstones belonging to family members and we photographed them. I took our children to Koronkowa Street where I had spent my summer vacations at the Fuchses. My elementary school was still standing. The building which housed the *Beis Yakov* was still there, as was the building in which I was born and had played as a child. The only place we could not find was the synagogue. It had burned down.

The next day, Sunday, we set out for Treblinka. We drove through the villages where people, dressed in their Sunday best, were walking home from church. Life for them was normal and undisturbed, yet they were living next to the largest graveyard in human history. In Treblinka we met a few Jews from Italy who had come to visit the place where their relatives had been murdered. A few buses carrying students from Australia, who were participating in the *March of the Living*, soon arrived.

From Treblinka we traveled to Maydanek, an hour and a half away. In Maydanek we had to go through strict security because the Israeli delegation had arrived at the same time as us. The students participating in the March of Living were also there. Prayers and *Kaddish* for the dead were recited. My children and I, holding onto each other, cried as we stood under the dome memorial. The young students looking on realized that I had been an inmate there. These innocent-faced students were seventeen years old, just as I was when I arrived in Maydanek. They were sitting on the steps leading to the dome memorial, walking around the grounds that were still surrounded with barbed wire and watch towers, and going in and out of the crematoria. They began to ask me questions. I pointed out to them that when I came here in May of 1943 that none of the buildings they could see today had existed. There had been only wooden barracks amid the vast empty fields where we worked. The young students asked me if the Holocaust could happen again. I replied, 'Yes.' They were not prepared for my answer. They did not want to believe it could happen again. Just as nobody had believed it could happen then. We did not believe it even as it happened to us. We only believed it when it was too late to save ourselves. As a living witness to those events who is well aware of what is going on in the world today, how could I deny them the truth? However, I added that Jews now have the State of Israel to secure our place in the world. We are no longer homeless and rootless.

The *March of the Living* was the largest international Jewish event dedicated to the memory of the Holocaust that had ever been organized. It marked the fiftieth year of our liberation from the death camps. It was organized by numerous Israeli organizations and by the Polish government. We had come from thirty-six countries around the globe to commemorate the victims of the Holocaust. Heading us was a delegation from Israel led by the Minister of Education and Culture, Amnon Rubinstein. The Vice President of Poland, Alexander Luczak and the President of Uruguay, Lois Alberto Lacalle De Herrera were also present. Delegations representing Holocaust study programs offered at numerous American universities were there, too. Ambulances were standing by near hospital tents, and doctors were in attendance in case of any medical emergencies. Security, to protect us from Polish hooligans and skinheads, was very tight and very visible. Fortunately, there were no incidents.

On April 7, 1994, more than 6,000 students and leaders of world Jewry participated in the principal ceremony of the *March of the Living*. We marched proudly holding both Israeli flags, and the flags from the countries in which we lived, as well as placards in Hebrew and English which read 'Remember'. We marched the three kilometers from Auschwitz to Birkenau. We marched along the same road where I had once been herded as a slave and guarded by the SS and their dogs. But this time I was marching with dignity as a free Jew surrounded by my children and proudly carrying a Torah presented to me by Rabbi Grussgot from the Montreal Shaar Hashomayim synagogue. In my wildest dreams of freedom I could never have envisioned that this would one day be possible. The Polish population looked on. Where they had once watched us as wretches marching to our deaths, they now watched us march for the living with our heads held high and our eyes triumphant.

As we marched past the Union munitions factory I recalled the heroism of Estusia Wajcblum, Regina Safirsztajn, Rosa Robota and Ala Gertner, the women who had smuggled out the gunpowder to blow up the crematoria. They were hanged before our very eyes on January 5, 1945, two weeks before we were evacuated on the horrific Death March. We marched past the railroad tracks along which the daily transports had arrived from all parts of Europe, bringing millions of our people to their deaths. We walked through the arched iron gate whose inscription reads: Arbeit Macht Frei. As we marched, memories and images came unbidden to my mind: the endless pre-dawn *appels* held in the rain and the cold snow, the weak and those who stumbled getting beaten or killed, and the terror of the endless selections. We marched towards the crematoria in Birkenau where the majority of Jews had perished.

Six thousand of us arrived and assembled for religious services around the ruins of the crematoria. Six torches were to be lit in honor of the six million Jews who had died in the Holocaust. Rabbi Mayer Lau led us in prayer. An octogenarian survivor, Jack Stromoza, a former Auschwitz inmate who had the macabre task of playing the lead violin in the camp orchestra that the Nazis used to lull the arriving transports, was there. He now played the same beautiful music, but this time for the living. The names of victims were read out over the loudspeakers.

As my children and I looked on, a woman survivor was called forward to light one of the six torches. I recognized her as Chanka Wajcblum, the sister of Estusia Wajcblum, one of the women whom the Nazis had hung before our eyes. I had not seen Chanka Wajcblum in fifty years. We embraced each other, weeping. Chanka pointed to the crowd and said, 'Look, you see, my sister is not forgotten.'

Once the dignitaries left we were allowed to enter the barracks. We went to Block 26 which was close to the crematoriums and adjacent to the Gypsy barracks. The Gypsy barracks were no longer there; they had since been removed. Chanka and I looked over the now-vacant field. We recalled the morning these barracks had been emptied of Gypsies, who were all taken away to their deaths during the night. We recalled our *blockeldeste* Editka, who had saved my life, and the endless selections we had gone through.

Again children of mine climbed up on the wooden *pritcha* in which I had slept. They said that although they had often heard about the suffering we had endured here, they had a different feeling and understanding of it now that they saw the place with their own eyes.

When we returned to Warsaw we visited the mass graves in the Gesia cemetery. We were accompanied by our cousin, Bolek Rojzman. At the mass graves, Rabbi Zale Newman from Toronto, Canada, stood surrounded by students as he led them in prayers. He recognized me from Maydanek, where I had spoken to the students. As my children lit candles at the plaque I had installed the previous year, in memory of my parents, Rabbi Zale Newman recited prayers.

Bolek Rojzman showed us the headstone he had prepared for himself in the Gesia cemetery. His headstone had the names of his entire family inscribed on it. Bolek wanted to make sure that when he died he would be buried as a Jew. His wish was honored when he died in 1997.

Today there are only a few thousand Jews still living in Poland. It is poignant to see the aged remnants of what was once the largest Jewish community in the world, now living on minimal pensions and on support from the Jewish Joint Distribution.

In the latter part of 1994 I was surprised to learn that all the surviving inmates of Ravensbruck and Sachsenhaussen had been invited by Manfred Stolpe, Minister President Des Landes Brandenburg to be guests of the German government at the remembrance ceremonies of the liberation of those concentration camps. My daughter, Evelyn, suggested that I accept the invitation. She offered to accompany me. To return to Germany was a difficult decision to make. As a survivor, I could not forget, nor forgive, those involved in the Holocaust. My curiosity about how modern Germany dealt with its Nazi past and its current neo-Nazism was not enough to persuade me to go, but the chance that I might find out something, from someone, about the fate of my best friend Sala Brezinski decided me. On April 23, 1995, Evelyn and I were among the survivors and their companions who flew to Germany.

Thousands of former concentration camp inmates had accepted the invitation and had flown in from all over the world. Groups of volunteers were waiting to receive us when we landed in Berlin. Evelyn and I were among a group lodged in the Hotel Deutschland in the town of Feldenberg, an hour's drive from Ravensbruck. The next day we were bused to Ravensbruck. We toured the camp, holding candles and flowers. The crematorium was overflowing with people praying for the victims who had been cremated there. Flowers were strewn over the Schwedtse Lake where the ashes from the crematorium had been dispersed. These events evoked strong memories of the terrors we had survived. A similar program was being held simultaneously at Sachsenhaussen. We were addressed by various people.

Gertrude Müller, a German woman who was imprisoned in Ravensbruck because of her opposition to the Nazis, and who was now the camp committee representative, greeted us at the site where fifty years ago 132,000 women and children had to endure such a heavy burden, where we had been 'only a number, where we were humiliated, degraded and tortured.' She warned that the fight against the evils of neo-fascism must continue, that Ravensbruck and other sites that were concentration camps must not be erased under the guise of development but must be turned into memorials. Memorials where the millions of innocent men, women and children, murdered by fascism are never to be forgotten. She also made a point of accusing Siemens, one of Germany's largest industrial groups, of still not having paid any reparations to the thousands of women that they had exploited as slave laborers. 'Our struggle against fascism and war must continue until the world has finally realized that all people have a right to live in peace and security. Never again fascism! Never again Ravensbruck! Never again war from German soil!'

Rose Guérin, another survivor of Ravensbruck and now President of the International Ravensbruck Committee, thanked the Allied Forces for conquering the Hitler regime, the Soviet Army for liberating the concentration camps, and the Swedish Red Cross for their efforts in liberating some prisoners. She stated that it was our responsibility to educate the younger generations to be vigilant against anti-Semitism, racism, fascism and war. 'We summon them to action everywhere in the defense of democracy, human rights and international friendship.' She asked all survivors ... 'to remember, to testify, to tell even the indescribable.'

Manfred Stolpe, Prime Minister of the Federal State of Brandenburg, thanked all of us who took this difficult personal path to return to Ravensbruck. He said, 'Ravensbruck was the only women's concentration camp on German soil. Concentration camps are the expression of a perverse ideology of extermination, of delusions about race, of terror and of lawlessness.' Girls, adolescents and women of every age, Jews, Sinti, and Roma, from twenty different countries that did not fit into the Nazi picture of society, were persecuted, tortured and murdered by the many thousands. He quoted Primo Levi, an Auschwitz survivor like myself, as saying, 'It has happened, and therefore it can happen again. That is the essence of what we have to say. It can happen anywhere.' He stated that we have to preserve history and remember what happened. 'That is why I would like to see your faces and hear your stories.'

It was inconceivable that one day I would be back in Ravensbruck, with my daughter at my side, amidst thousands of fellow survivors to hear a German government official admit the guilt and shame they felt for the suffering inflicted by their nation on us, the Jewish people, and on so many others. But I wondered, with all the resurgent neo-Nazism and xenophobia in Germany today, what the average German in the streets thought of the Holocaust today.

The next day we met our friends Dieter and Yolanda Birkenmeir in Berlin for a tour of the city. The highlight of our visit to Berlin was the magnificent golden-domed Centrum Judaicum on Oranienburger Strasse. It was a newly-built center for Jewish activities and education. Located inside it is the new Berlin Synagogue. Security precautions prevented our visiting the center's interior as preparations were underway for a ceremony to dedicate a plaque commemorating the bravery of Wilhelm Krotzfelds, the Berlin Police Chief, who had ordered that the fire, set by the Nazis to destroy the synagogue on Kristallnacht of November 1938, be put out.

Touring Berlin until late in the evening, we missed our train back to Feldenberg. We decided to take a taxi. The taxi driver, a young German, knew the purpose of our visit to Germany. Here was an opportunity to learn what he thought about the Holocaust. Our taxi drive from Berlin to Feldenberg was a two hour drive. There was plenty of time to talk to him.

'These Holocaust events in Ravensbruck and Sachsenhaussen were in all the papers,' he volunteered. I asked him, 'Are you or your family aware that only thirty kilometers from here in Sachsenhaussen thousands of people were murdered?' He replied that he was born in 1945, almost at the end of the war, and then pointed out the road which led to Sachsenhaussen and said, 'This road was called the Road to Death. Whoever went down that road, never came back.' I was sure that he was referring to Jews. But he went on to add, 'Germans who were suspected of sabotage, or were disapproved of by the Nazi regime, or people who were betrayed by their own family members were taken down this road, never to return.' I asked him if the Germans had known what was going on in Europe under their occupation. His answer was, 'Yes, but not to the degree we came to learn later. Occasionally there was talk, but people were embarrassed so they tried to suppress it.' He added, 'Like in every bushel of apples, you find a few rotten ones.' He was honest and frank about his views. They underscored the reasons that I had to finish writing my testimony. I now knew that I would redouble my writing efforts when I got home.

Our next commemoration was in Malchow, at the site of its former concentration camp. Sala Brezinski had been taken out of Malchow by the Swedish Red Cross and I had hoped to find some information about her there. The day we were to leave for Malchow, I became very ill and could not go. After more than fifty years, I still have not found her. I continue to search for her.

Upon my return to Canada I was interviewed by the Spielberg Survivors of the Shoa Visual History Foundation dedicated to remembering those who had perished in the Holocaust. The video crew from the Spielberg Foundation came to my home for the interview. They were courteous, considerate and extremely professional. This time I was not as nervous in front of the camera. We filmed for six hours. It was too long. After a couple of hours of taping I became emotionally exhausted. I should have stopped and continued another day, but I pressed on, because there was so much more that I wanted to say. For days afterwards I felt a disturbing anxiety. I realized that the more fatigued I had become, the more I compressed my description of the events that I had survived had been. Again I realized that the best way to record the details of the torrent of memories that rushed forth every time I started to talk about the Holocaust was to write them down. But I was writing in fits and starts. I wrote and stopped. Started again and stopped again. Willing myself to recall and hold all these painful memories as I struggled to write them down was a slow and emotionally torturous process. I could only do so much at a time. How can one describe the feelings, the emotions, one is going through when one is a witness to such events, or any single one of them?

The day is coming when voices of survivors will no longer be heard. Were my future descendants going to have to read about the Holocaust in a book written by someone who was not there, disputed by Holocaust deniers posing as historians?[9] It was important for me, as a survivor who had lived through the horrors of the Holocaust, to leave as detailed a testimony as I could for future generations. I pressed on with the painful and difficult task of writing my witness of the Holocaust.

My promise to my sister, made in the death camp of Maydanek, to live 'so that you can tell', has at last been fulfilled. Fulfilled not only to the generations of my immediate descendants but also to all those who wish to, or are compelled to, know what happened to us during the Holocaust.

Moishe and I with our five children. Simon and Holden are in front of me. Debbie is in Moishe's arms and in front of him are Evelyn and Annie.

Block 26, Birkenau. April 1993. This was the *pritcha* I shared with the other girls.

April 1994. An unimaginable triumph! On the very road where fifty years earlier I had been a slave laborer condemned to death for being a Jew, I now carry the Torah in freedom and dignity. To my left is Rabbi Sidney Shoham of Beth Zion Congregation of Cote St Luc and to my right is my niece Sarah Wajcer

Genealogy

Feigenblatt

- Channa m. Kanterovitch
  - Surka*
  - Son*
- Esther m. Cimbalist
  - Karl m. Regina Cukier both d. 1943
  - Efraim*
- Mindel m. Pacula
  - 4 Children d. 1943
- Sarah 1862-1940 (m. David d.1887)

Domb

- David d.1887 (m. Sarah 1862-1940)
- Berel
- Gicha
- Mair m. Ettel
  - Yetta m. Slak
    - Schmulek Slak*

Sarah

- m. (1885) David Domb d. 1887
  - **Chava Domb** 1887-1942
- m. (1888) Menashe Slak
  - Milech* m. d. 1918
    - 1 Child*
  - Shifra m. d.1952
  - Raizel m. Lazar Srebrenik both d.1943
    - Uteh 1927-1943
  - Rachel Leah d.1924

BURMAN FAMILY

Chava m. Mordechai

- David 1907-1907
- Chaim 1910-1943 m. Sourka 19??-1943
  - Sheva 1939-1943
- Channah 1914-1943 m. Max Szyldszrajber 19??-1943
  - Felunia 1937-1943
- Schloime 1916-1943
- Moishe 'Tusha' 1922-1943
- Menashe 1923-1925
- Faiga 1926-

Wajcer Family

Faiga 1926- m. Moishe Wajcer 1925-2003

- Simon 1946
- Evelyn 1950 m. Larry Vatch
  - Lisa
  - Mitchell
- Annie 1954 m. Rick Rubin
  - Michael
  - Jessica
  - Zoe
- Holden 1956 m. Nathalie Lessard
  - Justin
- Debbie 1958 m. Tarek Sharif
  - Omar Joseph

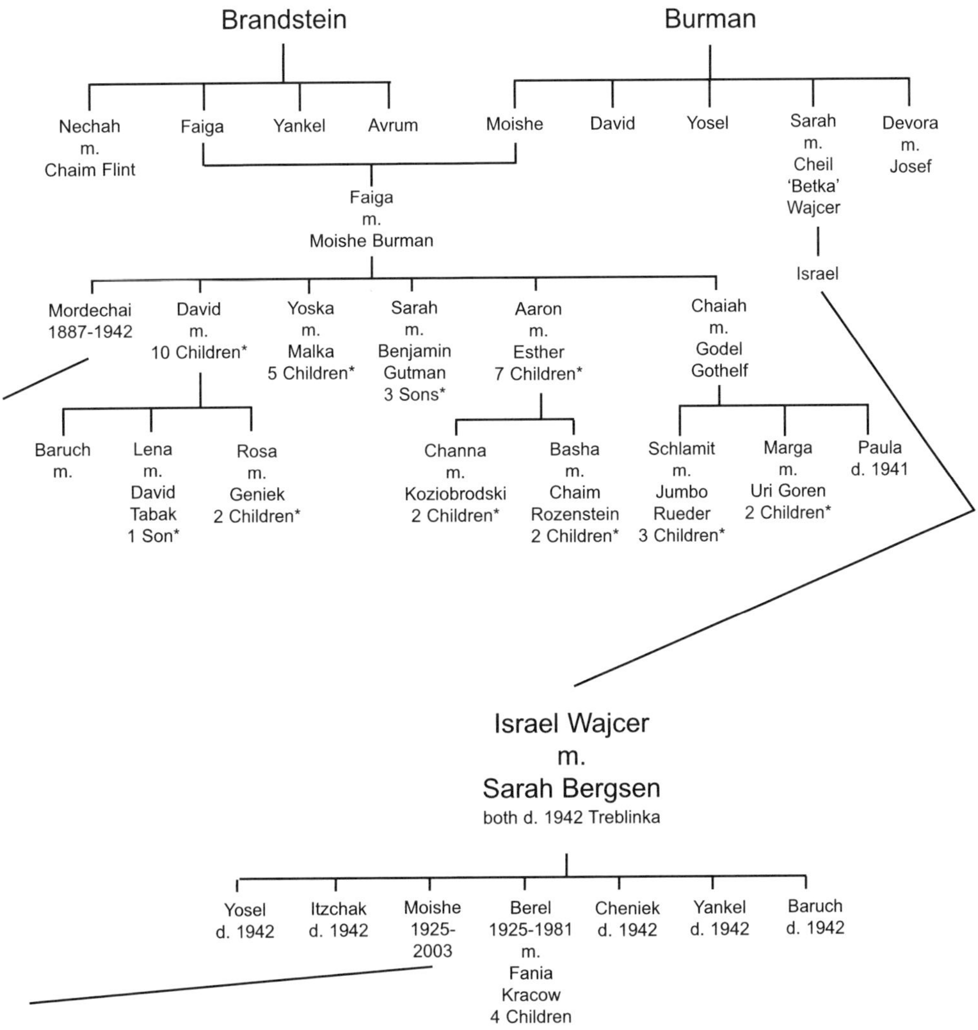

*** *see* Generations**

The grandchildren; Lisa, Mitchell, Justin, Michael, Zoe, Jessica and Omar.

GENERATIONS

And I will make thy seed to multiply as the stars of heaven, and will give unto thy seed all these countries; and in thy seed shall all the nations of the earth be blessed;

Genesis 26:4

From the day I accepted that I was the only survivor of my immediate family I began to search for my other relatives, any Burman, Domb, Slak and Feigenblatt that might have survived the Holocaust. They had all been very large families. Very few of us in Europe had survived. In the years following the war I did find some members of these families who had the good fortune to have emigrated from Poland before the war. In the late fifties I found Esther Domb and Peretz Eckstein in New York. They had married and left Grodzisk before the war. Peretz told me how he had adored my mother, and in their stories of her I could feel her love for me again. This is the fate that befell the Burmans, Dombs, Slaks and Feigenblatts during the Holocaust.

Chava and Mordechai had five children: Chaim, Channa, Schloime, Tusha and myself. They had one son-in-law and one daughter-in-law and two granddaughters, Felunia and Sheva. Only I, their youngest daughter, survived the Holocaust.

I wed Moishe, also a Holocaust survivor, and we brought into this world five children: Simon, Evelyn, Anne, Holden and Debbie. Evelyn married Larry and gave us two grandchildren: Lisa and Mitchell. Anne married Ricky and gave us three grandchildren: Michael, Jessica and Zoe. Holden married Natalie and gave us a grandson, Justin. Debbie married Tarek and gave us a grandson, Omar. We live in Canada.

My father Mordechai's five siblings were: David, Yoska, Sarah, Aaron and Chaiah.

David had ten children: Shloime, Channa, Herschel, Esther, Lena, Sarah, Faiga, Moshe, Rosa and Baruch. Of the ten, only Lena, Rosa and Baruch survived.

Lena wed David and they begot Chaim. Chaim wed Shifra and they had

Paz, Maytal, On, David and Ore. They live in Israel.

Rosa wed Geniek and they had two daughters: Chaya and Sara. Chaya married Baruch and they had David, Carmit, Orit, and Sheeri. David married Yael and they had Gal and Nir. Carmit married Yair and had Bar, Guy and Ziv. Orit married and had Noy. Sara married Eli and had Gili and Chen. They live in Israel.

Aaron had seven children: Channa, Faiga, Yohevet, Sara, Basha, David and Moishe. Basha and Channa survived.

Basha married Chaim and they had two daughters, Esther and Lilliane. Esther married Irving and had two children: Miriam and Alain. Lilliane married Camille and had two children: Aline and Gabriel. They live in Belgium and Germany.

Channa wed and had two children. Her descendants live in Australia.

Yoska and his wife, Malka, had five children. They moved to Brazil before the war and their descendants live there.

Sarah wed Benjamin Gutman. They had three sons: Schloime, David and Beryl. None survived.

Chaiah wed Godel Gothelf and had three daughters, Friedel, Marga and Paula. Friedel and Marga survived.

Friedel took the Hebrew name of Shlamit in Israel. Shlamit wed Jumbo and they had three children: Gaby, Ofra and Yonathan.

Gaby wed Esther and they had Ayelet, Noga and Liat. Noga wed Eyal and had Shlamit.

Ofra wed Eddy and they had Eran and Edit. Eran wed Nurit and had twins: Eetai and Ronnie.

Marga wed Uri and they had two sons, Gideon and Avner. Gideon married Nava and they had Heela and Erez. Avner wed Shoshie and they had Noa, Anat and twins Yoav and Eyal. They live in Israel.

My mother had a half brother and three half sisters: Milech, Schifra, Raizel and Rachael Leah. Milech and Rachael Leah died before the war. Raizel, her husband, Lazar, and their daughter, Uteh, did not survive the war. Only Schifra who had moved to Belgium survived the war. She was childless and died in

Israel.

My maternal grandmother, Sarah Feigenblatt, 'the Bubbeh', had three sisters. Their married names were Channa Kanterovitch, Esther Cimbalist and Mindel Pacula.

Mindel Pacula, her husband and four children perished in the Holocaust. Esther Cimbalist had two sons, Karl and Efraim, who had both emigrated to England. Karl, trapped in Poland on a visit, perished in the Holocaust. Efraim's descendants live in the United States.

Channa Kanterovitch survived in England. Her descendants live in England, Canada and the United States. She had a son and a daughter, Surka. Her son wed and fathered Leon and Gina. Leon married Cookie and they had a daughter.

Gina married Alfie and they had Laurence and Steven. Laurence wed and lives in England. Steven wed, has two daughters and lives in Canada.

Channa Kanterovitch's daughter, Surka, wed twice. With Diamond she had Yudele and with Boris Rayczki she had Rosa, Mary, Sophia, and Rita. After the Germans took France, Surka Rayczki and her daughter, Rita, fled Paris to Portugal. Mary's children did not survive the Holocaust. Sophia's only child, Denise, was taken by her father to Portugal; from there she was evacuated to the United States where she married and raised a family. Surka, Rita and Denise's father managed to get past the British naval blockade[1] and into Palestine.

After her husband, Avrum, was arrested and deported east to the concentration camps, Rosa and her two children, Yvette and Michael, fled to England. Rosa's descendants live in England.

Yudele wed Mary and fled France to Canada at the beginning of the war. He and Mary were childless.

Rita married Daniel and had Alan and Naomi. Together with Surka they settled in Canada. Alan married Rose and they had Adam. Naomi married Yitzhak and they had Adam, Daniella and Aviva.

Of the Dombs none in Poland survived the Holocaust. The only Domb I found was Esther, who had married Peretz Eckstein and left Poland for New York before the war. They raised three sons and their descendants live in the United States.

Of the Slaks none in Poland survived the Holocaust. In the fifties I located my cousin Schmulek Slak. After Handsome Yosel's accident Schmulek went on to Yugoslavia. There he married. During the war he went to Italy where he was interned. After the war he and his wife immigrated to Venezuela. They had two daughters. His descendants live in Venezuela.

There may have been other members of my family who survived the Holocaust, but neither I, nor anyone I know, have found them. It is still my hope that we may.

This promise made to our forefathers holds true also for us. For more than once have they risen against us desiring to destroy us; in every generation they rise against us and seek our destruction, but the Holy One, blessed be He, saves us from their hands.

The Haggadah

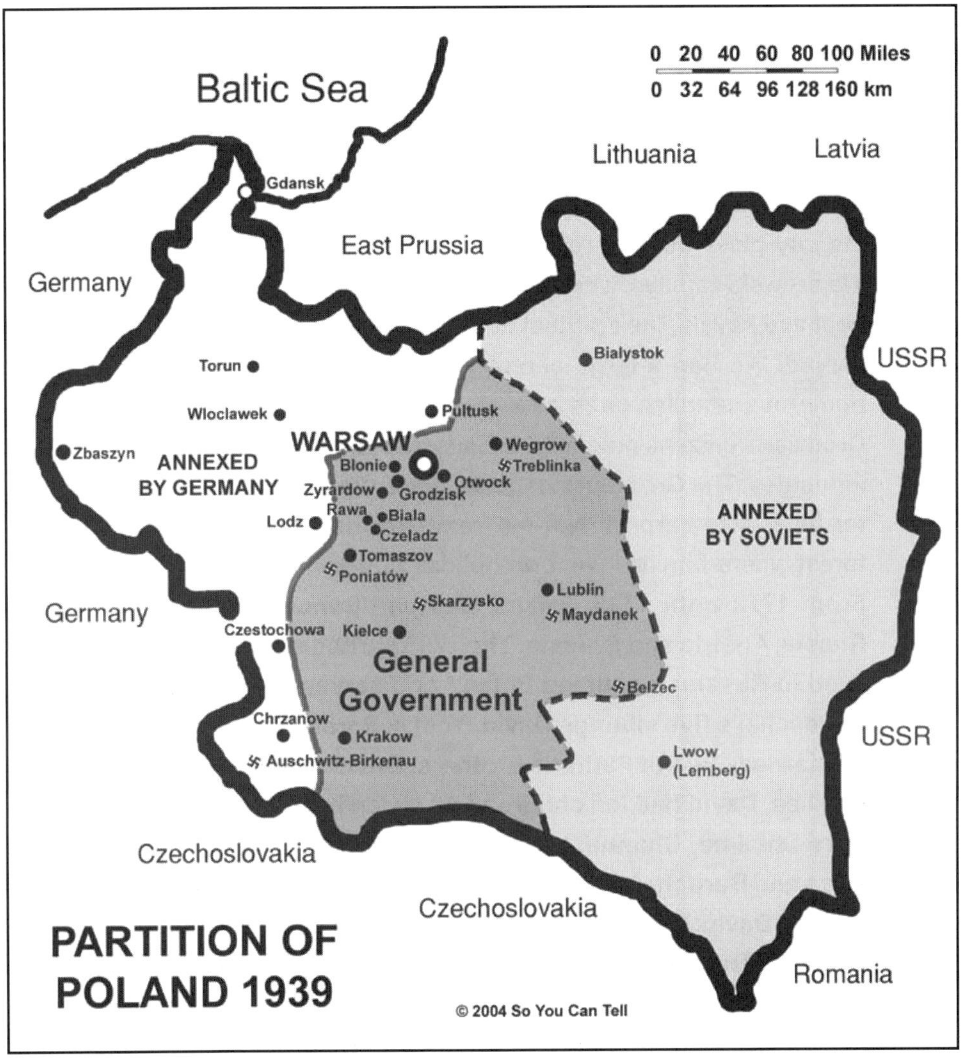
0 20 40 60 80 100 Miles
0 32 64 96 128 160 km
Baltic Sea
Lithuania
Latvia
Gdansk
East Prussia
Germany
Torun
Bialystok
USSR
Wloclawek
Pultusk
WARSAW
Wegrow
Treblinka
Zbaszyn
ANNEXED BY GERMANY
Blonie
Otwock
Zyrardow
Grodzisk
Rawa
Biala
Lodz
Czeladz
ANNEXED BY SOVIETS
Tomaszov
Poniatów
Skarzysko
Lublin
Maydanek
Germany
Czestochowa
Kielce
General Government
Belzec
Chrzanow
Krakow
USSR
Auschwitz-Birkenau
Lwow (Lemberg)
Czechoslovakia
Czechoslovakia
Romania
PARTITION OF POLAND 1939
© 2004 So You Can Tell

NOTES

BOOK ONE

1 Grodzisk had a post office, a well- equipped fire station, and a railroad station from which an electric train that ran into Warsaw, several public schools, and it boasted a *gymnazium*. Its medical community consisted of a hospital, a sanatorium and many pharmacists, doctors, and dentists. The city's cultural core was provided by its library, its two movie theaters, the Lux and the Venus, and its municipal orchestra, which performed in the city park. Several restaurants provided gourmet fare. The wealthy Walczewski family owned a man-made lake where people could swim, boat and kayak. The spiritual needs of Grodzisk's citizens were also well served. We had a large central synagogue on Synagogue Street and numerous smaller ones as well. The Poles had the Catholic Church. Grodzisk's citizens practiced various trades, professions, enterprises and industries. The Grodzisk Izdebskis factory was known throughout Poland for its quality carpets. Not far from Grodzisk was the Lesna Podkowa forest where families went on holiday outings.

2 From 1772 until 1795 Poland was partitioned three times between Russia, Austria and Prussia. The 1795 partition lasted until 1918. Motta lived in Russian occupied Poland and served in the Czar's army.

3 Mordechai's five siblings David, Yoska, Sarah, Aaron and Chaiah were all married. Two of Father's brothers, David and Aaron, had very large families. David had ten children and Aaron had seven. David's children were Shloime, Channa, Herschel, Esther, Lena, Sarah, Faiga, Moshe, Rosa and Baruch. Aaron's children were Channa, Faiga, Yohevet, Sara, Basha, David and Moishe. Father's sister, Sarah, married Benjamin Gutman. They had three sons, Schloime, David and Beryl. Schloime, the eldest was very close to Father. By the time I was born, Schloime himself was married and had two daughters. He was the managing director of a knitting factory in Warsaw and was always travelling to France or Germany on business. Schloime employed his family members whenever possible. These two uncles and aunt, with all my cousins lived in Warsaw.

Father's other sister, Chaiah, married Avram Godel Gothelf and had three daughters: Friedel, Marga and Paula. They lived in Brandenburg,

Germany. I never saw my Uncle Yoska. He, his wife Malka and their four children had emigrated to Brazil before my birth. Their fifth child, a son, was born there in 1926. I often heard that he was a handsome charmer and an actor whose portrayal of the Dybbick in local Yiddish theatre was hailed as a definitive performance and lauded for many years. The Dybbick is a famous Yiddish play written by S.Z. Rapoport under the pen name of S. Ansky. It is a classic of the Yiddish theatre repertoire and continues to be performed around the world in many different languages.

4 Mother's half-brother Milech had married and moved to Russia. Her three maternal aunts: Channa, Esther, and Mindel, the Bubbeh's sisters, had all married. Their married names were, Channa Kanterovitch, Esther Cimbalist, and Mindel Pacula. Channa Kanterovitch and her family emigrated to England. Esther Cimbalist and her family lived in the small city of Tomashov, and Mindel Pacula and her family lived in Rawa.

5 Gramophones, radios or telephones were not found in the average Polish home during the 1930's. Gramophones and radios were luxury items. Poland's telephone network covered its major cities and essential government, military and police installations. The more prosperous businesses and individuals in the cities could also afford them.

6 Betar is a Zionist youth movement founded by Ze'ev Vladimir Jabotinsky in Riga, Latvia in 1923, in response to the deadly pogroms against the Jews in Eastern Europe. The pogroms in the western Ukraine during 1918 – 1920 saw 85,000 Jews massacred. Another 2,658 Jews were recorded killed in pogroms between 1920 and 1932. The greatest number of these murders occurred primarily in the Ukraine, Poland and Hungary. Betar advocated self defense and a return to a Jewish state that included both banks of the Jordan. The term Betar was commonly used to refer to any one of the Jabotinsky-inspired Zionist organizations.

7 Ze'ev Vladimir Jabotinsky strongly opposed the policies of Chaim Weizmann and World Zionist Organization. One issue that he took great exception to was the refusal by the 17th Zionist Congress in 1931 to define the aim of Zionism as the establishment of the Jewish state. By 1935 Jabotinsky and his supporters, the Union of Zionist

Revisionists, disagreed with the World Zionist Organization to the point that they walked out of it and started the New Zionist Organization.

8 Anti-Semitism, the spiritual malaise that manifests itself as an irrational hatred of Jews, has been a fundamental plank in the platforms of many European politicians and nationalist groups for centuries. This has not changed. Today we need look no further than; Jean Le Pen of the National Front in France, Jorge Haider of the Freedom Party in Austria, Vladimir Zhirinovsky the Russian ultra-nationalist; the Ba'ath Party in Syria, the many Arab Islamic fundamentalists groups; Louis Farrakan's American Nation of Islam; and the countless neo-Nazi groups mushrooming throughout the western world. They all blame and hate Jews for their problems, both real and imagined. Nor have Church leaders entirely stopped advocating anti-Semitism. The Archbishop of Gdansk, Poland, Father Henry Jankowski was suspended for one year for stating that the Foreign Minister of Poland, Bronislaw Geremek did not have the right to represent the nation because he is of Jewish descent.

9 The Jewish Question was the politically correct way of stating that the Jews living in a particular country were not welcome there. Their 'hosts' considered them as aliens, regardless of how many centuries they had lived there or their contributions to its culture, economy and defense, and were seeking a way to get rid of them. For centuries the Jews wrestled with the problem of making themselves acceptable to their host populations. Their options ran from being model citizens, to cultural assimilation, to conversion to Christianity or Islam. Conversion was unacceptable to the great majority of Jews. Cultural assimilation and being model citizens met with limited success because nothing Jews did could ever be an antidote to the spiritual malaise that causes the irrational hatred of Jews. The only acceptable solution for the Jews lay, as always, in the annals of early Jewish history, the Bible. The return of the Jews to Israel from exile in Babylon was more than just a Biblical story or a liturgical prayer. It was the road map for Zionism. A mass return to Zion, the Jewish Homeland, became the goal of Rabbi Zvi Hirsh Kalisher in 1836. At that time a mass return to Biblical Israel was impossible; it was occupied by the Ottoman Empire. However, he had planted the seeds of modern day Zionism.

In 1903 the British proposed to establish a Jewish homeland in Uganda.

The Zionist movement refused the offer. With the collapse of the Ottoman Empire, Biblical Israel, which had been renamed Palestine by its Roman conquerors, became a British protectorate. For a brief period during the British mandate of Palestine was open to Jewish immigration.

10 Biro-bidjan was a Soviet scheme to solve the Jewish Question by creating a Jewish Autonomous Region in eastern Siberia on the Manchurian border. It was a totally undeveloped area of over 14,000 square miles of primeval taiga, coniferous forest. The Soviets expected at least 500,000 Jews to resettle there making it possible to establish the region as a Soviet Republic.

11 May 1st has been a holiday since ancient times, usually one having to do with spring fertility rites; however, in 1889 the 2nd Socialist International designated May 1st as a labor holiday. Since then it has been celebrated with parades and demonstrations at which labor union leaders and leftist party officials give speeches. These activities are usually capped with a picnic.

12 Field Marshall Josef Pilsudski became Poland's great national hero and president when his Polish Legion finally liberated Poland from Russian territorial claims in 1920. Many Jews fought in his army because he promised them absolute equality with Poles. Even though he was already head of state and commander in chief of the military, in 1926 he carried out a coup d'etat that made him a quasi-dictator. He abolished anti-Jewish laws but did not grant Jewish rights. Pilsudski kept the more rabid anti-Semitic politicians and churchmen at bay during his reign.

13 Marshal Edward Smigly Rydz, head of Poland's pro-German and anti-Semitic forces, became the fascist leader of Poland after Pilsudski's death. He unleashed an economic, patriotic and religious crusade against the Jews. He passed anti-Jewish laws. Jewish students in universities had to sit on special benches. Jews could no longer work in government, the police nor municipal jobs. Jews could only be officers in non-combat, medical and engineer units. Many churchmen openly preached against Jews. In his pastoral letter of 1936 Cardinal Hlond, Primate of Poland, said, 'It is also true that Jews are committing frauds, practicing usury and dealing in white slavery ... one does well to prefer his own kind in dealings and to avoid Jewish stores and Jewish

stalls in the markets.' Marshal Smigly Rydz's institutionalized anti-Semitism did not advocate physical violence against Jews and was referred to as a cold pogrom; however, in 1937 Jewish shops were not only picketed but bombed, and 79 Jews were killed and 500 injured.

When Germany invaded Poland Smigly Rydz fled to Romania where he was briefly interned. He died in Warsaw in 1941.

14 Endeckkes is the Polish pronunciation for the National Democrats acronym. They were one of the many anti-Semitic parties that Smigly Rydz used in his crusade against the Jews. When they picketed Jewish businesses they sang the following:

"Don't buy from Jews, not food nor wine
We'll drive them out to Palestine."

"Buy just from Poles, leave Jew boys be
We'll make the dirty Yidd'n flee."

15 Fascism as a political social system came into existence in Italy after WWI. It was an anti-democratic reaction to the enlightenment, laissez-faire economics, and any form of liberalism. Fascism is based on nationalism, racism, authoritarianism and militarism. It advocates conformity, racial purity, and an absolute leader. Hitler expressed this with his rallying cry of, Ein Reich, Ein Volk, Ein Führer (one state, one nation, one leader). By the late thirties Fascist parties were on the ascendancy in almost every country of the western world. Fascist parties were in power in Germany, Austria, Poland, Italy, Hungary, Greece, Spain, Portugal and Argentina. The fascists in Germany were called Nazis, the acronym for National Socialists.

The United States Fascist party had close ties to the American branch of the Nazi Party of Germany (the Bund). American Fascism had many powerful and wealthy supporters, among them Henry Ford, and the Duponts. They funded groups like the Black Legion, Silver Shirts, Christian Crusaders, American Vigilantes and others. Their agenda was modeled on Hitler's, to establish a dictatorship that would eliminate democracy, unions, socialists, communists, all dissent, and non-Aryan people. Rev Charles E Coughlin, head of the Christian Front, openly preached anti-Semitism on his national radio show.

Canada fascist parties were numerous; there were more than twenty Fascist organizations in Quebec alone, the largest of them being the *Parti National Social Chrétien* (National Social Christian Party) led by Adrien Arcand. He tried to organize an economic boycott of Jewish businesses.

16 In October, 1938, Smigly Rydz's Polish government announced that the 15,000 Polish-born Jews who had lived outside Poland for more than five years would have their passports revoked and would become 'Stateless Jews'. The Nazis immediately announced that there would be no place in Germany for 'Stateless Jews'. On October the 18th the round up of 'Stateless Jews' began. 10,000 German Jews were deported to the Polish–German border town of Zbaszyn.

17 Youth Aliya was established by the Jewish Agency in the 1935 to rescue Jewish children from Germany and to bring them to Israel. With the financial aid of women's Zionist organizations such as Hadassah, Mizrachi Women's Organization, and others, Youth Aliya was able to rescue 60,000 boys and girls from the Holocaust.

Rescue operations of the children were hampered by the British White Paper of May 17, 1939, which limited Jewish immigration to its Palestinian Mandate to no more than 15,000 Jews a year for the next five years. Britain had ceded to pressure from the oil-rich Arab states. They committed their naval resources to a blockade that trapped the Jews of Europe, leaving them with nowhere to go to escape the German genocide.

18 *Kristallnacht*, 'the Night of the Broken Glass', occurred on the 9th of November, 1938. Hitler had already prepared to attack the Jews throughout Germany. The assassination of the minor Nazi embassy official, Ernst Vom Rath in Paris, by seventeen-year-old Herschel Grynszpan gave Hitler the pretext to launch his attack. That night hundreds of synagogues were set on fire, 91 Jews were killed, hundreds of others were brutalized in the streets, and thousands of Jewish shops had their plate-glass windows broken and were ransacked. By the next morning 35,000 Jews had been arrested and sent to concentration camps. It was all the shattered plate glass in the streets that gave the night of terror its name.

BOOK TWO

1 The German Luftwaffe had been ordered to designate Warsaw's Jewish quarter as a priority target. 3,000 Jewish residents of Warsaw were killed during the bombing of Warsaw.

2 Warsaw fell to the Germans on September 27, 1939. On October 1st German troops occupied the city. All Polish military resistance was over by October 5, 1939.

3 In addition to the laws already passed against the Jews by Smigly Rydz's fascist government, the Germans added their own anti-Jewish legislation: the Nuremberg Laws, various decrees and a series of prohibitive rules and regulations were issued. 'Educational camps' were established for Jews; every Jew over twelve years old had to wear a white armband with a blue Star of David on it; all Jewish assets in excess of 2,000 zlotys per family were appropriated; Jews were forbidden to earn more than 500 zlotys a month, Jews were forbidden to ride on public transportation; Jews were forbidden to travel without permit; Jews were forbidden to own gold or jewelry; Jews were forbidden to work as bakers; Jews were forbidden to conduct business with non-Jews; Jews were forbidden to be treated by non-Jewish doctors; and Jewish doctors were forbidden to treat non-Jewish patients. The list of anti-Jewish legislation was endless, its purpose was to disenfranchise, impoverish, diminish and humiliate the Jews: to break them physically, morally and spiritually.

4 Stalin and Hitler had come to an agreement known as the Ribbentrop-Molotov Pact. It stated that: Russia would not ally with England in the coming war between Germany and England, and that Germany and Russia would divide Poland between them. Soviet troops began their take over of eastern Poland on September 17, 1939. They completed their annexation by September 28, 1939.

5 Approximately 250,000 Polish Jews fled into Russian occupied Poland during the first two months after partition. From there many of them were sent into the interior of Russia, primarily central Asia, where they suffered the same deprivations as did the local populations, but most of them survived the war. They became the largest surviving segment of Polish Jewry.

6 Chaiah Korcarz and her family survived the war in Russia, as did the

Goldfarbs. The Beckers also survived but had the misfortune to lose a child to starvation.

7 6,000 Jewish soldiers gave their lives in the defense of Poland. 61,000 Jewish soldiers were taken prisoners of war. They were immediately separated from the other prisoners, denied their basic rights as prisoners of war, and were brutalized. As concentration camp inmates, they were worked to the point of death, gassed and burned.

8 Belzec was located about 270 kilometers SE of Warsaw on the Bug river close to the new Russian border. Tusha and the other boys from Grodzisk were used as slave labor to drain marshes dig anti-tank ditches and build fortifications that made up the Germans' Otto defense line against the Soviets. Belzec became an extermination camp in 1942.

9 The Warsaw Ghetto became a reality on October 1st 1940 and was sealed by mid-November. The wall surrounding the Ghetto was three meters high and topped with broken glass and barbed wire. It was eleven miles long and had thirteen gates in it. Jews were not only used as forced labor to build it, but they had to pay for it as well. The Gestapo coerced the *Judenrat* to collect the cost of its construction.

10 Rations for Jews were 183 calories per day. In comparison: Poles received 934 calories/day, foreigners 1,790 calories/day and Germans 2,310 calories/day. In addition, Jews paid twice as much per calorie as did Poles, and twenty times as much as did Germans.

11 The Germans ordered the Judenrat, the Jewish Community Council, to form a 1,000 man Jewish Police unit to police the Ghetto. They were to enforce German orders, collect taxes, and to round up Jews for forced labor and for transport east. Being a Jewish policeman quickly became a position from which to secure one's own survival, albeit at the expense of one's fellow Jews. For the less scrupulous ones it was a very exploitable position. Before long, positions were being bought. By July of 1942 the force numbered 2,500 men and had become a haven for the most corrupt and criminal elements in the Ghetto. Many of its leadership and top officers were Jews who had converted to Christianity. Chief of the Jewish Police was Colonel Jozef Szerynski, a convert and violent anti-Semite, who had been a former Polish police inspector. He, and others like him, were assassinated by Jewish resistance groups.

12 The Polish thugs and hooligans that preyed on Jews were called

schmaltzers because they demanded that their victims hand over their 'fat'. The reward for turning in a Jew to the Germans varied; it could be three kilos of sugar, or one liter of vodka and one kilo of sugar, or one liter of vodka and some bread. The *schmaltzers* were the dregs of society. They operated in gangs and divided the city into districts in which to hunt down Jews. Others like shop-keepers, neighbors, tradesmen, school mates, customers and competitors informed on the Jews they knew.

13 The poem 'The Little Smuggler' written by Henryka Lazowert in the Warsaw Ghetto reflects the motivation and risks taken by those young children.

THE LITTLE SMUGGLER

Through a hole, through a cranny,
Starving yet stubborn and canny,
Sneaky and speedy like a cat
I daily risk my youthful neck.

And if faith will turn against me,
In that game of life and bread,
Do not weep for me Mother, do not cry,
Are we not all marked to die?

Only one worry besets me,
Laying in agony, so near death,
Who will care for you tomorrow,
Who will bring you dear Mom
A slice of bread.

14 Frankenstein was a German officer who took great pleasure in killing young smugglers. He patrolled the Ghetto's walls in a jeep mounted with a machine gun hunting for his victims. When he could not catch someone in the act of smuggling, he would kill someone at random. He had to kill someone every day.

15 The Nazis requisitioned everything of value. All metals and materials of value such as gold, silver and furs were confiscated. All works of

art had to be surrendered. Anyone owning a radio had to turn it in; not to do so was punishable by death.

BOOK THREE

1 By February of 1941 the decree of November, 1940, stating that any Jew found outside the Ghetto without a pass was to be shot, was being officially enforced. Those Jews that were not immediately shot when discovered outside the Ghetto walls were arrested, brought back into the Ghetto and jailed. The official executions of these people began on February 22, 1941. Special posters announcing the executions were signed by Dr Auerswald, the German Commissioner of the Ghetto.

2 Despite the conditions in the Ghetto, religious, educational and cultural activities were maintained for as long as possible. Cafes, restaurants and night clubs existed. Their customers were the small minority of profiteers, smugglers, blackmailers, collaborators, gangsters and others who could afford them.

3 The Gestapo established the *Judenrat* of Warsaw to replace the Jewish Community Council. The Germans picked its members from among the wealthy and prominent Jews of Warsaw and appointed Adam Czerniakow as its president. Any appointments to the *Judenrat* made by Czerniakow required the approval of the Gestapo. All *Judenrat* members were held personally responsible for any disorder. The *Judenrat* had to collect taxes for the Gestapo and to provide them with forced labor and deportees. The Gestapo ordered the *Judenrat* to create the Jewish Police as a means to enforce their demands. The Gestapo used the *Judenrat* to control the Jewish population. Through the Judenrat the Gestapo disseminated disinformation that kept the Ghetto population divided, confused and passive with the false hope that those who co-operated or were useful would survive. These 'snares of hope' were extremely effective.

The Germans succeeded in creating several divisions among the Jews; the first group were the Judenrat members themselves, who at their peak numbered some 6,000 and their dependents; then came the Jewish Police, Gestapo agents and collaborators, and their families;

a third group were the war workers who saw themselves as necessary to the German war effort; another group were the wealthy who believed they could buy their way until the war ended; and finally there were those who were to be sacrificed to pacify the incessant German demands for labor and resettlement in the east.

The German control of all newspapers, radio and travel made it impossible for anyone to know what was going on anywhere else. Everything was seen in isolation. There were rumors and stories of various atrocities that occurred in different places, not unlike disastrous events that had happened to Jews in the past. No one knew of the mass systematic murder of Jews by the *Einsatzgruppen* operating right behind the Wermacht's victorious advance into Russia. While it was happening very few individuals were able to grasp the big picture: to realize that the Germans were carrying out their plan to exterminate all the Jews. That plan had been finalized at the Wannsee Conference on January 20th 1942. Eight of the conference's fifteen participants were PhDs.

When Czerniakow finally faced the reality that all of the Ghetto's Jews were to be liquidated, he could no longer bear being the Gestapo's tool and took his own life.

4 The Germans posted a proclamation throughout the Ghetto ordering all Jews not working in their factories to report for transport to the east where they would be resettled and usefully employed for the war effort. In the east they would have ample food and better living conditions.

5 Treblinka was a death camp a mere eighty kilometers north east of Warsaw. Being sent to Treblinka was an automatic death sentence. Everyone arriving there was immediately stripped, gassed and burned. It was run by the German SS and Ukrainian guards. By November, 1943, all Treblinka had been razed. Heinrich Himmler, Chief of the SS and all the police apparatus of the Third Reich, had ordered that all visible signs of the killings be removed.

6 Poniatow was a slave labor camp approximately 130 kilometers east of Warsaw.

7 Ukrainian and Lithuanian soldiers were volunteers who served with the German SS: they were not draftees. Their countries, the Ukraine and Lithuania, were Axis partners.

8 From July 29, 1943 to August 4, 1943 the Nazis lured the starving Jews

of the Ghetto with three kilos of bread and one kilo of jam for those who volunteered for deportation. For too many it was an irresistible offer, if only to fill the bellies of their starving children one more time.

9 The German policy to any act of resistance was one of immediate reprisal carried out by collective punishment. It did not matter who carried out the act of resistance, everyone was held responsible. In 1940 when a German soldier was found assassinated in the Ghetto, the Germans summarily shot the first 100 Jews they could find. When Jewish smugglers killed a Polish policeman the first 110 Jews the Germans found were executed in reprisal. This German policy succeeded in deterring acts of individual resistance throughout Europe.

The young Jews who advocated resistance realized it needed to be organized. This proved to be no easy task. The *Judenrat* and public opinion were against them. The *Judenrat* led the public into believing that resistance would only bring terrible reprisals, that the reports of death camps were exaggerated, that the Germans did not have genocidal plans, and that the war would end soon. The Jewish Police and the Gestapo's collaborators and agents worked very diligently to suppress any resistance to the Germans. In addition to these problems the young Jews who wanted to resist lacked arms, lacked the funds to buy them with, lacked suppliers to buy them from and lacked training in their use. Support from the Polish underground was not merely negligible but shameful in its anti-Semitic bias. When arms were available the prices were extortionate.

Despite all these formidable obstacles, by January 18, 1943 the first organized resistance had been carried out in the Ghetto. Poorly armed and untrained, the Jewish Resistance fighters engaged German troops in large-scale street fighting. Although they inflicted losses on the Germans, it was a costly battle for them as well; their casualties were also very high. They changed tactics and began house to house fighting. The fighting lasted until the 22nd of January. The fighting had the desired galvanizing effect on the remnants of the Ghetto population; many were now determined to resist. The Germans could no longer enter the Ghetto with impunity. It had become a war zone.

10 The Warsaw Ghetto Uprising began on April 19, 1943. It was the first urban uprising in Europe against the Germans. By the time of the

uprising it was too late for the great majority of the Jews. They had already been deported from the Ghetto to their deaths in Treblinka and other death camps. The fighting lasted until mid-May. A group of young men and women, armed with pistols, Molotov cocktails, a few rifles and limited ammunition, had defended the Ghetto against the power of the German Army's elite SS units. Despite being armed with automatic weapons, flame throwers, tanks, artillery, airplanes and limitless ammunition, the Germans had to burn down the Ghetto block by block to suppress the Warsaw Ghetto Uprising.

11 Maydanek was a slave labor and death camp situated approximately 260 kilometers south of Warsaw in the Lublin area. It was run by the Waffen SS. It had gas chambers and a crematorium. In 1943 it was out in the country, isolated and surrounded by empty fields and swamps. Today development is threatening to engulf it and obliterate it both as a historical site that is hard physical evidence of the Holocaust and as an important Holocaust memorial.

BOOK FOUR

1 Emmanuel Ringelbaum, a social historian and noted archivist of 'Notes From The Warsaw Ghetto', wrote that, '...each day was like a decade in the Ghetto'. Faiga Burman states that, 'Each day in the death camps was like a lifetime.'

2 After the war, Brigida, the SS woman, married an American and became Helen Braunsteiner-Ryan, an American citizen. She was discovered and stripped of her American citizenship and returned to Germany where she was tried, convicted and sentenced to life imprisonment.

3 Birkenau was one part of the Auschwitz concentration camp complex. It was the women's camp and referred to as Auschwitz II. It had four gas chambers and a crematorium, built in 1942. Monowitz was the men's camp and referred to as Auschwitz III. The Auschwitz concentration camp complex was the largest of the Nazi extermination camps.

4,000,000 Jews were murdered there. Those who were not gassed immediately on arrival were used as slave laborers. The more fortunate ones were put to work in the German factories producing war materials.

Among the many German corporations that exploited this slave labor were: Siemens, Bayer, Krupp and I.G. Farben.

4 The cynical motto *'Arbeit Macht Frei'* (work makes free) was wrought in iron and arched over the entrance gate to Auschwitz.

5 The Nazis considered the Roma (Gypsy people) and Sinti (German tribe of Gypsies) as inferior human species and murdered over 500,000 of them.

6 Camp Commandant Franz Hoessler was the commander of the women's camp. He was a glib talker and was almost always on hand to greet the arriving transports. He always succeeded in reassuring the frightened arrivals that all was well and that their skills were highly valued and required for the German war effort. He easily swayed them into believing that being asked to undress for the showers was only a standard hygienic procedure which everyone followed. He was so convincing that people passively walked into the gas chambers disguised as showers. Hoessler was the one who devised this murderous deception that worked so well. The *sondercommandos*, those who witnessed him plying his skills, called him 'Moishe Liar'. After the war he was tried and convicted at the Belsen Trial. He was executed by hanging in 1945.

7 The infamous Dr Josef Mengele was an SS physician and held a PhD in anthropology. His thesis argued that one could differentiate racial groups by the slope of a person's jaw. He became the senior doctor at Auschwitz in May 1943. He was in charge of all medical experimentation and personally conducted many on his specialty, twins. He escaped justice and lived in South America supported by his wealthy family in Germany. He is rumored to have drowned in 1978 and was officially declared dead in 1979.

8 SS Tauber was Hoessler's second-in-command. 'He was a tall, thin, bold man. A man who I avoided looking at for fear of attracting his attention, for on the slightest whim he would send people to their death.' *Faiga Burman*

9 Non-Jewish prisoners in Auschwitz lived in separate barracks. They received the same starvation rations but did not suffer the same brutalities, work-to-death policies and selections that the Jewish prisoners did. In addition they were permitted to receive help from their families and medical attention from the Red Cross.

10 The Union munitions factory at the Auschwitz concentration camp complex was a Siemens plant that made up one cog of the vast war industries complex that was run using slave labor.

11 The Nuremberg Laws were a body of 400 anti-Jewish laws legislated by the Germans between 1933 and 1939. They defined a person as non-Jewish if their lineage did not have any Jews in it for at least three generations on both sides of their family tree. If a person was more than ¼ Jewish from either side of their lineage, they were not entitled to the privilege of German citizenship and were treated as a Jew. As a result assimilated Jews and converted Jews did not receive any consideration by the Germans. For a time during the Warsaw Ghetto some converted Jews, protected by their churches, lived better than the rest of the Ghetto. But they were still Jews in German eyes and when the deportations started they were taken away and murdered.

12 The orchestra at Auschwitz, led by the violinist Jack Stromoza, was the crowning touch of Hoessler's' deception. Arriving transports, hearing the orchestra and seeing the misleading signage, would be very susceptible to Hoessler's reassurances that all was going to be well.

13 The crematorium was blown up on Oct 7, 1944 by the *sondercommando.* The *sondercommando* and the Polish Resistance had been planning an uprising at Auschwitz. The Polish Resistance not only postponed the initial revolt but also did not participate as planned when it did happen. Most of the *sondercommando* were killed in the battle. The rest, with very few exceptions, were murdered immediately after. This was the only armed uprising to have occurred in Auschwitz.

BOOK FIVE

1 The prisoners were split into smaller groups and marched off on different circuitous routes with the sole purpose of killing them through exhaustion and starvation. The Nazis wanted to kill as many Jews as they could and leave as little evidence of their murder as possible by strewing their corpses all across Germany.

2 Hungary was Germany's ally during the Second World War. Hungarian troops served the German cause faithfully. Anti-Semitism in Hungary

did not require any mentoring from the Germans; it had been endemic to their political and social culture for centuries.

3 Ravensbruck was the only woman's concentration camp in Germany, situated approximately 100 kilometers north of Berlin. It became a stop over and dumping ground for dying prisoners as the Nazis tried frantically to complete their genocide of the Jews.

4 The Polish Revolt in Warsaw began on August 1, 1944, more than a year after the end of the Warsaw Ghetto Uprising. The Polish insurgents were crushed by the Wermacht. Warsaw's population was evacuated, many to internment camps and Warsaw was totally flattened, house by house, street by street.

5 Malchow is situated approximately 200 kilometers north of Berlin.

6 Up until the very end of the war the Red Cross had not been allowed to see any of the Jewish prisoners in the camps. With the loss of the war imminent and accountability looming the Germans tried to deceive the Red Cross as to the nature of their regime towards the Jews. The German camp commander had no illusions as to his fate if captured by the Russians; either he would be executed on the spot or sent to a brutal death in a labor camp for German POWs. In the hours and days immediately after liberation many starving concentration camp prisoners died from their attempts to eat the food given to them by the Allied and Soviet soldiers that had freed them. Their wasted bodies could not metabolize the food. After everything that they had survived, this was a cruel death.

7 Hitler Youth was the youth branch of the Nazi Party.

BOOK SIX

1 In the two years after the war one thousand Jews were killed in Poland due to anti-Semitic violence. In one day of July 1946, forty-one Jews were murdered during a pogrom in the Polish city of Kielce. This was the last straw for the majority of Jews who thought to rebuild their lives in Eastern Europe. Most of them left for Israel or for the west.

BOOK SEVEN

1 The Children of Survivors seminars were an off-shoot of the book, Children of the Holocaust written by Helen Epstein. She was the first lay person to write about the effects of the Holocaust on herself and other children of survivors.

2 New arrivals to Treblinka, being unloaded from the cattle cars, saw a narrow street containing men working at various jobs. They saw signs directing them to the showers. Everything was set up to reassure them that they were being asked to get undressed for routine showers prior to being processed for work. They were then walked naked from the train platform to the gas chambers. This path was cynically referred to by the Jewish prisoners who worked in Treblinka as the *Himmel Strasse,* the Street to Heaven.

3 Franz 'Lalka' Kurt was Treblinka's deputy commander. His attack dog was called 'Barry'. In addition to setting his dog on people, his other sadistic practices included using inmates to practice his boxing skills on, and braining young children by swinging them against a wall. He evaded capture until 1959. He was found living in Dusseldorf under his own name. In his possession was a photo album of his Treblinka experiences. It was titled 'The Best Years of My Life'. He was tried and imprisoned for the murder of 139 prisoners and complicity in the murder of 300,000 Jews. The German government released him in 1993 when he was 79 years old. He died a free man.

4 When Jerzy and his mother found out that Stashek was Jewish they continued to shelter him, despite the risk to themselves. The punishment they faced for harboring a Jew was death.

5 The Rappaport Monument is a sculpture titled, 'Defenders of the Ghetto'. It was created by the Israeli sculptor Nathan Rappaport, who was born in Warsaw.

6 Zygelblom, Szmul Arthur, was a Polish Jew who escaped the Warsaw Ghetto and embarked on a mission to England to personally seek the assistance of the Polish Government in exile to implore Allied Government intervention to prevent the destruction of Polish Jewry. As a member of the Polish National Council and a Representative of the Bund (Socialists) in London he had access to the top levels of power. His efforts and pleas fell on deaf ears. When the destruction of

the Warsaw Ghetto by the German Army was complete he committed suicide in protest against the indifference he had encountered and in solidarity with his fellow Polish Jews. '...By my death I wish to make my final protest against the passivity with which the world is looking on and permitting the extermination of the Jewish people.'

7 The *March of the Living* is an event that takes place each spring. It begins in Poland on *Yom Hashoah,* Holocaust Memorial Day. It is the day during which the memory of the millions of Jews who perished at the hands of the Nazis, and their collaborators, is honored. Thousands of Jewish teenagers from communities around the world participate in the commemorative activities that take place on the grounds of Auschwitz, Treblinka and Maydanek. It gives them a deep and personal understanding of the Holocaust, how it happened and where it took place. From Poland, the *March of the Living* goes to Israel for *Yom Hazikaron*, Israel Memorial Day and *Yom Ha'Atzmaut*, Israel Independence Day.

8 Gentiles who risked their lives, and by extension their families' lives, to save a Jew from death during the Holocaust are honored for their courage and humanitarianism by the Jewish people in a ceremony at *Yad Vashem* as a Righteous Gentile Among the Nations. Their names are inscribed in *Yad Vashem*'s park on Mount Herzl in Jerusalem and their deeds recorded in their archives.

9 Leading Holocaust denier David Irving claims that the Holocaust of the Jews never happened. David Irving holds a doctorate degree in history from a well-known British university. He has spawned a slew of imitators posing as historians and basing their thinly veiled anti-Semitic tracts of Holocaust denial on his thesis. In 1994, Penguin Books of Britain published Denying the Holocaust: The Growing Assault On Truth and Memory by Professor Deborah Lipstadt of Emory University in Atlanta, Georgia. David Irving had the *chutzpah* to sue Professor Lipstadt and her British publisher for libel. The case went to trial and Irving lost; he was found to have deliberately and willfully ignored, omitted and misused the information that he had referred to.

GENERATIONS

1 In response to years of relentless Arab terror opposing Jewish immigration to British Mandated Palestine, the British government issued a White Paper in May, 1939. This infamous document limited Jewish immigration to Palestine to 15,000 per year. The immediate enforcement of this edict by the British Navy until May, 1948, resulted in catastrophe for millions of Jews trapped in Europe. The Jews of Palestine responded in two ways. One was a policy of illegal immigration that managed to bring in just over 113,000 Jews by December 1947. The other response was one of resistance and terror against the British Mandatory Government carried out by the Irgun and the Stern gang.

As far as pacifying Arab terror the White Paper was an abysmal failure. Even though the British had exiled the principal leader of Arab terror, the mufti of Jerusalem, Hajj Amin Al-Husseini, whom they had appointed to the post, he continued to incite Arab terror against the Jews and the British in Palestine. This incitement continued from Iraq and Germany throughout the Second World War. Hajj Amin Al-Husseini allied with the Nazis. Among his many services to the Nazis he recruited and organized some 20,000 men into the SS Bosnian Muslim battalions which served in the Waffen SS.

GLOSSARY

Appel	A call to assembly
Befielshtelle	Command quarters
Beis Midrash	A synagogue, or any place of study and prayer.
Beis Yakov	A girl's Hebrew school, where young Jewish girls received their Hebrew education.
Blockeldeste,	The block elder in charge of and responsible for the entire block. The Germans appointed her to execute their orders.
Canada commando	The slave labor group that collected and sorted all the property and effects left behind by the people arriving on the transports after they were stripped and marched off to the gas chambers. They had their own group of blocks.
Chaider	A school where Jewish boys, starting as young as three years old, begin their Hebrew education. They study Torah, the five books of Moses.
Challa	An egg enriched, braided white flour bread.
Chassidim	(The Pious) The followers of Israel Baal Shem, who in the eighteenth century founded a mystical movement in Judaism distinguished by its simplicity and religious ecstasy. It placed more value on doing good among men than on formal Talmudic studies and rabbinical strictures. It replaced a wrathful God with a warm loving God who was celebrated with laughter, dance, song and the joy of life. They wear distinctive garb.

Chish	A person whose intellectual processes, and consequently his priorities, are addled. A Chish is totally oblivious to his condition.
Chulent	Beans, potatoes, meat, marrow bones and water are placed in a large pot and set in an oven to slowly bake overnight.
Chuppah	A traditional wedding canopy of a fine white cloth under which the bride and groom are wed.
Chutzpah	A Yiddish word for behavior that is: in your face, shows nerve, or gall, and that totally disregards another's sensibilities.
Combineer	To scheme and manipulate in order to stay alive. See *organize*.
Einschrieberen	The block registrar or block clerk, responsible for keeping the meticulous records that the Germans demanded.
Einsatzgruppen	They were the Special Operations Groups operating on the eastern front behind the Germany army as it rapidly advanced into Russia in the summer of 1942. Their task was to immediately round up and murder all the Jews in the newly conquered territories.
Gefilte fish	A fish cake or fish loaf made from several different types of fish minced together. One of the fish is traditionally carp. *Gefilte fish* is served with *challa*.
Grieben	Is chicken skin fried up into small crusty clumps and is usually added to the *schmaltz*. Cracklings.
Gymnazium	A secondary school that combines the curriculums of both a high school and junior college.

Glossary

Hiding	A place of refuge from an enemy. It could be an impromptu contrivance for one or two people or a highly organized shelter for any number of people.
Kaddish	The Mourner's Prayer. Its recitation is led by the eldest male child of the deceased.
Kapo	A person in charge of a work detail. In concentration camps *kapos* were selected from among the prisoners. It was very advantageous to be a *kapo*, but not everyone could be that ruthless to a fellow prisoner.
Kosher	Food which conforms to Judaism's ritual dietary laws which dictate: what Jews can and cannot eat, how to prepare it, and when to eat it.
Kibbutz	A collective community run on Zionist and socialist principals. Initially *kibbutzim* were engaged in agriculture, but later ventured into other enterprises to support their members.
Klaidenskammer	The place where all the clothing and packages collected by the *Canada commando* was taken to and processed.
Litvack	Any Jew from Lithuania.
March of the Living	An event organized by world Jewry. Its purpose is to educate Jewish youth about the Holocaust by bringing them to the death and slave camps where these horrors occurred.
Musselman	A slave laborer who had been starved into a skeletal state and had lost her ability to struggle and will to live. They could no longer work, walk or stand straight.

Mezuzah A *mezuzah* is small, hollow, cylindrical object that is attached at a diagonal to the right side of the front door post of every Jewish home. A *mezuzah's* ornamentation may range from the very simple to works of art. In the hollow is contained a piece of parchment on which is inscribed specific scriptures, usually Deuteronomy 6:9.

Nahora The evil eye, a curse, or a spell.

Ofzayeren An overseer, a supervisor. A high ranking *kapo*.

Organize To devise a way to get food or anything that could be exchanged for food or anything that could help one survive.

Papuskas Felt slippers worn by poor peasants.

Pasiaks Literally meaning stripes, which described the prisoners' black and white striped uniform.

Pritcha The plank shelving three tiers high that served as beds for the concentration camp prisoners.

Puskai A Slavic term meaning 'let go'.

Rassenshande Means race disgrace. It was part of the Nuremberg laws which prohibited Germans from marrying or having extra-marital relations with Jews.

Righteous Gentiles A term used to describe those non-Jews that risked their lives and their families' lives to save a Jew from the Germans. Such an individual is considered as one of the Righteous Among the Nations. They are recognized and honored by *Yad Vashem*. A medal, bearing their name, is struck, they are awarded a certificate of honor, and their name is inscribed on

	the Wall of Honor in the Garden of the Righteous Among the Nations at Yad Vashem.
Rosh Hashanah	Is the day of the Hebrew Year that commemorates the anniversary of the creation of the world and of God as judge, dispensing mercy or justice to all. The *shofar*, ram's horn, is blown to mark the beginning of *Rosh Hashanah* which starts the period known as the High Holidays. It is a ten day period that ends with *Yom Kippur*, the Day of Atonement.
Schlep	A Yiddish word meaning to drag.
Shma Israel	A prayer recited by Jews several times daily and when they are about to die. It proclaims his faith: 'Hear O Israel, the Lord our God, the Lord is One....'
Schmaltz	Yiddish for rendered chicken fat.
Schtetl	Is the Yiddish word for a small city, town or village.
Schtubeneldeste	A subordinate to the *blockeldeste*.
Sondercommando	A 'special' group. These were the slave laborers who helped disembark the arriving victims, took their possessions from them and stood by helplessly as they were led away to their deaths. They then emptied the gas chambers of the dead, pulled their gold teeth, fillings, crowns and dentures, shaved the hair off the dead women, and put the corpses into the crematorium ovens. The Germans killed off the *Sondercommados* at regular intervals and replaced them with newly arrived prisoners; they did not want witnesses.
Striemel	A fur trimmed hat favored by the *Chassidim*.

Tsimmis Is a traditional sweet dish of assorted vegetables grated and cooked with fruit.

Umschlagplatz Its literal meaning is a transfer or trading place. It was located just outside the Ghetto.

Volksdeutsche Is the term for ethnic Germans living as foreign nationals.

Yad Vashem An institute headquartered on Har Hazikaron, the Mount of Remembrance, in Jerusalem. It was established by an act of the Knesset in 1953 as the Holocaust martyrs' and Heroes' Remembrance Authority. It commemorates those who were victims of the Holocaust, archives its history, supports its study and honors the *Righteous Gentiles*.

Yom Ha'Atzmaut Celebrates May 14, 1948, the day Israel declared its independence. On that day the armies of Egypt, Syria, Jordan, Iraq, Lebanon and Yemen invaded her.

Yom Hashoah Holocaust Memorial Day.

Yom Hazikaron Israel's Memorial Day. When all who have fallen in her defense are remembered and honored.

Yom Kippur The Day of Atonement. A twenty four hour period of prayer and fasting. *Yom Kippur* of that year was on October 9, 1943.

ACKNOWLEDGEMENTS

Preparing my mother's testimony, about the murder of our family and of millions of others, for publication was an emotionally wrenching journey. A great amount of thanks goes to Celine Boucher for getting me under way by keying in my mother's hand written text. Thanks go also to my niece, Lisa Vatch, for her invaluable grammatical assistance. My siblings, Evelyn, Anne and Holden, and my nephews Mitchell Vatch and Omar Joseph Sharif, all proof read the manuscript before I placed it in the competent hands of professor Paul Hedlin for editing. Thanks Paul. Another thank you goes to Radu Stratulat for his digital preparation of all the book's images and its layout and design. And last but not least I thank my mother for her patience with my endless questions about places, events and people that were painful to recall. If there are any errors or omissions in this book the fault lies solely with myself.

Simon Wajcer

Montreal, Quebec
Canada

INDEX

A

B

C

D

E

F

G

L

M

N

O

P

Q

R

S

T

Y

Z